MODELS OF RELIGIOUS EDUCATION

Theory and Practice in Historical and Contemporary Perspective

HAROLD W. BURGESS

Evangel
Publishing House
Nappanee, Indiana

Toll-free Order Line: (800) 253-9315
Internet Website: www.evangelpublishing.com

First edition published by Victor Books/SP Publications, ISBN: 1-56476-443-5.

Publisher's Cataloging-in-Pubication
(Provided by Quality Books, Inc.)

    Models of religious education : theory and practice in historical and contemporary perspective / Harold W. Burgess. – 1st ed., rev.
    p. cm.
    Includes index.
    LCCN: 00-108288
    ISBN: 1-928915-14-0

    1. Christian education–Philosophy–History.
2. Christian education–Philosophy.   I. Title.
BV1464.B87 2001   268'.01
                    QBI00-893

Printed in the United States of America
5 4 3 2 1

This book
is dedicated to
Marcia Kay Burgess
my wife
and my encourager

CONTENTS

FOREWORD

The Christian church has flourished for twenty centuries. In all that time it has never been more than one generation from extinction. The church is renewed and sustained as members enter, grow in "the faith," and eventually assume roles of leadership. Recruitment, evangelization, and education have been the principal means of sustaining the church and insuring its future. This accords with the "Great Commission" in which Jesus commanded his followers to reach out to all the world and make disciples by baptizing and teaching them to practice the principles he had commanded. Quite obviously, education (together with its cognates: teaching, discipling, spiritual formation, etc.) is the primary ongoing activity addressed to those who have been identified as new or future members. Because of the importance attached to forming new members, the church's most influential leaders have directed their best energies toward the development of educational strategies.

My interest in strategies for teaching new generations of Christians was piqued while teaching a "required frosh religion" class. It was immediately obvious that many of my 125 students had been effectively inoculated against a vital Christian faith. The Sunday schools and youth groups of their local churches had not served them well. This realization fostered an awareness that I had better understand what was truly happening to students in my class. I certainly did not wish to contribute to an even more profound level of inoculation. So I began an earnest search for understanding the dynamics of teaching new Christians. My search actually led to a new career, Christian educator.

My inclination was to look to the experience of the early church for direction. I have always believed the substance of the happily stated aphorism: "If you don't know history, you don't know anything. You're a leaf that doesn't know it's a part of a tree." Accordingly, this study begins with an historical survey that employs six categories (aim, content, teacher, learner, environment, and evaluation) to ascertain the shape and dynamic of the early church's educational endeavors. As a backdrop to its eventual focus on developing more effective strategies for the twenty-first century, the study applies these categories to the educational writings of sixteen thinkers from Clement of Alexandria (third century) to John Henry Newman (nineteenth century). Along the way I discovered such impressive thinkers as Cyril of Jerusalem (fourth century) with his curiously modern insights and John Comenius (seventh century) with his burden to reconstruct educational processes that "mangle the mind."

From the writings of the sixteen historic educators, a prototypical model emerges. It has proven extremely helpful in understanding current as well as historic issues. In this book, the prototype provides benchmarks for considering the views of more than thirty twentieth-century thinkers such as George Coe, Randolph Crump Miller, Sara Little, James Michael Lee, and Kenneth Gangel. Four major twentieth-century models surface. For three of these, theological considerations are normative. For the fourth, norms fall largely within the field of teaching-learning psychology. For the twentieth century, then, the results of this study may be presented in an analytical chart in which the six categories mentioned above describe four, historically progressive models: the classical liberal model, the mid-century mainline model, the evangelical/kerygmatic model, and the social-science model. The primary writings of fifty-three writers were analyzed in the course of the study. In the present book I have sought to preserve a sense of the times in which each of these writers lived by using their own terminology whenever possible. Thus the spirit and tone of their understanding relative to aim, content, teaching, and learning is one of the intentional contributions of the book. Theological changes are shown in sharp relief, demonstrating the importance of developing a thorough theological understanding. The potential for incorporating a clearer understanding of teaching-learning psychology is the focus of the chapter on social sciences.

At its entry into the twenty-first century, the church obviously faces issues it has never faced in exactly the same way. However, because we are "leaves of the same tree," I believe it will prove helpful to address twenty-first century issues with all of the wisdom that can be gleaned from historical educators such as Augustine, Luther, Calvin, and Wesley. We also benefit from attending to twentieth-century writers such as Miller, Cully, Edge, and Lee. Still, changes are bound to occur. For example, the Sunday school that has served Protestantism so well for two hundred years is currently finding waning support in the literature. Consider that the church existed for eighteen centuries without the Sunday school and that it fulfilled the principles of the Great Commission quite well. It may be that twenty-first century innovators will be obliged to find an alternative. Nonetheless, no alternative to Sunday school is suitable unless it accomplishes the educational task that the Master Educator defined in the "Great Commission."

As a contribution to effective educational thinking, strategizing, planning, and teaching, this book is offered through Evangel Publishing House, a developing enterprise dedicated to providing resources for assisting effective ministries throughout the church. I am especially happy that Evangel has chosen this book as its first professional offering in the field of Christian Education.

Harold Burgess
Wilmore, Kentucky
Summer 2000

This study employs six categories (aim, content, teacher, learner, environment, and evaluation) for ascertaining the shape of religious education endeavors throughout the church's history. As a backdrop to its focus on the twentieth century, the study applies these categories to the educational writings of sixteen thinkers from Clement of Alexandria (third century) to John Henry Newman (nineteenth century); including Augustine, Martin Luther, John Calvin, and John Comenius. A historic, prototypical model emerges from their writings. This prototype provides benchmarks for considering the views of more than thirty twentieth-century thinkers and theorists, including George Coe, Randolph Crump Miller, Sara Little, Lois LeBar, Johannes Hofinger, and James Michael Lee. Four major twentieth-century models surface. For three of these, theological considerations are normative; for the fourth, norms fall largely within the social-science field of teaching-learning psychology. For the twentieth century, then, the results of this study may be represented pictorially by a 6 x 4 analytical matrix in which the six categories describe four, historically progressive, models: the classical liberal model, the mid-century mainline model, the evangelical/kerygmatic model, and the social-science model. Little effort is expended in an evaluation of the several models in that the purpose of this study is to promote consideration of theory and its application in practice.

Harold W. Burgess
Wilmore, Kentucky
Advent 1994

CHAPTER 1

THE RELATIONSHIP BETWEEN THEORY AND PRACTICE:

An Introduction

THE SETTING

The roots of this book go back to a January day early in my teaching career. Just six days before the spring semester, the dean reassigned me to a section of "required frosh religion." In my naiveté the prospect of teaching this particular course was actually quite exhilarating. After all, these students had elected to matriculate in a college with a reputation for taking its religious commitments seriously. Hoping to serve them well, I worked diligently for six days to organize the entire corpus of Christian doctrine. The whole was properly outlined; every point was placed in its appropriate cubbyhole. As the new semester commenced, I began inflicting my outline upon the more than 100 students.

It soon became clear that certain class members didn't even know that the Ten Commandments were imbedded in the biblical narrative. Moreover, they did not care that they did not know. This discovery merely stiffened my resolve to make sure that we were covering all the bases, covering them so thoroughly that any serious student could repeat every item from the above mentioned outline on my increasingly detailed tests. A number of students dropped the course. Looking back, I am indeed grateful that one of them was candid enough to write on the drop slip: BORING. Understandably, these matters provoked considerable reflection.

Such reflection eventually included the religious education to which that Vietnam-war generation of students had been exposed in the conservative, evangelical subculture from which most of them, and I myself, had come. My judgment was that, in their early religious training, a significant number had been more effectively inoculated than educated. Furthermore, it seemed clear that to simply barge ahead with my teaching plan involved the risk of inflicting yet a deeper level of inoculation, one which would continue working against these students becoming vitally religious persons. Out of this process there arose a consciousness-raising gestalt: "As a teacher, I had better understand what I am doing to my students."

Accordingly, I began earnestly seeking a better understanding of the dynamics of religious education. At a practical level, I was looking for better instructional methods. The first glimmer of genuine hope came during a chance reading of D. Campbell Wyckoff's *The Gospel and Christian Education*. Three of Wyckoff's sentences offered a new perspective on the understanding I was looking for: "The most critical problem that faces Christian education, however, is the need to understand itself—to gain deep insight into what it is about. It needs to see how it is related to the cultural situation, to the church's life and thought, and to the educational process. This problem of self-understanding is the problem of theory."[1]

Wyckoff's counsel seemed prophetic. It connected solidly with a viewpoint embraced by James Michael Lee, with whose works I became acquainted in the process of my ongoing search. Lee's stance is nicely encapsulated in his own words.

> *I firmly believe that one major cause for the relative inefficacy of much of contemporary religious instruction lies in the fact that most religion teachers hold one theory of religious instruction while at the same time they utilize pedagogical practices drawn from another highly conflicting theory. Consistency in the relationship between theory and practice is absolutely*

indispensable for the effectiveness, expansiveness, and fruitfulness of a practice in any domain whatsoever.[2]

Perhaps the most important thing that developed out of the situation I have been describing is that the scope of my attention broadened. It shifted from a narrow focus upon subject-matter content to include actual religious-life outcomes. This acquired consciousness provided a much more concrete standard of judgment for evaluating and adjusting my own teaching. Constructs related directly to the teaching-learning act became useful in planning learning sequences. These proved far more effective than those based upon analysis of subject-matter content, such as my outline described above. Very good things began to happen in my classes. The students grew in both grasp and application of their espoused Christian faith. However, they taught me more than I taught them.

With a new appreciation for the vital relationship between theory and practice, I began to read the writings of those creative individuals who have long been at the forefront of the church's educational endeavors. I discovered Cyril of Jerusalem, with his curiously modern insights; Thomas Aquinas, with his awe-inspiring capacity to organize theological data; Martin Luther, with his incredible creativity in applying old ideas to new situations; John Comenius, with his burden to reconstruct educational processes that "mangle the mind"; and George Coe, with his disturbing proposal for a "democracy of God."

The writings of these thinkers, together with many others, constitute the intellectual milieu out of which this book had its birth. Of course, religious educators do not all agree. The times in which we live, together with our dissimilar cultural and religious environments, contribute to diverse perspectives. Even so, it seems worth nurturing a dream that we can learn to communicate in ways that will enable us to help one another become more effective in the church's cardinal ministry of religious education. Accordingly, one driving interest in offering this book is to do my part to advance the developing sense of history within the professional community of religious educators and among students taking courses in the field. A concomitant interest is to encourage a thorough reading of the truly exciting original sources by offering brief introductions to the thinking of more than fifty men and women who have written influential books on religious education. These interests, intentionally, impose an important limitation on this book: it draws almost exclusively upon the writings of selected authors who have published books that contribute substantially to the theory of Christian religious education. These writers have been selected (1) out of my own reading; (2) in consultation with other religious educators; (3) through interaction with students in the classroom; and (4) by following up conversations, comments, and criticisms generated by my earlier book, *An Invitation to Religious Education* (1975).

THEORY AND PRACTICE

Terminology is an important consideration throughout this book. In an effort to employ as broad a term as possible, and to accommodate the varied nomenclature employed within the schools of thought to be considered, the term "religious education" will commonly be used. In two chapters, "Christian education" will most accurately reflect the intention of writers who consciously chose this term to express their theological commitments and their educational philosophy. In one chapter, "religious instruction" properly focuses the discussion on the teaching-learning act. Again, "Christian religious education" most happily conveys what I believe to be the intention of a number of writers. In all instances, my choice of terminology is intended to reflect practical judgments necessary to maintain objectivity.[3]

Despite numerous attempts to define the field, religious education continues to have a critical problem with its identity. Even the authorities in the field—those who write the books, journal articles, and denominational handbooks—seem quite unable to satisfactorily answer the question of "what is religious education." One factor contributing to this perplexity concerning nature and purposes seems to be that no common methodology for analysis and synthesis has been fully established.[4]

By way of contrast, in the field of science it can be boldly asserted that everyone knows what science is because everyone knows what science does. Science observes, discovers, measures, experiments, and frames theories about the way and why of things. A typical scientist in any of the scientific disciplines is trained in a rigorous system whereby he or she has become confident and skillful. A scientific education, it may be assumed, assists the learning scientist to acquire (1) a knowledge of theory and (2) skill in applying theory in practice. The designation "scientist" suggests one who knows how to state appropriate goals as well as how to develop and test ways of working toward them. It is also assumed that any scientist should be able to communicate clearly with other scientists, even those from other cultures.

Clearly, the term "religious educator" is not accompanied by such positive assumptions. Indeed, as a field of study, religious education tends to be rather lightly regarded.[5] I believe that a conscious attention to theory can move us in the direction of establishing better definitions, and greater recognition, for the field.

One extremely important factor is that the notion of "theory" is somewhat slippery. The term is derived from the Greek word θεωρια signifying "a beholding" or a "speculation." In common contemporary usage, theory refers to a verified explanation of a set of facts as they relate to one another. By extension, theory provides a plausible explanation of the principles underlying a practice.

The central purpose of this book, accordingly, is to respond to the widely recognized need to deal with religious education theory. Although my preferences may show from time to time, it is not my intention to defend a particular theory or model. Rather, I hope to make more explicit the elements which tend to characterize certain models of religious education that are discernible in the literature. As alluded to earlier, a subsidiary purpose is to offer a broad historical introduction to the field as a backdrop for the more defined theoretical contributions of twentieth-century thinkers.

Finally, this book is an effort to promote fruitful communication across the several ideological barriers that separate those of us who work in the field. To this latter end, selected schools of thought will be analyzed to assess the extent to which they agree or disagree with respect to constructs, definitions, and propositions which constitute the more observable elements in religious education theory. Obviously, the task of ordering and disciplining the wealth of knowledge already in existence will not be exhausted, but this present labor seems well worth the effort.

RELATIONSHIP OF THEORY AND PRACTICE IN THE FIELD

For me, it was Charles Melchert who originally brought the theory-practice relationship into usable focus. In a seminal article he pinpointed a "bias toward the practical" as the fundamental crisis in the field. In his view this crisis is rooted in the lack of theoretical and conceptual clarity on the part of religious educators. Melchert thus argued that a decision to change a practice often means little more than that it will be done differently. Such a change process affords no room for serious consideration of theoretical grounds which might justify either the change or the new practice. One obvious problem with any practice not solidly based on theory is that there is little encouragement for educational enrichment and reconstruction on bases more solid than whim and fancy.[6]

The establishment of an appropriate relationship between theory and practice is a perennial problem in many of life's arenas. The ancient Greeks first advanced the notion of a possible connection between these concepts. For them, theory and practice referred to modes of life, which, though polar opposites, were not separate. "Theoretical" life included much of what today would be called "scientific inquiry." Such "inquiry" was rooted neither in curiosity nor in practical necessity. It was rather to escape ignorance. "Practical" life was concerned with the performing of activities.

Twentieth-century language contributes to a somewhat different popular understanding. "Practice" is characteristically contrasted with "abstract ideas." "Mere thinking and reflecting" are placed in an unfavorable juxtaposition to "action." This habit of mind has the effect of making "practice" seem more valuable and more useful than "theory."[7]

Even a cursory examination of the literature suggests that religious educators have not always been committed to examining issues theoretically. Influenced, it seems, by the popular attitude described above (i.e., that theory is not very useful), it has been more usual than not for practice to be elevated above theory. Certain statements drawn from professional documents are indeed startling in this regard. Consider the following passage from the "Introductory" to the first issue of *Religious Education* (April 1906): "Religious education has no academic problem. There are plenty of philosophers who will take care of the theoretical aspects of the subject. The Religious Education Association stands for practice rather than speculation."[8] This sentiment is echoed in a very wide range of literature. Admittedly, this genre of thinking, with its emphasis upon usefulness and immediacy, does have a certain attractiveness. After all, the specific concerns which motivate many of us to enter the field of religious education as area of serious inquiry are practical.

USING SCIENTIFIC RESOURCES

The direct applicability of social-science methodology to the investigation of issues relevant to religious education was demonstrated early in the twentieth century by such studies as the Character Education Inquiry. Also known as the Yale Studies, this project was directed during the 1920s by Hugh Hartshorne and Mark A. May. By challenging a number of assumptions that had long influenced religious education practice, these studies suggested that certain common practices should, at the very least, be reconsidered. For example, the Yale studies raised serious questions about the validity of one assumption evident in the literature, at least as far back as Augustine. This assumption, upon which many religious educators have commonly placed much confidence, is that mere knowledge of morals and religious ideals is almost always transferred into one's personal lifestyle. In fact, the studies found very little correlation between knowledge of religious ideals and actual moral behavior.[9]

As will be developed more thoroughly in a later chapter, James Michael Lee has for some time played a leading role in applying the findings of social-science research to the improvement of religious education. His widely read trilogy,[10] probably constitutes the only full-blown macrotheory in the field. Lee employs the findings and methods of the social sciences, while respecting and utilizing the theological commitments of varied religious traditions. To my knowledge, no other religious educator has yet advanced a complete theory on the scale developed by Lee. Nonetheless, a number of theorists of differing traditions have employed the findings of the social sciences for the advancement of religious education theory in very significant ways. Witness the different uses of social-science findings evident in James Fowler's seminal offerings on faith development, in *Stages of Faith*;[11] in Timothy Lines' creative wrestlings to define paradigms for understanding the process of religious education, in *Functional Images of the Religious Educator*;[12] and in Larry Richards' widely read, but little heeded, proposals for including the family within the locus of religious education, in *Christian Education*.[13]

MODELS OF RELIGIOUS EDUCATION

The thrust of the term "model" is closely related to "theory." Indeed, some writers employ these terms interchangeably. However, the notion of change seems more integrally related to modeling than to theorizing. For more than fifty centuries, possibly beginning in ancient Egypt, models have been employed *first*, as keys to understanding the past and *second*, as bridges leading to the future. Through their focus upon structures rather than upon subject matter, models tend to evoke consciousness of relationships, particularly the relationships that pertain among any given model's variable elements. In addition, because of their dynamic organization of data, models are exceptionally useful in communicating specific properties that affect relationships among variable elements.[14]

The religious education enterprise quite often requires one to initiate changes which affect the future. Such changes, of course, ought to rest upon responsible interpretations of prior history and experience. Models powerfully assist in this kind of strategic thinking process and, as Martin Heidegger reminds us, the nature of our age seems to require good thinking more than other ages.[15] The utilization of models, then, offers significant promise for helping religious educators to seize appropriate opportunities for better understanding, for fostering desirable change, and for communicating with one another. Accordingly, this study will employ the term "model" to describe four twentieth-century schools of thought regarding the nature and processes of religious education. Taken together, these relatively discrete models offer potential support for that disciplined thinking so needful for the development of fruitful religious education strategies.

MODEL ELEMENTS

One reason for the relatively slow development of a framework for theorizing, model-making, and hypothesis testing in the field of religious education is that the necessary descriptive research underlying this phase of theorizing has not been accomplished. Research progress in a given field may wait more on sound theory, developed from the process of "descriptive analysis," than it does upon instrumentation. Accordingly, in addition to previously stated aims, this book proposes to engage in a descriptive, analytical study of the writings of representative religious educators concerning fundamental units of religious education theory. Since literature in the field is often criticized for lack of clarity, it seems helpful to employ a category system in order to facilitate the analysis and description of the several models analyzed in this book. Some such system has often been proposed as an important early step in bringing better order to communication within the field.[16]

The notion of a category system as a device for exploring religious education theory is not a new one. As early as 1917, George Coe employed an effective set of categories in his well-known book, *A Social Theory of Religious Education*. Coe's categories are: (1) an indication of the *kind of society* that is regarded as a desirable end result of religious education, (2) a notion of the *original nature of the student*, (3) an idea of the *kinds of educational experiences* that will most surely bring about the desired result, and (4) some means by which *progress* is evaluated. There is good reason to believe that Coe's continuing influence rests in large part on the cogent ordering of his views made possible by his careful and consistent ordering of his theory according to its elements.[17]

During the 1940s, Lewis Sherrill distinguished among four perennial efforts of religious thinkers to provide a basis for a comparative study of religious beliefs and education: "the attempt to discern the nature of the Supreme Being, the attempt to discover how he manifests himself most significantly, the attempt to know what his will for men is, and the attempt to identify and secure the ultimate values of the universe."[18] Sherrill's categories, though not employed precisely as model elements, did contribute significantly to the usefulness of his influential history, *The Rise of Christian Education*.

D. Campbell Wyckoff has offered a useful category framework consisting of six basic units as a means of understanding and expressing religious education theory. His very helpful units are: (1) objective, (2) scope, (3) context, (4) process, (5) personnel, and (6) timing. He argues that the use and further development of this, or some other similar categorization, is a necessary step in the development of religious education as a discipline.[19]

Jack Seymour and Donald Miller have experimented with the potential for explicating approaches to religious education in descriptive terms that function somewhat as categories. Their *Contemporary Approaches to Christian Education* (1982) organizes an exploration of the field in terms of five "approaches": (1) religious instruction, (2) faith community, (3) spiritual development, (4) liberation, and (5) interpretation.[20] *Theological Approaches to Christian Education* continues the Seymour and Miller exploration. It seeks to "reclaim the dialectic between theology and teaching" by offering a perspective which considers "teaching as a theological activity." The summative categories by which Seymour and Miller present the results of this latter study are: (1) tradition, (2) church, (3) person, (4) mission, and (5) method.[21]

James Michael Lee proposed an elegant, yet dynamic, four-part model for teaching religion based on his analysis of the teaching-learning act: (1) environment, (2) learner, (3) teacher, and (4) subject matter. Lee's categories are applicable for objective analysis of teaching and learning in any domain. In the context of religious instruction, they enjoy a distinct advantage in that they are not affected by specifically theological, or even religious, connotations.[22]

The several styles of categorization suggested by these writers express their individual thought patterns and expository notions regarding the religious education enterprise. For this reason, and in the absence of a universally agreed-upon set of units, I will employ the following categories to facilitate my description and analysis of selected models of religious education: (1) aim, (2) subject-matter content, (3) teacher, (4) learner, (5) environment, and (6) evaluation. These categories obviously do not exhaust the possibilities, but they do embody a number of the more important ideas developed in the category frameworks reviewed above. Furthermore, in a slightly different form they have enjoyed wide use in my earlier book, *An Invitation to Religious Education.*[23]

THE MODELS IN BRIEF

The historic prototype reflects the prevailing worldview and religious convictions of the church during the first nineteen centuries of its existence as these were applied to the related problems of (1) educating succeeding generations for vital Christian living and (2) incorporating individuals into the church. Wayne Rood suggests that, throughout these centuries, the faith of the church was fixed upon a metaphysical object and a biblical cosmology, even through the scientific advances that marked the eighteenth and nineteenth centuries. Thus questions of aim, process, and evaluation were generally considered matters to be decided upon the basis of constructs that presupposed a God who had spoken to humankind through a "word-oriented," saving message. Teaching practices commonly included a strong element of verbal transmission. Although these convictions were not elevated to the status of a truly discrete model, a number of historic educators seem to have given attention to learners and learning outcomes in a manner that presaged at least some elements of twentieth-century paradigms.[24]

The liberal model is rooted in the classical, liberal theology characteristic of the early twentieth century. It is buttressed by the progressive educational theories explicated in the writings of such theorists as John Dewey, George Coe, and William Clayton Bower. Rood's assessment is again helpful. He argues that this model reflects not so much the "fading of faith as its transfer from a metaphysical to a scientific object."[25] Accordingly, a primary difference is that salvation is believed to occur through processes solely, or almost solely, related to this world; and it is for *the many*, as contrasted with *the individual*. From the perspective of the liberal model, determining religious education aim, procedure, and evaluation requires theological judgments amenable to a decision process transferred from a metaphysical to an empirical perspective. Teaching practices generated by this model are typically oriented to life through social action.

The *mid-century mainline model* grew out of a reassessment of the assumptional underpinnings of the liberal model on the part of a number of theologians and religious educators. These included such thinkers as Reinhold Niebuhr, H. Shelton Smith, and Randolph Crump Miller. The theological position adopted by some, but not all, of the earlier thinkers working from this model was "neo-orthodoxy." This perspective perceives religious education to occur most effectively through a dynamic interaction within the Christian (religious) community. Practices developed directly out of this model typically feature relational group activities. The group is often considered a microcosm of the church.

The *evangelical/kerygmatic model* might be regarded as a renewal of certain commitments that characterized the historic prototype. Since renewal movements typically go beyond a former pattern that is held up as an ideal, it should not be surprising that certain aspects of this proclamatory model seem to represent a set of mind that is more inflexible than the historic understanding. Thus, this model is energized by the vision of a revealed message that must be faithfully communicated. The model itself gives rise to the lecture, even preaching, as the ideal teaching paradigm.

The *social-science model* is rooted in the teaching-learning process. It consciously sustains a value-free relationship to theology, but accepts and inserts it, as appropriate, into the process of teaching religion. Since particular attention is given to understanding how learners learn best, teaching practices generated by the model have a high degree of specificity to individual situations. Theoretically, then, teaching acts flow from the religion teacher's deliberative efforts to achieve learning goals by weaving together biblical, social, cultural, and environmental factors in the here-and-now learning process.

SUMMARY

This chapter addresses the important relationship between theory and practice in the field of religious education. Theoretical advances on many fronts have provided powerful tools for improving practices in the field, but these tools have seldom been adequately employed. To heighten awareness of possibilities, the chapter proposes an analytical matrix consisting of six categories (aim, content, teacher, learner, environment, and evaluation). It is projected that this matrix might be profitably applied to four schools of twentieth-century religious educational thought (liberal, mainline, evangelical/kerygmatic, and social-science). Further, since twentieth-century practices are deeply linked to practices in earlier centuries, it is proposed that it might also be helpful to apply the analytical categories to earlier understandings of Christian religious education. Accordingly, chapter 2 describes a prototypical model distilled from the writings of sixteen thinkers who lived during the first nineteen centuries of the Christian era. Few of these writers would be considered theorists today. Still, each contributed in a unique way to the development of religious education practice as we know it. It is important for the reader to keep in mind that the following chapter functions as a backdrop to chapters 3–6. Each of these addresses a distinctive twentieth-century way of viewing the religious education task.

CHAPTER 2

THE HISTORIC PROTOTYPE OF RELIGIOUS EDUCATION:
A Backdrop to Twentieth-Century Models

PROTOTYPICAL MODEL

For the first nineteen centuries of the present era, Christian religious education functioned according to a relatively well-defined model, or, more accurately, "prototype." This prototypical model was profoundly influenced by the perceived educational ideals of Jesus and the writers of the New Testament, but its deeper roots were in the Hebrew world of the Old Testament and in Greco-Roman culture. Most importantly it reflected a worldview that prevailed for the greater part of the Christian era prior to the twentieth century. This view posited the existence of a personal God who communicated with humankind essentially through saving acts, as recorded in the Scriptures.

In most instances in this chapter, I have elected to use the term "prototype" rather than the term "model." In the case of the sixteen thinkers whose works will be considered, the term "model" conveys the notion of a conscious structuring of elements that goes somewhat beyond the facts. "Prototype" is used in the sense of "exhibiting the essential features of a later, more carefully defined, type or model."[1]

Compactly stated, the historic prototype assumes (1) that religious education is fundamentally concerned with communicating a divinely given message; (2) that aims and subject matter are best ascertained from the Bible and from carefully preserved doctrines rooted in it; (3) that the teacher's role is to communicate the spirit and facts of the saving message as well as to assist the learner's assimilation into the church; and (4) that learners will live out the implications of the message with respect to their participation in the church, as well as their eternal destiny.[2]

The period under consideration in this chapter is a very long one. Thus, while it seems fair to conclude that there was indeed an operative prototype (model) of Christian religious education, it is also fair to note that it was not always interpreted by the rather brittle set of mind that came to characterize certain writers in the sixteenth, nineteenth, and even twentieth centuries. Then too, it is well worth keeping in mind that, even though it can be helpful to identify handles for research by reducing complex phenomena to rather simplistic categories, simplicity itself can be misleading. Accordingly, while surveying the underpinnings of the prototype, this chapter will seek to promote insight into "how multiform Christian education actually is."[3]

BIBLICAL ROOTS OF THE HISTORIC PROTOTYPE

The Old Testament

The centerpiece for understanding the Old Testament contribution to Christian religious education is that remarkable pronouncement, "the Shema," ostensibly given by Moses during the closing period of Israel's wilderness wanderings.

> *Hear, O Israel: The Lord is our God, the Lord alone. You shall love the Lord your God with all your heart, and with all your soul, and with all your might. Keep these words that I am commanding today in your heart. Recite them to your children and talk about them when you are at home and when you are away, when you lie down and when you rise. Bind them as a sign on your hand, fix them as an emblem on your forehead, and write them on the doorposts of your house and on your gates (Deut. 6:4-9).*

The principles enunciated in the Shema express something of the intense national spirit that undergirded a powerful system of education centered in the Hebrew home. In considering the Old Testament contribution to Christian religious education, it is important to remember that its concept of education was not dependent on schools. In many cultures, laws, customs, patterns of life, and religion are communicated through the home and family. The home is the environment of almost every child's earliest learning. Accordingly, it should not be surprising that few traces of formal schooling are easily discernible in earlier Hebrew history. The Hebrew family provided the needed structures within which training in morals, religious knowledge, and social obligations occurred. As schooling eventually became more formalized, children entered school having already learned the elements of literacy and the principles of the Hebrew religion.

In the more public arena, those events by which God was believed to have communicated with His people were kept alive by temple rites and national feasts. A product of the centuries just preceding the birth of the Christian church, the synagogue was above all else a place where the Scriptures were read and interpreted. In some sense a precursor of the local church, the synagogue combined religious instruction with worship. It was a powerful preserver of Hebrew culture and values. During later centuries, especially with the rise of the synagogue and the formalization of schools, the role and status of the teacher was elevated to a position of highest honor.[4]

The New Testament

Consequently, teaching was a primary instrument through which Jesus carried on his ministry. This was in agreement with the tradition of his people. A master of the story, Jesus was equally effective when learners were numbered in "multitudes"; when they were a band of closely linked disciples; or when, as in the case of Nicodemus, a searching individual came with a poorly conceived question. To the student of teaching, the most impressive aspect of Jesus' teaching may well be the way in which He seems to have consciously employed strategies that accounted for the developmental stage of the learner.

Sadly, Jesus' practice has at times served as a pattern for a rather wooden version of the historic prototype. In actuality, his teaching was so conscious of the learner, of the learner's growth needs, and of the broader criteria for evaluating learning, that he was much more than a mere representative of the historic prototype. As interpreted by reform-minded educators in later cultural contexts, the outlines of the historic prototype seem to have served as a limiting model. Ulich observes that Jesus' attitude toward teaching was so advanced that it took many hundreds of years, at least up to the period of Comenius, for the wisdom inherent in his attitude to be fully realized. Jesus was a great teacher, at least in part, because he gave the learner priority. He obviously concerned himself with providing information, but his greater burden was to meet specific personal needs.[5] The Apostle Paul is probably less remembered for his pedagogy than for the content of his proclamation and defense of the Gospel. Consequently, there has been a popular conception that as a teacher he was rather rigid. However, a careful examination of Paul's strategy suggests a teacher who was quite aware of the learner and who was responsive to the learner's needs. As a matter of fact, Paul mindfully varied his teaching methods as required for the sake of desired outcomes. As a theologian, Paul indeed seems to have been quite in harmony with the historic prototype. Nevertheless, his creative teaching strategies never gripped later educators in quite the way that Jesus' strategies did. Accordingly, Paul's influence on the course of Christian religious education seems to have been more in the use of his writings as a source of subject matter than as a model for the role of teacher.[6]

The Greco-Roman World as a Nurturing Factor in the Development of the Historic Prototype

The Christian church began in a world governed politically by Rome; however, it was governed intellectually by Greek patterns of thought. Well before the Christian era, Greek thinking had been spread over almost all of the Mediterranean world and deep into Europe, Asia, and Africa. There is no simple way to briefly encapsulate the impact of Greek schooling and thought on Christian education. A cultural mix, that included a passion for intellectual independence coupled with a disciplined curiosity, owed much to the Greeks. This kind of curiosity brought a richness to the education of many early Christians that gave a certain helpful dimension to their relationship with the world at large. But such curiosity also created a number of problems, in that the boundaries of orthodoxy were continually threatened by educational adventurers such as Philo and Origen.

Greek thought patterns nurtured the idea of schooling and created a climate in which the teacher was easily regarded as the "spiritual father" of learners. In ancient Greek schools it was intended that learning would be fostered through constant companionship with the teacher ("pedagogue"). This perception of schooling blended nicely with Jesus' peripatetic mode of life and teaching. Its impact in the church fitted easily with the way in which Christians of the first three centuries were sometimes forced to live as wanderers.

The Greek view of education was closely related to that of the Jews.[7] Both views recognized the importance of learning through the teacher and also through imitation of the teacher. It appears that, over time, the seeking, dynamic, and relational dimensions of education present in both the Hebrew and Greek paradigms were short-circuited in some historic expressions of Christian religious education. The outcome was that learning came to be perceived as a static, receptive listening, rather than a firsthand experience with reality, a wrestling with truth that could be fully owned. Indeed, as one of the legacies of the later stages of Greek schooling, there is considerable evidence that teaching evolved as "a telling and a learning by heart."[8]

During the approximate period of time that the Hebrews and Greeks were engaged in developing their respective models and processes of education, Roman education arrived at certain similar structures, at least insofar as schools were concerned. However, Roman schools were targeted to develop quite a different kind of individual. In contrast to the active, imaginative, creative, independent individual idealized in Greek schools, Roman schools sought to produce a practical, concrete, managerial kind of person. The Romans valued colorful personality and the capacity for authoritative leadership much more than the reflective qualities admired by the Greeks. The church, then, seems deeply indebted to Roman education for its part in developing the kind of leadership that the church needed to hold it steady during the Middle Ages when the surrounding culture was in disarray.

It is sometimes avowed that Rome adopted and eventually perpetuated Greek ideals in education. Yet it also seems true that the Romans contributed a long-range vision for this world that neither the Greeks nor the Hebrews were able to achieve. In the context of the needs of the Christian church, these three streams (Hebrew, Greek, and Roman), together with the original contributions of Jesus and the New Testament writers, did bring about a kind of educational amalgam that, overall, served the needs of the church well.[9]

THE FIRST FOUR CENTURIES

Perhaps the early church's single most important contribution to educational theory was the notion of the essential equality of every person. The church, unlike the state, acknowledged the absolute necessity of educating everyone. Nonetheless, comparatively little is known of educational practices as regards direct church involvement in educating children from Christian homes. What evidence is available indicates that it was considered incumbent upon Christian parents to educate their children in the primary facts of the faith. This focus on the home as the functional center of educational experience followed the Jewish ideal. It does seem interesting that no formal treatise to assist parents in their educational task has yet been discovered in the literature of the earliest centuries. Of course, extant sermons and informal tracts do admonish parents to bring their children up in the faith.

The fundamental educational emphasis during these early centuries seems to have been on what today we might call "adult education." With little doubt this emphasis grew out of such pressures as (1) the threat of heresy from within the church and (2) the threat of persecution, even death, from without. The former threat was met by redoubled efforts to define "the faith" in terms which could be employed defensively. In the process of educating and assimilating new converts into the church, the latter threat meant that every individual must be encouraged to seriously weigh the consequences of becoming identified as a Christian.

Although a variety of emphases in early church education might be classified, the mention of but two serves the purpose of this chapter. *First*, the notion of kerygma, or announcement of the facts of the Gospel, played an important role in educational thinking. The kerygma encompassed a threefold theme of Christ's death, burial, and resurrection appearances, highlighting the facts of the Gospel. Beyond that, in clear images it reminded the early Christian that the hard way of the cross was for every follower of Christ. At the same time it was underscored that this was a way with hope. The idea of kerygma is closely related to the core concepts of the historic prototype where the teacher functions as herald, announcer, and proclaimer. *Second*, didache, as a concept (as well as a document) in early Christian religious education, developed a number of steps in the direction of credal formulation. From this discussion it should be apparent that it is by no means easy to make a radical distinction between preaching and teaching as educational practices in the early church.[10]

The Catechumenate

By the beginning of the third century a catechumenal system was operational in at least the larger local church settings. The catechumenate was not so much an effort to educate children of Christian families as it was a means of integrating new converts into the life of the church. Catechumens often met in the teacher's home where they were systematically instructed in the biblical and doctrinal content of the Christian faith. The catechumenate was clearly not intended to provide academic training. Its obvious goal was to morally and spiritually prepare candidates for membership and meaningful participation in the life of the church.

The importance of the catechumenate takes on greater significance when one pauses to consider what an awesome step it was to profess faith and receive baptism in the primitive church. It was like choosing sides in warfare. One might very well be called upon to give up life itself for the sake of such a choice. The period of preparation for the catechumen to become a full communicant member was about three years. During this time catechumens were moved along in a growing relationship with the church. Following a statement of intention they were permitted to listen to the Scripture reading and the sermon during the early part of the worship service. Later on, after they had received basic instruction and had demonstrated fidelity to the faith, catechumens were allowed to remain for prayers. Finally, upon having been judged worthy, they were instructed in the liturgical life of the church in final preparation for baptism and full membership.[11]

It seems obvious that the catechumenate was based upon tenets that are strikingly similar in many important respects to the historic prototype. The *aim* seems to have been to underscore the transmission of a body of biblical and doctrinal *content* through the medium of a *teacher* perceived to have been both called and gifted for the task of faithful communication to the *listener/learner*. In a number of ways, then, the catechumenate appears more educationally sophisticated than the prototype as it eventually evolved in sixteenth-century catechisms, or even in the nineteenth-century American Sunday School. Accordingly, *environment* was taken seriously and seems to have been carefully structured so as to move the learner along the path of cognitive and affective commitment to, and development in, the Christian faith. Then too, *evaluation* was taken seriously; having been conceived in such a manner that the entire lifestyle of the catechumen was considered in the final judgment as to readiness for full participation in the church.[12]

Catechetical Schools

Whereas modern confirmation classes are in some sense a continuation of the catechumenate, it is apparent that Christian higher education (colleges, seminaries, universities) grew out of another form of early church education, namely the catechetical school. That the catechumenate was limited to the religious task of preparing seekers for baptism and membership in the Christian church might suggest that early Christians disdained what today we might call a liberal education, and indeed some did. However, overall there was a high regard for education together with a legitimate concern that Christians might be advanced to a more competitive relationship with other educated individuals. One particular goal seems to have been to establish a standpoint for defending the Christian faith in the marketplace.[13]

The catechetical schools approached the matter of education quite differently than did the catechumenate. The curriculum was deliberately rooted in the prevailing Greek disciplines, especially philosophy. Biblical and theological studies were pursued along academic lines and were informed by the best scientific and critical tools available. To be sure, catechetical schools came in for their share of criticism by some conservative segments of the growing institutional church.

The best known of these schools was the one in Alexandria, Egypt. One long-standing tradition has it that, after he left Rome following Paul's martyrdom, Mark, the writer of the second Gospel, actually laid the groundwork for this eventually powerful institution. Under any condition, Alexandria began to achieve eminence under Pantaenus in the late second century. Mostly scattered around the shores of the Mediterranean, the catechetical schools probably contributed little to the historic model of education as defined in this chapter. However, these schools did contribute much to the glorious story of education in the Christian church. In almost every case the catechetical schools were led by one principal teacher who was responsible for the whole range of learning. A number of these teachers rank high on any list of third- and fourth-century "movers and shakers," whether the list be assembled from the perspective of church, or from the perspective of general education.

REPRESENTATIVE EDUCATORS OF THE FIRST FOUR CENTURIES

Clement of Alexandria (ca. 150-215)

Clement, "the first great Christian scholar," was born in Athens and educated in the standard university curriculum of his day. He apparently converted to Christianity in his mature years, possibly under the influence of Pantaenus. Upon Pantaenus' death in 190, Clement succeeded him, bringing his own broad learning to the chair of the principal teacher. Clement's aims were ambitious to say the least. He sought to educate Christian scholar/philosophers ("true Christian gnostics") who would integrate secular and sacred knowledge in defense of the faith. Clement's classrooms were crowded as he sought to bring his students "to the feet of the Incarnate Word." While he valued scholarship, it was only purposeful scholarship offered in the service of the church. He despised meaningless knowledge and useless information.[14]

Clement's legacy to the church is very great. He brought the catechetical school, as an educational concept, well along the way toward its third-century zenith, and he contributed still extant works such as *Christ the Educator*[15] and *Miscellanies*.[16] These works show that, based on earlier Greek university traditions, Clement contrived a definite course of instruction that some scholars think mildly resembles Herbart's contributions in the nineteenth century. Perhaps the way in which he contributed most significantly to the development of the historic prototype was that he deliberately incorporated the Christian revelation into his system of epistemology. Clement's educational notions were definitely a blend of Greek and Christian thought, but his deepest loyalties were on the side of the church.

Origen (182-254)

Origen was among the most able, accomplished, and versatile leaders in the early church. Before the age of twenty he had been appointed head of the Alexandrian school. At the beginning of the third century this school seems to have had a broad, mostly lay-oriented, curriculum. However, Origen took his duties as chief catechist so seriously that he sold his library, gave up his scholarly pursuits, adopted an ascetic style of life, and devoted himself almost exclusively to exhaustive Bible study. According to Eusebius, Origen's fame as a teacher eventually drew "thousands" under his influence, many of them of the intelligentsia. His writings have left Origen with an enduring reputation (1) as the first true textual critic, (2) as the most influential commentator of the early church, (3) as the first theologian to offer a systematic exposition of the Christian faith, and (4) as one of history's most effective apologists.

Origen is popularly remembered for his allegorical method of interpreting Scripture, but his own literalistic interpretation of

Matthew 19:12 influenced his decision to castrate himself so as to allay suspicions about his relationship with the numerous women who attended his lectures. His writings and asceticism also seem to have spawned and nurtured the monastic movement that flourished in succeeding centuries. Still, Origen is one of the church's most memorable teachers. He profoundly shaped the course of history from his study and from his classroom. One would, of course, not associate Origen with the historic prototype at all points, but his focus upon the Bible as a primary source of content left an enduring mark, especially upon higher education in the Christian context.[17]

Cyril of Jerusalem (ca. 310-386)

Cyril was born somewhere near Jerusalem early in the fourth century. Of his developing years little is known, but it is certain that he was elevated to the Jerusalem episcopacy relatively early in his life, near the middle of the century. On the whole, Cyril's theology was conservative, but he was not enthusiastic about the brittle character of Nicean theology making its way into the mainstream of church life. With pressure from both sides over his moderate position on certain questions relating to the Arian controversy, he was for a time deposed. Restored to his bishop's chair in 379, Cyril was eventually acclaimed "Confessor of the Faith" and thus recognized as a champion of the faith.

Living in momentous times, Cyril shared the Christian theological stage with such greats as the three Cappadocian saints, Basil the Great, Gregory of Nyssa, and Gregory of Nazianzus. However, his greatest contributions to the church fall within the pastoral realm, especially in the area that today we would define as religious education. Even before he became bishop, Cyril seems to have gained some reputation for his sermonic discourses on the shape of the Christian faith. Shortly after he became Bishop of Jerusalem, one series of such discourses was transcribed by a nameless recorder who provided a priceless service to the church and to history. These sermons, dating from about 348, comprise one of the most important documents surviving from the early church. In its entire compass, the series includes eighteen sermons delivered to catechumens preparing for baptism and five "mystagogical" discourses to newly baptized believers seeking to learn the Christian way. Cyril's "catechetical discourses" were widely circulated during the last half of the fourth century. Not only so, they have been revived and widely used as catechetical and spiritual formation models from time to time in the intervening centuries. The substance of Cyril's lectures has to do with doctrines, sacraments, rites, and practices. He also delivered at least a "fair share" of exhortation.[18]

Cyril's discourses can hardly be described as original. As a matter of fact he followed a kind of syllabus, or standard curriculum, for baptismal catechesis that appears to have been current in the fourth century. The indications are that baptism required an extensive orientation into the Christian community, still recovering from intense persecution. These discourses are quite obviously patterned according to the historic prototype. Cyril took theological doctrines that he found in the Scriptures and expounded them to his hearers with the expectation that the content, once internalized, would foster the qualities that he envisioned as necessary for becoming a true member of the mystical and eternal community, the church.[19]

Chrysostom (ca. 347-407)

John of Constantinople was probably the most prominent scholar/preacher of the ancient Greek church. He is often credited as being one of the greatest Christian preachers who ever lived. The name by which John is most often remembered, "Chrysostom," means "golden mouthed." It was obviously given as a tribute to his eloquence. His treatise *Address on Vainglory and the Right Way for Parents to Bring Up Their Children*[20] has exercised a salutary influence upon church education at several junctures in history. Beyond that small, but important, contribution to religious education, numerous passages in his voluminous works dwell upon the responsibilities of parents to provide a Christian education for their children.

One would be hard-pressed to defend classifying Chrysostom as a full-blown proponent of the historic understanding of religious education. His wise, "spiritually turned" thinking dwelt more upon broad Christian life goals than upon the process of reaching them.

Even so, his works demonstrate a deep and sympathetic understanding of the developing Christian's mind.[21]

Augustine (354-430)

Augustine grew up in what is now Algeria, North Africa. He received a thorough Christian training from his zealous Christian mother, Monica. While searching for "truth" in his late teens, he experienced a kind of conversion away from his childhood faith to philosophy. After spending a portion of his early adult life teaching rhetoric, Augustine traveled to Milan, Italy where he came under the powerful preaching of Ambrose. Converting back to Christianity, he was baptized by Ambrose in 387. After abandoning his teaching profession he eventually returned to Africa where, in 395, he was consecrated Bishop of Hippo. From this small Numidian city, Augustine became one of the most important figures in history.

Although he is most often recalled as a theologian, a number of Augustine's works played major roles in shaping the way that the church educates its converts, as well as its young. With considerable insight, *The Teacher* (ca. 389), cast as a dialogue with his son Adeodatus, Augustine addresses the issue of how the learner learns. He observes that one learns not merely from words, but as God works within the learner.[22] *First Catechetical Instruction* (ca. 400) is a practical statement of Augustine's method for instructing new converts. He argues that the effective teacher must (1) know the topic, (2) know the learner, (3) vary the method according to circumstances, and (4) engage the learner's response.[23]

Augustine's understanding of the nature and role of education in incorporating new members into the church is so insightful that Sloyan suggests, "No one, actually, who teaches religion can afford to be unfamiliar with Augustine's uncanny analysis of the apostolate. His insights into the characters of teacher and taught are beyond price."[24] His model of religious education required a commitment to the content of the Scriptures and to a theology that was rooted in revelation as God's message. In some ways, Augustine's works on Christian education mark the high point of the catechumenate and set a standard to which reformers seeking renewal along the lines of the early church have often sought to return. Thus Augustine's writings seem to have informed the curriculum developers of both Lutheran and Catholic catechisms during the Reformation and Counter-Reformation more than 1,000 years after his death. Again, during the intellectual ferment at the beginning of the twentieth century, traditional theorists rediscovered in the works of the Bishop of Hippo a resource for restating the historic prototype along the lines that we will later discuss under the evangelical/kerygmatic model.[25]

THE FIFTH THROUGH THE FIFTEENTH CENTURIES

The creative energy that had sustained the church's educational efforts during earlier centuries, when it was facing the twin threats of heresy from within and persecution from without, began to dissipate during the fifth century. Thus the catechumenate, that had been so important to the basic education of succeeding generations for more than three centuries, began to lose its vitality. By the seventh century it seems to have all but disappeared as a viable institution. just as the disintegration of the Roman Empire undermined appreciation of learning and scholarship, so it also contributed to a kind of intellectual stagnation in Christian education. Of course this stagnation may have been related to the lessened dynamic in the instructional situation. In another idiom, powerful instructional processes such as the catechumenate, originally intended to prepare a new Christian to resist both heresy and persecution, seem to have given way to milder processes such as token memorization of the creeds and commandments. These processes were better fitted to prepare the individual for a relatively passive participation in the prevailing Christian culture.

Beginning in the fifth century, the challenge of expansion into Europe and the British Isles did produce some revivals of educational fervor. Thus such evangelist/educators as Patrick, Columban, Augustine of Canterbury, and Boniface occasionally revived concepts that were reminiscent of the catechumenate. Even so, these educational leaders, responding to their own cultural situation, commonly simplified the catechumenate both as to process and content. Those sketchy outlines of Christian instruction that survive from the period suggest that topics of special interest included: (1) the futility of idol worship; (2) the need to believe in the Creator God who sent His Son for our salvation; (3) the obligation of personally accepting the "Gospel"; (4) the codification of Christian beliefs through memorization of the creed and the "Our Father"; and (5) if not baptized beforehand as an infant, to seal these beliefs in baptism. It is surely not difficult to discern the primary structures of the historic prototype operating in these practices.[26]

By the middle of the ninth century a developing attitude, which later blossomed into scholasticism, began to be felt in the evolution of the question and answer format. Alcuin, for example, composed a series of nearly 300 such queries for his commentary, *Interrogationes et responsiones in Genesin*. The organizing principle of question and answer was later expanded still further with considerable indebtedness to Origen and other scholars of earlier centuries. Some of the work of this genre has been judged it analytical to the point of pedantry…orderly, exhaustive, removed from the spirit of Christ's preaching, repellant to the youthful mind."[27] Much of this curriculum, it should be noted, was reserved for episcopal schools intending to prepare clergy rather than to educate Christians generally.

The tenth and eleventh centuries witnessed educational processes with a growing sacramental flavor that appear catechetical only in a remote sense. Much popular religious education seems to have been primarily rote memorization of the creed, the Our Father, the Hail Mary, and the Ten Commandments with some enrichment through the use of pictures and "spiritual stories." This process was supplemented in an important way by that modest exposure to doctrine to which the ordinary Christian was granted through the architecture and art in cathedrals and churches, as well as through celebrations relating to the Christian year.

During the twelfth through the fifteenth centuries the church was near the pinnacle of that vision of an earthly kingdom of God articulated by Augustine in his *City of God*.[28] Perhaps related to the developing awareness of the worth and value of individual human beings, some modest efforts were made by the church to insure the proper religious education of its young. For example, in 1186 the synod of Dublin issued an order reminding priests of their responsibility under God to faithfully catechize children and, in 1254, the synod of Albi ruled that children of seven or older must be fittingly instructed in Christian doctrine.[29]

With the evolution of commercial life in Europe there was a rapidly growing need for literacy. As schools were raised up to meet this need, instruction in Christian doctrine was sometimes added to the secular core of reading, writing, and arithmetic. Even so, Jesuit liturgist Josef Jungmann observes, the most powerful education "came from the formative influence of a world imbued with a Christian spirit." This environmental dimension, identified and elaborated by Jungmann, certainly does seem worth thinking about. The evidence seems to support him in that, during significant portions of the later medieval period, Christian rites were observed with more seriousness of purpose than in some earlier centuries. Baptism, for example, was treated with greater solemnity as a point of entry into the Christian community. In this connection, by the fourteenth century, the role of godparents had become a keystone element in the religious education process.[30]

REPRESENTATIVE EDUCATORS: FIFTH THROUGH FIFTEENTH CENTURIES

Benedict of Nursia (480-543)

Benedict was born at Nursia, Umbria. Early in his life he pursued a formal education in Rome. Shocked at the undisciplined and dissolute living of his fellows, he left school to live in a cave. Benedict's example of single-minded dedication to the Christian faith brought a number of invitations for him to found a cloister. Eventually, in 529, he made his famous journey to a picturesque mountain between Rome and Naples where he organized the Monte Cassino. It was expressly intended as a "school for the Lord's service." Here Benedict devised the ideals and practices which became the basis for the "Benedictine Rule."[31] The Rule reflects Benedict's organizational genius, his acute insight into human nature, and his balance between the "contemplative" and the "active." The Benedictine Rule institutionalized monastic life and set the standard that has continued from the sixth century to the present.

The aims of education under monasticism were determined by the aims of monastic life itself. Such aims included physical and moral discipline under the overarching goal of the soul's salvation. An underlying notion which affected the monastic approach to education was that the material world was pernicious. Thus salvation could be certain only through rigorous self-discipline, celibacy, self-denial, and devotion. Monks exercised ("asceticism" is linguistically linked with the notion of exercise in the gymnastic disciplines) by disciplining desires and renouncing the world, including claims of family and society. From another perspective, the monasteries contributed to the preservation of learning, especially in the early Middle Ages when they were the only secure places where scholars could retreat to study, meditate, and write. Thus, institutions such as the Monte Cassino played a major role in the preservation of learning in an age of cultural decline. The fact is much of the treasure of Western learning was preserved as a heritage for later ages by disciplined monks.

One of Benedict's distinctive contributions was that manual labor was dignified. Benedictines were required to till the soil as well as to pray and to study. Under the Rule, distinct times were reserved for labor, for sacred reading, and for prayer. Idleness was considered the great enemy of the soul. Although his detractors have criticized Benedict for his austerity, it seems a fair judgment that the disciplines he imposed on his followers did much to insure the continuity of the church during the more disruptive periods of the Middle Ages. Indeed, it could be argued that the surfacing of Benedictine values in Europe during the later Middle Ages gave sticking power to the dreams of a more industrialized culture.[32]

Alcuin (735-804)

Alcuin received his formal education at the famous cathedral school at York under the mentorship of its headmaster, Ethelbert. Here he was imbued with a passion for study and a wholehearted reverence for the Roman tradition. He succeeded Ethelbert as York's headmaster in 766. Later, with the support and encouragement of the pope, he accepted a call from Emperor Charlemagne to become master of the palace school at Aachen in 781. Breaking with tradition, Alcuin chose not to serve within the palace as teacher, but rather to address his energies to the Empire's need for both sacred and secular learning. He initiated and superintended a movement for learning that was to some extent focused in Charlemagne's proclamation of 787. In this declaration, Charlemagne called upon bishops to cultivate the study of letters so as to provide a better basis for decisions and to undergird right actions on the part of educated persons. The resulting "Carolingian Renaissance" found much of its inspiration both in a return to classical scholarship and to early Christianity for its models. One important by-product of Alcuin's reforms was the revived theological vigor which grew out of the renewed intellectual activity.

With respect to his specific contributions to Christian religious education, Alcuin is sometimes credited with having been the originator of the catechetical or "question-and-answer" method of instruction. Whether or not he was the originator, he did use the catechetical method in the palace school as a primary means of instructing students in the seven liberal arts. Whatever his direct benefactions to Christian education might have been, he does seem to have been a major contributor to the then growing European vision for a program of broad-based fundamental education available to the general citizenry. Late in Alcuin's career he was appointed abbot of St. Martins, Tours. Under his leadership the school at Tours became the "nursery" of ecclesiastical and liberal education for much of Europe.[33]

Hrabanus Maurus (776-856)

Hrabanus Maurus entered the Benedictine order about the turn of the ninth century to become a monk in the monastery which had been founded at Fulda by St. Boniface. He was sent to Tours where he spent a year studying and absorbing something of Alcuin's enthusiasm for scholarship. He was elected abbot in 802, and under his rule Fulda rose to occupy the place of eminence in learning that had belonged to Tours a generation earlier. As a thinker and educational innovator, Maurus was more vigorous and independent than Alcuin.

Prominent in the resurgence of learning that was continuing to spread across Europe, Maurus' writings were widely read and respected. He was also highly regarded for his "efficiency" as an educator. As with others of his age, though, his attention focused more intently upon religious and professional matters than upon strictly educational ones. Maurus' best known work, *On the Education of Clergy*,[34] deals largely with church organization, with orders of clergy, and with details of ritual. Marique quotes a brief passage from this work which gives some insight into Maurus' imaginative understanding of teaching and scholarship: "All the useful knowledge that lies in the books of the heathen, and the salutary truths of the Scriptures as well are to be used for one purpose and referred to one end—that is—the perfect knowledge of truth and of the highest wisdom."[35]

It is clear that Maurus was the most important Christian religious educator of the ninth century. Although he contributed only sparsely to what might be called educational theory, he did contribute energy and vision for an educational process that offered a broader base for the church, and for Western culture, than was the case with educators in the centuries immediately preceding his life.

Thomas Aquinas (ca. 1225-1274)

Thomas Aquinas was born near Naples and received his earlier education at the Benedictine monastery of Monte Cassino. Eventually he entered the Order of Preachers (Dominicans) and pursued a higher education at the University of Paris where his mentor was Albert the Great. Albert exposed his student to Aristotelian thought which blossomed in the structures and tenor of Thomas' mature intellectual life. The pinnacle of Thomas' thought was surely his *Summa Theologica*[36] with its "magnificent dialectical architecture." This work was the summit of more than a century of rapid intellectual growth on the European continent. Ulich observes that it would be difficult to find any other period in history with which to compare its progress toward classical mastership.[37]

With the exception of the very modest contribution of his work, "De Magistro,"[38] even the genius of Thomas Aquinas was not highly productive in regard to the direct development of useful educational theory. As was true of his contemporaries, most of Aquinas' theorizing was largely borrowed from models dependent upon ancient sources. Then too, in order to do justice to the role of

Aquinas as an educator, one must include in the standard of judgment his important contributions to the education of the Catholic clergy. Even though his primary work was only obliquely related to education, Aquinas' original work in metaphysics, psychology, and epistemology provided the categories of thought which have informed and shaped the course of Christian education for more than eight centuries. In this regard, Thomas' convictions were based upon Aristotelian principles of causality in which God, as ultimate cause, is the end toward which all being is directed. Accordingly, his was a theocentric view of man which fit in quite nicely with the historic model.[39]

Thomas Aquinas and the Dominicans have often been identified with a method of inquiry and also of teaching known as "the disputation." His *Quaestiones Disputatae*[40] remains the best known, most complete, and probably finest example of the disputation employed as an academic exercise. Although little known today, the disputation with its formalized process of analysis and synthesis through structured questioning affords a potentially healthy tension between faith and reason. As such it offers a certain power to deal with, and to rethink, significant religious issues in a spirit of balanced earnestness and tolerance.[41]

John Gerson (1363-1429)

Scattered through histories of both secular and Christian education, one finds numerous references to the contributions of John Gerson. Gerson's life and work is well worth considering from the perspective of any serious Christian. Shortly after having completed his formal studies in theology, Gerson succeeded to the powerful position of chancellor of the University of Paris. During the early years of the fifteenth century, while at the height of his power, he exerted a formative influence upon both academic and religious instruction. Although a true Roman Catholic, Gerson argued for change along a number of lines that became hallmarks of the sixteenth-century Reformation. For example, he regarded the Bible as the proper foundation of Christian knowledge and he argued that a General Council was superior to the pope.

Gerson's most often mentioned work is *On Leading the Young Toward Christ*. This defense of the dignity of teaching, and analysis of the conditions under which meaningful religious learning occurs, is indeed impressive. Observe Gerson's argument: "But where there is no love, what good is instruction, as one neither likes to listen to it nor properly believes the words heard, nor follows the commandment! Therefore it is best to forego all false dignity and to become a child among children." Some scholars regard this rather unknown work as the finest piece of medieval educational literature.[42]

Gerson faithfully reserved major blocks of time for teaching the catechism to children, even during the busy years of his chancellorship. He also sought reform in the presentation of theological matters to laypersons. Accordingly, Gerson required his theological faculty to give attention to providing books "for simple folk." His own effort along these lines resulted in a number of widely circulated pieces bearing on such themes as the commandments, confession, and how to die well. Gerson is probably best remembered for his emphasis on love as the beginning and end of Christian experience, the true tie between God and humankind.[43]

THE SIXTEENTH CENTURY

One fruit of the Renaissance that flowered in the fourteenth and fifteenth centuries was a humanistically energized self-assertion against tradition. The mood in Europe at the beginning of the sixteenth century demanded a more empirical testing of values than had earlier ages. This ethos unveiled a new conception of education, wherein an important goal was to produce an independent, self-disciplined person. Doctrinally, the notion of original sin gave way to a tolerant interpretation of human nature which was in accord with the more lenient pedagogy. The great Rotterdam humanist, Erasmus, gathered up one version of this mentality in his vision for a society that could appreciate the true meaning and simplicity of religion. He wanted schools to awaken the mind and soul of the learner, with maturity as a goal. Erasmus argued that such an education would bring about the learner's commitment to the Christian faith along with needed skills in speaking, writing, and living.

Alongside this liberalizing spirit there was a growing movement stressing the need for a return to the ancient church's purity. Moved by these restorationist sentiments, the Protestant Reformers merely served to hasten the already approaching end of tolerance in matters of religion. By mid-century the spirit of the times had become decidedly unfriendly to liberal thought. The Roman Catholic response was a return to severe discipline with a fixation upon traditional dogma. In the context of this rapidly changing environment, humanism was pitched out of the religious arena to find its energies renewed in later centuries through its influence upon philosophy, aesthetics, and modern science. Erasmus seemed the only major figure able to bridge the gulf between Renaissance and Reformation. He poured considerable energy into his search for a middle road, but in the end found himself distrusted by Catholics and scorned by Luther.[44]

In some ways the Reformation has exerted a controlling influence on the course of religious education well into the twentieth century. The need to define one's version of Christianity, and to present it in a defensible form, was reminiscent of the way that Christians of the early church defined and defended their faith before a pagan world. The need of the times was for heroes. Such heroes arose to forcefully lead a wide variety of educational endeavors calculated to produce faithful adherents of the faith on both sides of the Protestant/Catholic divide. Three of these heroic leaders, more than any others, seem to have decided the future of Christian religious education during the earlier years of the Reformation: Martin Luther and John Calvin on the Protestant side, with Ignatius Loyola on the Catholic side.[45]

REPRESENTATIVE SIXTEENTH-CENTURY RELIGIOUS EDUCATORS

Martin Luther (1483-1546)

Born of peasant stock at Eisleben, Germany, Martin Luther was given an early classical education that was later sharpened at the University of Erfurt. In 1505, a profound religious experience, precipitated by a narrow escape from death, moved Luther to become an Augustinian monk. Here Luther exercised his considerable intellect in studying the Bible under his mentor, Johann von Staupitz. Luther suffered from a tremendous sense of guilt during his early years as a monk. This was not an uncommon phenomenon; guilt was deliberately employed as a formative tool by the late medieval church. Eventually his studies of the Apostle Paul's writings brought freedom through a life-changing insight into the central significance of faith. This insight armed Luther with a passionate personal faith. It also turned him away from scholastic Aristotelianism, with its rationality to a "truth that reveals itself in faith." Equipped with this understanding, Luther came to perceive that the individual can be reconciled to God and that God can be reconciled to the individual.[46]

The humanistic thought that was abroad in the early sixteenth century functioned as a catalyst for Luther to capture the minds of the people with his message of individual salvation through "faith alone." Apparently, at the beginning of his protest he did not intend to become a revolutionary. His intention was decidedly conservative, namely to recover and preserve a "pure faith" and a "Pure church." Under any condition, through Luther's efforts major segments of the church experienced a redirection toward emphasizing a more personal relationship between the individual and God. One consequence of this chain of events was that Christian religious teaching assumed a new shape in both lower and higher education. In brief, the dialectic of Scholasticism was rejected for an attempt to discover the original message of the Scriptures. Biblical languages replaced Latin as a vehicle of thought in accord with Luther's often quoted statement: "The languages are the scabbard in which the Word of God is sheathed."[47] In time, the scholarly energies unleashed by Luther and the Reformation caused the humanists to fear that their own endeavor was being put in the shade.

To Luther, nothing seemed of greater importance than good schools. The right kind of schools, he argued, would not only prepare individuals for the tasks of industry and government, but they would accomplish the greater goal of teaching every Christian to read the Bible. His "Letter to Mayors and Aldermen of All the

Cities of Germany in Behalf of Christian Schools"[48] is but one example of Luther's culture-changing writings on education.

On any list of Luther's contributions to Christian religious education, one must surely include the following four. (1) His translation of the Bible may well have been his most noble achievement, for he successfully rendered the biblical idiom into the Germanic way of thinking.[49] (2) His large and small catechisms were apparently motivated by the low level of Christian consciousness he discovered while on his pastoral rounds. In the spring of 1529, as a direct effort to lift his followers to a higher plane of Christian life, he published a "large catechism," intended for pastors and adult leaders.[50] This was followed a few months later by the "small catechism," intended as a guide for home-based instruction. A number of scholars consider this smaller catechism to be among the greatest masterpieces in Christian religious education.[51] (3) His creation and popularization of the Protestant hymn taught almost all Christians to sing. The singing of hymns was also a recommended part of the Lutheran family's catechetical hour. Indeed, one Jesuit is reported to have mourned that Luther's hymns killed more souls than his sermons.[52] (4) Finally, he profoundly influenced the establishment of Christian schools. From one perspective, Luther's primary impact upon the course of European culture was in the educational arena as he directly involved secular authorities in casting a new shape for education. Even so, Luther's primary concern was a religious one, rooted in his concept of the priesthood of all believers. This concern energized his emphasis upon biblical learning.[53]

In many ways Luther's educational contributions amounted to a revival and refocusing of the historic model that had reached its literary peak in the writings of Augustine more than 1,100 years before Luther's period of greatest influence. Accordingly, it is important to remember that Augustine's thought was among the shaping influences on Luther in his formative years.[54]

John Calvin (1509-1564)

Born in Picardy, France, John Calvin received his early education at the University of Paris. Later, he acceded to his father's wishes and pursued the study of law at the University of Orleans. Following his father's death in 1531, and intent on becoming a "man of letters," Calvin returned to Paris to follow the study of his first love, the humanities. In 1533, when he was twenty-four years old, Calvin experienced a "sudden conversion" that resulted in a conviction both of God's sovereignty and of the utmost importance of living according to His will. At first he seems to have given little thought to leaving the Catholic Church, but he was shortly preaching and teaching elements of his new faith. Influenced by Nicholas Cop, Calvin's increasingly evangelical messages created such a stir that he was forced to flee from France. Following a period of itinerate ministry intermixed with scholarly pursuits, he made his home in Geneva, Switzerland, where he found the environment to support his life's work as the key shaper of Protestantism.

Calvin's *Institutes of the Christian Religion*,[55] first published in 1536 and in a number of revisions thereafter, earned him a rightful place among the great system-builders of the Christian faith. He had much in common with Luther, especially (1) in their agreement that the Bible is a "never-to-be-doubted" religious authority and (2) in their affirmation of the value of education in moving Christians toward a unity with God and with each other. On the other hand, Calvin was a more logical thinker than Luther. His mind carried any premise to its ultimate conclusion. Thus, while Calvin and Luther had similar underlying convictions concerning humankind's dependence upon divine dispensation, it was Calvin's development of the doctrine of God's sovereignty that effected the greatest difference in the development of Reformed theology.

For more than four centuries, Protestant education has been profoundly influenced by the philosophy that Calvin developed through his "Geneva experiment" during the middle decades of the sixteenth century. In 1536, shortly after Guillaume Farel prevailed upon him to cease from his itineracy and to make Geneva his home, Calvin outlined for the citizens a constitution which included a school. Attendance was intended to be compulsory, the poor paying no fees. By 1538, Calvin's early plans had gone awry. He was expelled from the city by Geneva's citizens, once they perceived the radical nature of his planned political and educational reforms.

Calvin was recalled in 1541 and, in addition to extensive political authority, given the power to effect his educational plan. He implemented his plan through the development of an academy to the extent possible in an environment where much of his energy had to be diverted to theological and political issues. His clear goal was to develop Geneva along the lines of a theocracy in which the kingdom of God could be fully realized. The academy, which was evolved during the 1540s and 1550s, offered an education which was in some respects quite humanistic. For example, disciplines in which instruction was offered included reading, writing, and arithmetic as well as classical languages, arts, and rhetoric. However the core of the curriculum was the Bible. "Now, in order that true religion may shine upon us," Calvin states, "we ought to hold that it must take its beginning from heavenly doctrine and that no one can get even the slightest taste of right and sound doctrine unless he be a pupil of scripture."[56] In contrast to Luther's model where the school was under the state, Calvin's model brought the school directly under the control of the church. Every teacher taught under strict ecclesiastical discipline. All were required to subscribe to the Confession of Faith. In turn, teachers were expected to exercise close supervision of their students' beliefs and styles of life.[57]

It should be obvious that the model of education from which Calvin worked is closely linked to the historic prototype. His profound influence toward conserving and firming of this model in succeeding centuries is probably due not only to his educational theory, but also to the impact his theology has had upon the development of the church in Switzerland as well as in Holland, Scotland, Germany, and the United States.

Ignatius of Loyola (1491-1556)

Ignatius of Loyola was born into a noble, yet relatively obscure, family from northern Spain. Although he was early on dedicated to the service of the church, his formative years were invested as a page in the court of Ferdinand and Isabella.[58] His early adult years were spent as a soldier. Ignatius was enamored of the chivalric tradition and caught the passion, common among Spaniards of the period, to become a knight in the service of God. The catalytic events that brought his life into focus began with his reading of *The Life of*

Christ by Lodolph of Saxony and *Legena aurea*, a book relating stories of the saints' lives. This occurred while he was recuperating from a laming wound inflicted by a French cannonball. The above mentioned readings had such a deep effect that Ignatius experienced a profound spiritual conversion. This conversion, in turn, issued in his resolve to live as a soldier/knight wholly devoted to Christ.

When he had sufficiently recovered from his wound, Ignatius withdrew to a cave at Manresa, near Barcelona, where he engaged in a year of prayer and penance. At Manresa, Ignatius experienced private and indescribable encounters with God, often in the form of blinding, ecstatic visions. His reflections on his spiritual journey, together with his insights on organizing and making sense of religious experience, became the primary substance of his *Spiritual Exercises*.[59] First published in 1548, the Exercises insured that Ignatius would be remembered among the giants of Spanish mysticism and of formative spirituality.

In 1524, after he had come to a clearer insight in regard to his own journey, Ignatius seriously began his proper education with the study of Latin. Eventually he settled at the University of Paris from 1528-1535 where he earned his M.A. degree. Ignatius also recruited six of the "brightest and best" (Francis Xavier, Peter Faber, Diego Laynez, Alfonso Salmeron, Simon Rodriguez, and Nicholas de Bobadilla). These joined him in the vows that consequently led to the formation of the "Society of Jesus," popularly known as the Jesuits. By order of Pope Paul III, the Society was formally established in 1540. Ignatius was elected superior general. In this office, he devoted the last fifteen years of his life to shaping the growing order from its headquarters in Rome. An elitist corps from its inception, the Jesuits recruited and accepted only physically strong men of sound character. Prospective Jesuits were required to progress through a rigorous twelve-year program that climaxed with a special vow of obedience to the pope.

As was the case with Luther and Calvin, Ignatius sensed a need to return to the purity of the ancient church. But his answer to this perceived need was his attempt to revive Catholic piety by militantly affirming traditional dogma and by paying attention "to the cultivation of the heart." Marching, as it were, under their motto "All for the greater glory of God" (*Omnia ad Majorem Del Gloriam*), Jesuits did much to restore Catholicism's fighting spirit. Using their four major tools, the pulpit, the confessional, the mission, and the school, Jesuits played an important role in controlling the expansion of Protestantism. Furthermore they defined and spread the Catholic faith in large portions of Africa, the Americas, and the Orient.

The school, functioning under educational principles first articulated by Ignatius and refined in practice, became a kind of spine for the entire Jesuit enterprise. Ignatius was not a creator of educational theory, but he recognized what worked and he was a superb organizer of what he absorbed from others. The most mature expression of Ignatius' educational thought is in his *Constitutions*,[60] which, after official approval in 1558, became "both the inspiring force and the official law" in Jesuit schools. This treatise made it abundantly clear that Ignatius and the Jesuits: (1) aimed first of all to bring students to a knowledge of God and the salvation of their souls; (2) intended to integrate the major branches of learning in such a way that they would be illuminated by God's revelation; (3) relied heavily upon theology as the branch of study which ties other branches into a unity, all other disciplines being regarded as "handmaids"; (4) sought a balance of intellect and acquisition of good habits; (5) placed a high estimate on the formative role of the faithful teacher; and (6) expected to pour capable leaders into the social order.[61]

The Jesuits seem to have been the first major religious order to undertake the development of a complete system of Christian schooling as one of its major ministries. Within a very few years, Jesuit schools were located in many countries. They were governed by common principles, and they followed a standard curriculum. Jesuit schools were able to exchange teachers when needed and they were subject to evaluation based on an established norm. Furthermore, they did not exist to perfect the individual so much as to lead him (Jesuit schools were for males) to accept without question the dogma of the Catholic Church. The limited curriculum did aim to produce readiness of speech, a quick wit, and a good memory. The boy who left even a lower level school was thoroughly trained to feel at ease in many situations and "to be in control." Even Protestant families often sent their boys to Jesuit schools because of the excellence of the training.[62]

As to its specifically religious content, the thrust of Jesuit schooling was clearly along the lines of the historic theological model of religious education. Succeeding generations of Jesuits, such as Peter Canisius (1521-1597), have drawn support from and given shape to this model. Canisius, by the way, is best remembered for his monumental catechism first published in 1555, and in a number of versions thereafter.[63]

THE SEVENTEENTH THROUGH THE NINETEENTH CENTURIES

Beginning about the middle of the seventeenth century, for the first time in at least 1,000 years, a deliberate attempt was made to organize a religiously neutral civilization intellectually independent of the Christian church. This great transformation was largely accomplished during the course of the seventeenth and eighteenth centuries and is commonly described as the *Enlightenment*. One key feature of the Enlightenment was the rise of an awareness of individuals as autonomous personalities. Something within the human spirit arose to seize and to exercise freedom in a way that had been unknown before. To be sure, the passage of time, especially the arrival of the nineteenth century, brought periods of criticism with respect to Enlightenment thought. On the whole, though, the sense of individual identity and the appetite for freedom that were awakened during the seventeenth and eighteenth centuries have never been reversed.

The nascent patterns of thought described above seem to have created the religious, cultural, and political environment that made possible the "Peace of Westphalia" (1648) which ended the Thirty Years' War. This war was among the later fruits of the Reformation, which had fostered such sharp distinctions among perspectives on the Christian faith. Thus, at least ostensibly, the Thirty Years' War was pursued in the interests of the particular religious group (church) identified with the individual European states involved in that debilitating conflict. The Peace represented a military stalemate between the states and signified a religious stalemate for the Reformation and the Counter-Reformation movements. The medieval spirit which persisted somewhat beyond the Reformation had largely dissipated by the middle of the seventeenth century. Thus, Westphalia brought us to the threshold of the modern world. This was a world in which, among other things, questions of war and peace would be settled criteria far removed from theological conviction.[64]

For the historian of thought, the Enlightenment represents the arrival of a new form of subjectivism for which earlier expressions of nominalism and humanism had paved the way. Breaking with the boundaries imposed by various forms of institutionalism, seventeenth- and eighteenth-century thinkers generated a passion for inquiry which to a significant degree laicized culture. This contributed to the breaking up of the aristocratic court society and introduced the patterns of thought that characterized the bourgeois nineteenth century in which the working class gained significant freedom to grow and to express. Relatedly, the growing passion for fulfillment which eventually filtered down to the lower classes contributed to a growing appetite for education. From one perspective within the church, Enlightenment thought spawned John Wesley's Methodism with its vision of a perfected society rooted in a new application of historic Christian doctrine. At the same time, from a point of view located outside of the church, the Enlightenment encouraged the perspective enunciated by David Hume that also regarded humankind as perfectible, but in this case through the use of reason, science, and natural rights.[65]

A number of the more important theological and psychological trends that contributed to the development of religious educational theory in the twentieth century will be discussed in the succeeding chapter. At this point, a churchman educator from each of the three centuries touched upon in this segment has been selected as a representative religious educator from this period. These are John Amos Comenius, a bishop of the Czech Brethren in the seventeenth century; John Wesley, leader of the Methodist revival in the eighteenth century; and John Henry Cardinal Newman, a leader in the Oxford (tractarian) movement and later Roman Catholic

Cardinal in the nineteenth century. None of these would today be considered professional religious educators, but each contributed significantly to religious education practice within his own century as well as with continuing effect into the twentieth century. Also, each of these thinkers contributed at least modestly to the development of religious education theory well beyond the particular denomination with which they were identified.

REPRESENTATIVE EDUCATORS: THE SEVENTEENTH THROUGH THE NINETEENTH CENTURIES

John Amos Comenius (1592-1670)

In his early years Comenius was surrounded by the legendary strength of a pietistic family associated with the Czech Brethren. Though orphaned at the age of twelve, he was fortunate in having faithful family friends who arranged for his basic Latin education. These friends also helped him enter the excellent Reformed gymnasium at Herborn and later supported him as he matriculated at the University of Heidelburg. In 1614, with his essential education in hand, Comenius returned to Moravia to enter the ministry among the Czech Brethren. Later known as Moravians, the Brethren traced their ecclesiastical lineage from John Hus, the martyred fifteenth-century reformer.

Comenius accomplished much of his most creative work during the troublous times of the Thirty Years' War. Early in the war he lost his wife and children to the plague and almost all of his earlier scholarly work was destroyed by invading forces. In the turmoil surrounding the war, Comenius became an itinerate scholar-preacher, later a bishop. Having lost his native land and most of the structures of his church, he became a citizen of the world and a pastor within the larger church. Comenius was thus among the first true ecumenists. Few facts from the sparse records prior to the "Peace of Westphalia" in 1648 satisfy scholars inquiring into reasons for the eventual greatness of his influential life. Spinka's assessment is that Comenius "was the sort of man whom the old stories would have liked: who since he was unable to control external circumstances, strives to rule that which is subject to his own will—the citadel of *his own soul.*"[66]

Nourished beyond his own distress through his developing convictions about how to shape the future, Comenius was struck by the power of education to transform children into mature adults. He was convinced that through properly ordering education, competent and morally responsible adults could be developed who would make right decisions about their own lives and the lives of others. These were the ones, he believed, who would determine what manner of world would come into being. Spinka believes that Comenius was "an educator who in defiance of the sorry present, dreamed a better future which would be built only by better men."[67]

Comenius reflected the typical educational understandings of his times, but he was also far ahead of his times. (1) He was among the first to emphasize the power of learning by doing: "What has to be done must be learned by practice."[68] (2) He was a pioneer in advancing the notion of individual differences. (3) He combated those schools of his day that operated as "slaughterhouses of the mind" by appealing for an education that was vital and pleasurable: "education shall be conducted without blows...as gently and pleasantly as possible."[69] (4) He anticipated the developmental emphases which would come to characterize certain facts of modern religious education theory. "The seeds of knowledge, of virtue, and of piety are...naturally implanted in us; but the actual knowledge, virtue, and piety are not so given. These must be acquired by prayer, by education, and by action."[70] (5) He advocated that free education be made available to male and female, rich and poor. (6) He revolutionized the teaching of languages through his 1631 publication of *Janua Linguarium Reserata* (The Gate of Languages Unlocked).[71] This work shifted the emphasis in language learning from rote learning of words to making connections between words and things. (7) Finally, Comenius ambitiously proposed to work out a system for classifying and relating all of human knowledge according to a scheme anchored by three principles: induction, reason, and revelation.[72]

In a number of ways, Comenius' thought was compatible with the historic prototype of religious education. For example, his views on revelation were about the same as those of the reformers. However, with his crusade against meaningless words, his emphasis upon the practical, his attention focused upon the "real," and his insistence upon firsthand experience, Comenius softened the sharper edges of the prototype and laid at least some of the foundations upon which contemporary theories have been erected.

John Wesley (1703-1791)

John Wesley was born in the rectory of the Church of England at Epworth. His father, Samuel, was deeply influenced by Puritan sentiments, but loyal to the established church. John's mother, Susanna, apparently possessed an even stronger personality than did Samuel. She seems to have had gifts for both scholarship and leadership, but her place in history is secured by her reputation as both mother and teacher to the large family of Wesley children. Susanna reportedly spent a full hour every week alone with each of her children to assure their religious development and academic progress. Later, having earned their way into Oxford University, John and his brother Charles began to practice the disciplined lifestyle , in part absorbed from the environment of the Epworth parsonage, that eventually earned for them the cynical nickname, "Methodist." The Methodist movement, as such, began in earnest with John's religious awakening on May 24, 1738. Before the middle of the century, Methodist societies were in evidence throughout England; by the end of John's long life, in 1791, they were known throughout much of the world.

John Wesley's place in religious education was secured during the tumultuous years in the middle of the eighteenth century when England was in the grip of the early Industrial Revolution. Wesley's Methodists focused their ministry mainly upon the unlearned, poorer levels of English society. They worked precisely among those most affected by the dreary quality of life offered in the sweatshop culture of the times. It is reported that in the England of Wesley's early ministry only one child in twenty-five attended any kind of school.[73] Wesley was convinced that the results of Methodist revivalism could be made permanent only as new members could be properly educated. Accomplishing his broad vision required addressing the need for basic education including essentials of such topics as hygiene and medicine. For Wesley, education was not secondary to evangelism, it was bound together with it. Methodist preachers were charged to "diligently and earnestly instruct the children" and to make a place for them to grow within the Methodist societal structure.[74]

Wesley gave considerable attention to the educational thinkers of his day, especially Locke, Milton, and Rousseau. He was also acquainted with at least some aspects of Comenius' thought. While not an especially original theorist himself, Wesley was quite willing to experiment with new ideas. Wesley's long interest in education may be observed most easily in his development of a number of schools. The most prominent among these was Kingswood, founded in 1739 near Bristol. The stated aim for Kingswood was to teach children "how to think, and judge, and act according to the strictest rules of Christianity."[75] In addition to his interest in boarding and day schools, Wesley was among the first religious leaders to incorporate the Sunday School into his ministry plans. The accepted date for Robert Raikes' founding of the Sunday School is usually 1780. Consider, then, Wesley's journal entry for July 18, 1784: "Before service I stepped into the S.S. which contains 240 children.... Perhaps God may have a deeper end therein than men are aware of. Who knows but what these schools may become nurseries for Christians."[76] Wesley's influence is commonly judged to have been among the primary reasons for the rapid rise of the Sunday School during the late eighteenth century. In many ways Wesley was a child of the Enlightenment. The radical individualism implied by Methodism's organization that functioned almost entirely outside of the established church would have been quite unthinkable before the time in which he lived. Nonetheless, the theoretical weight of Wesley's ideals were rooted in his understanding of the authority of the Bible. Thus it seems fair to judge that, in most respects, Wesley was a key eighteenth-century proponent of the historic prototype.

John Henry Cardinal Newman (1801-1890)

John Henry Newman's father was a London banker. His mother, a pious woman of French Huguenot descent, seems to have been a primary influence upon the development of his spiritually sensitive nature. But it was under the influence of the headmaster at Ealing that, at the age of fifteen, Newman experienced the evangelical conversion that so deeply affected his later life. He entered Oxford in 1817 and was elected fellow at Oriel College in 1822. In this setting, Newman blossomed as a scholar and thinker. Having taken Holy Orders in the Church of England, he was named vicar of St. Mary's, The University Church, in 1828. Here his associates included such names as Richard Hurrell Froude and John Keble. These were among the founders of the Oxford Movement which purposed to bring renewal to the Church of England, at the time in considerable disarray. Newman emerged as the intellectual and spiritual leader of the movement, but his studies and writing brought about his eventual conversion to Roman Catholicism in 1845. Because of the peculiar journey of his life, Newman has been honored by a wide range of Protestants as well as by Catholics.

Some Christian leaders founded movements bearing their name so that followers call themselves, for example, Lutherans or Wesleyans. This was not the case with Newman. His influence within the church came not through a movement or through institutions, but through ideas that have given flavor to the church and effected the shape of its being in the world. Such is especially true in regard to Newman's influence as an educator. After his conversion to Catholicism, Newman became convinced that there was a primary need for an educational program that would enable Catholics to compete in the modern world. Accordingly, with the opportunity to shape the University of Dublin, "Newman was anxious to establish not merely a Catholic institution but a Catholic institution whose policy was shaped to meet the battle of the modern world."[77] That Newman's attempted development of an institution passed fruitlessly does little to negate the results of his effort. For example, the point of view expressed in Newman's lectures, given in association with the attempt to found the university, has influenced the shape of the Western educational system both structurally and spiritually. Newman later published these lectures under the title of *The Idea of a University*.[78]

Newman, of course, did not think in idioms that square precisely with the historic prototype. Nonetheless, in many ways his works are supportive of that viewpoint because he took historic Christianity so seriously. Chadwick reminds us, for example, that

Newman actually "revered the age of early Christians."[79] Never content with the baldness of woodenly stated doctrinal fare, Newman presented his understanding of Christianity in sermons and lectures that require being weighed, or perhaps measured, in the mind. The result is that one need not fully agree with Newman to be confronted with a faith-enriching dimension of reality.

ANALYSIS OF THE HISTORIC PROTOTYPE

As suggested at the beginning of this chapter, the historic prototype (model) played a major role in shaping the educational endeavors of the Christian church from its earliest days until near the dawn of the twentieth century. It should be kept in mind that this was not a consciously structured model. Rather, it seems to have been maintained across the centuries as an amalgam of theological convictions and beliefs about human nature. This amalgam was shaped largely through the effects of the prevailing worldview which assumed that a revelatory communication from God was the cornerstone of Christian religious education.

Obviously the prototype was not preserved in a static, pristine state across these many Christian centuries. Winds of change were felt, but not always consciously worked through. These sometimes contributed to a sense of uneasiness in the church's educational milieu. For example, this uneasiness was acutely felt in the church when Origen introduced Greek thought patterns into Christian religious education and again when Comenius began raising the importance of the learner to the level of revealed subject matter. On the other hand, it seems clear that, because it was so deeply imbedded in the Christian psyche, the historic prototype played a conservative role. As such it exerted considerable force to preserve and promote the perceived character of primitive Christianity in the lives of succeeding generations of Christians.

For the purposes of our study, it should be borne in mind that an analysis of the four models described in succeeding chapters of this book may be pursued with the luxury of knowing that twentieth-century theorists, however disparate their point of view, typically follow certain linguistic conventions in explicating their respective theories. Almost all of them employ expressions that more or less equate with the six analytical categories delineated in the first chapter: aim, content, teacher, learner, environment, and evaluation.

No such luxury applies to a descriptive analysis of the prototype. Historic thinkers do appear conscious of a considered pattern in the thinking that underlies their efforts to provide sound educational assistance for their readers. However, the educational standard from which these intrepid educationists worked is much less distinct than the term *model* commonly implies. Of the sixteen selected writers spanning the second through the nineteenth centuries, Augustine in the fifth and Comenius in the seventeenth seem to have given the most conscious attention to theory as theory. In the writings of these two theorists, at least, the categories of aim, content, teacher (method), learner, and evaluation are given relatively clear definition. Other educator/ theorists selected in this chapter seem consistent in the way their understandings find root in the primary structures of the prototype, albeit their energies were not directed to the kind of theoretical reflection that might influence them to directly address the categories that guide the analyses in the later chapters of this book. Nonetheless, the following analysis is important as a means of establishing benchmarks to assist in comparing twentieth-century models with earlier points of view.[80]

Aim

Perhaps the defining aspect of aim most evident in the literature of the historic prototype is an acute sense of Christian mission. Religious education was intended to promote both Christian faith and faithfulness to Christian values. Faithful Christians, in turn, were regarded as a primary resource for pursuing the broader goals of the church. In brief, the faithful were to have been inwardly converted through their response to the revealed message which had been received from apostolic times, and they were to live out its implications in the world.

Cyril of Jerusalem underscores this notion of inward conversion quite clearly when he claims at the outset of his catechetical discourses that "I bring you as it were the stones of knowledge; you must be instructed in the doctrine of the living God."[81] He pinpoints the reason for such instruction by arguing that it alone has the capacity to bring about "the spiritual regeneration of the soul."[82] Augustine, likewise, maintains that a fundamental theoretical issue in aim is to "discover how suitably to present that truth, the belief in which makes us Christians" with the larger goal in mind "that the Christian life and profession are maintained."[83] Augustine's essential perspective, quite nicely sketched above, profoundly influenced the structural features of the historic prototype.

In the century following Augustine's seminal contributions, Benedict formulated the principles governing educational aim in the introduction to the Rule that has since governed Benedictine schooling: "Therefore we intend to establish a school for the Lord's service.... Never swerving from his instructions...we shall through patience share in the sufferings of Christ that we may deserve also to share in his kingdom. Amen."[84] In the heart of the Middle Ages, Maurus stated his aim in essential harmony with the historic perspective: "Above all it is necessary that he, who aims to attain the summit of wisdom, should be converted to the fear of the Lord."[85] Then in the period just before the Reformation, Gerson, obviously defending his personal practice of taking time from his chancellorship of the University of Paris to teach the catechism, states: "I do not know if there be anything greater to which to devote my modesty more profitably than, with the help of God, to snatch souls from the very doors of Hell.... It is the children of whom I am thinking, bearing in mind that Christ gives them growth. But I am assured that by my preaching publicly (in the opinion of some) I should reach this aim in a more splendid manner."[86]

With probable indebtedness to Augustine, Luther argues with his usual bluntness, that children, servants, and other citizens are to be exposed to the kind of missional education that will lead them to the knowledge of "the truth and to the knowledge of the Word, and thus above all things the soul have its nourishment, in order that men may become godly and pious, and thus be saved."[87] There is nothing on earth so important, his argument continues, as that "we bring other people, and in particular those who are entrusted to us, to the knowledge of God and the holy gospel"...to the end that "they receive the doctrine and become godly."[88] Though as a

Catholic heartily opposing Luther on ecclesiastical grounds, Ignatius seems in essential agreement with Luther's educational convictions, as well as with earlier expressions of the historic perspective. Indeed, Ignatius' educational efforts served to revitalize the historic perspective within Catholicism. Throughout his *Constitutions* and other writings, but especially through his actions, Ignatius seems to demonstrate his conviction that the proper aim of education must be "the salvation and perfection of the students that they in turn might promote the salvation and perfection of their fellowmen," thus leavening society with "the spirit of the Kingdom of Christ."[89]

Living in the century following the Reformation, Comenius was evidently affected by the streams of thought that eventually led to the Enlightenment. Thus, in considering aims, he gave serious attention to the learner as a citizen of time and space, as well as of eternity. A thoroughgoing realist, he nevertheless combined this perspective with fervent evangelical convictions as to the need to bring all persons to a converting faith. Accordingly, Comenius' biographer, Laurie, argues that his whole educational aim "was to lead youth to God through *things*—to God as the source of all, and as the crown of knowledge and end of life."[90] Comenius' educational concerns were so encyclopedic that an encapsulation of his views on the aim of religious education from his own writings runs the risk of oversimplification. Nonetheless, a passage from his chapter titled "Religious Education" in his *School of Infancy*, appears clearly grounded in the historic prototype. Here Comenius suggests that, undergirded by proper exposure to doctrine and the Scriptures, we may implant in children "the foundations of piety, through prayer...surrendering them in holy dedication, to Christ the Redeemer, imploring likewise for them the care of the Eternal Teacher, the Holy Spirit."[91] Comenius seems always jealous to understand aim in such a way that religious education effects are not static. Thus he states: "From the very beginning it is necessary to form practical and not theoretical Christians...religion is a real thing and not a reflection of reality, and should prove its reality by the practical results that it produces."[92] Though avowedly influenced in some measure by Comenius' rather progressive educational thought, John Wesley demonstrates his rigid, religious reformer's viewpoint when he declares that the aim for his school at Kingswood is to teach children "how to think, and judge, and act according to the strictest rules of Christianity."[93]

Content

The historic perception of content seems to have been deeply influenced by a number of catechetical syllabi that circulated in the early church. None of these survive, but their existence is evident from the standardized structure of published catechetical lectures, such as those of Cyril and Augustine, which have been preserved. These syllabi seem to have been grounded in a common view of the Bible, regarded as the fountain of proper religious education content. They also appear to have found their organizing principles in the creed, the commandments, the "Our Father" prayer, and the biblical institution of the sacraments. With these features serving as an underlying structure, individuals seeking to improve education practices used their own creativity in shaping the notion of content to the particular needs of the age in which they lived.

Thus, as mentioned earlier in this chapter, Clement of Alexandria sought to integrate secular and sacred knowledge in defense of the Christian faith. He directed his attention not merely toward educating the individual seeking to enter the church, but also toward the Christian seeking to be educated so as to become a more productive member of the prevailing Greek culture. Consequently his notion of content found a role for elements of Greek philosophy, but its roots were in the Christian revelation. In an essay on instruction in spiritual perfection, Clement suggests that the educational process might well proceed according to the appropriate educational level of the individual with "a sketch of the Christian religion." This "sketch" need not be broken in its "discourse by constant reference to the scriptures" since the object "is to set forth, not their phraseology but their meaning only."[94] Cyril nicely encapsulates a certain dimension of the historic perception of content: "True religion consists of two elements: pious doctrines and virtuous actions."[95] He moves from this statement to a consideration of a number of standard doctrines and then to the creed, designating the knowledge of such matters,

together with their scriptural underpinnings, a "precious possession."[96]

In what may be his major statement on the content of religious
education, Augustine prefaces his key remarks by taking the time to
list all of the books in the canon as he understood it. Then he states:
"in all of these books those fearing God and made meek in piety
seek the will of God. And the first rule of this, understanding and
labor is, as we have said, to know these books even if they are not
understood."[97] Once one is familiar with the Scriptures, he
continues, "we should turn to those obscure things which must be
opened up and explained so that we may take examples from those
things that are manifest to illuminate those things which are
obscure."[98] "The narration is complete," Augustine declares in
another passage, only "when the beginner is first instructed from
the text: *In the beginning God created heaven and earth*, down to the
present period of Church history."[99] Augustine notes in the context
that he is not calling for a verbatim on every book or passage in the
Bible, but that the story be woven together.

Benedict placed a high value of the formative role of Scripture
in the education and development of the monks in his order.
Benedict's rule sets forth some very high standards in this regard.
Consider, for example: "For monks who in a week's time say less
than the full psalter with the customary canticles betray extreme
indolence and lack of devotion in their service."[100] Maurus likewise
viewed accumulation of scriptural content as the fundamental task
in the education of clergy: "The foundation, the content, and the
perfection of all wisdom is the Holy Scripture, which has taken its
origin from that unchangeable and eternal Wisdom, which streams
from the mouth of the Most High."[101]

Luther envisioned the future leaders of Germany, and of the
church, as children sitting in the classrooms of the schools for
whose existence he argued. He maintained that all other subject-
matter content offered to these future leaders must be subordinate
to the Bible, which was in his understanding the core content of an
adequate preparation for leading the nation and the church. Thus
Luther states: "Above all, in schools of all kinds the chief and most
common lesson should be the Scriptures.... Should not every

Christian be expected by his ninth or tenth year to know all the holy Gospels, containing as they do his very name and life?"[102] Luther understood the catechism essentially as a tool for adding to one's fund of basic scriptural knowledge. Thus he suggests to those teaching the young that they "keep ever to one form and teach them, first of all, the Ten Commandments, the Creed, the Lord's Prayer, etc., word for word according to the text, that thus they may easily repeat and remember them."[103] Calvin's views on content are essentially similar to those of Luther. In the by-laws of the Geneva Academy he writes, "These (public-scholars) shall likewise write each month on what are known as the fixed points of doctrine, all sophistry, all curiosity, all sacrilegious boldness in corrupting the word of God, all evil contention and obstinacy shall be ruled out. All shall be discussed pro and con in a spirit of reverence and holiness."[104]

Comenius, who found a place for all kinds of content in a rounded Christian education, still believed that "the Holy Scriptures must be the Alpha and Omega of Christian schools.… In Christian schools therefore, God's Book should rank before all other books; that like Timothy, all the Christian youth may, from boyhood, know the sacred writings which are able to make them wise unto salvation."[105] In spite of his wide-ranging interests, and his desire to organize all knowledge so that it could be useful to humankind, Comenius could yet write, "Whatever is taught to the young in addition to the scriptures (sciences, arts, languages, etc.) should be taught as purely subordinate subjects."[106] Newman argued that theology must be included as a matter of course in the liberal education of Christians so as to enable them to take their proper place in the totality of commerce. "I will say, then," he states, "that if a university be, from the nature of the case, a place of instruction, where universal knowledge is professed…the subject of religion is excluded, one of two conclusions is inevitable—either on the one hand that the province of religion is very barren of real knowledge, or on the other hand, that in such a university one special and important branch of knowledge is omitted."[107]

Teacher

Teaching, as perceived by most historic writers, is a function of an individual, almost always identified in the context as a man.

There is relatively little reflection upon teaching in relation to learning, as such. Good teaching is more or less equated with good presentation of scriptural and doctrinal material properly arranged to meet the learner's religious needs. One common, though not universal, characteristic of this school of thought is that God is the true teacher. Thus the notion of teaching is sometimes given a mystical dimension by historic writers.

Clement accordingly suggests that, "our educator is the holy God, Jesus, the Word guiding all mankind."[108] He expands and seeks to clarify his position thus: "Just…as the helmsman pilots his ship conscious of his responsibility for the lives of his passengers, so the Educator (Christ), in his concern for us, leads His children along a way of life that ensures salvation."[109] Obviously, Clement's view of this matter is rather complex. In brief, his understanding is that the Word, as (1) teacher instructs the mind; as (2) educator, he is practical—oriented toward the religious rather than the purely cognitive domain.[110]

Augustine experimented with a number of images of the teacher. But, overall, his preferred image seems to be that the teacher is one who makes a doctrinally and scripturally complete presentation of the fullness of the Christian message that yet sets the learner free to grow. Thus Augustine states: "He who explains to listeners what he understands in the Scriptures is like a reader who pronounces words he knows, but he who teaches how the Scriptures are to be understood is like a teacher who advises how the words are to be read." And again, "He who receives the precepts we wish to teach will not need another to reveal those things that need explaining…since he has certain rules…in his understanding."[111] Augustine believed that an attitude characterized by optimism and hope functioned as a catalyst to enable the religion teacher's goals to come alive in the personality of the learner.[112] Furthermore, he mentions in a number of passages his fundamental conviction that teaching will be undermined when the teacher forgets that words are not, in and of themselves, reality. Accordingly, effective religion teaching requires that the teacher keep clearly in mind the reality that even carefully chosen words seek to convey. The teacher consciously strives to vary words and modality so as to communicate that reality. Even so, it is not the words themselves that teach, but Christ the teacher. Thus, Augustine states: "By means of words, therefore, we learn nothing but words. For if things which are not signs cannot be words, even though I have already heard a word, I do not know it is a word until I know what it signifies. Consequently with the knowledge of realities there comes also the knowledge of the words, whereas when the words are heard, not even the words are learned."[113] Augustine's argument continues: "Regarding, however, all those things which we understand, it is not a speaker who utters sounds exteriorly whom we consult, but it is the truth that presides within…He it is who teaches—Christ."[114]

Living in a culture in which teachers found plenty of occasions to use the rod on children, Luther denounced flogging as a teaching tool. In opposition to harsh teaching methods, he argued: "A well-informed and faithful teacher on the other hand, mingles gentle admonition with punishment, and incites his pupils to diligence in their studies, and to a laudable emulation among themselves; and so they become rooted in all kinds of desirable knowledge."[115] In the by-laws of the Geneva Academy, Calvin offered this rather cryptic advice: "While teaching, the instructors shall observe decorum both in dress and manner. They shall offer no adverse criticism of the authors whom they are to interpret but faithfully explain their meaning…. They shall teach especially the love of God and hatred of vice…. They shall cultivate a mutual and truly Christian harmony among themselves."[116]

Comenius envisioned a number of the concepts underlying the contemporary perception of the teacher as a professional. Decrying what he perceived as a pervasive dysfunction in schools, Comenius counseled those who would hear him to consider "that the teacher should know all the methods by which understanding may be sharpened, and should put them into practice skillfully."[117] To clarify his meaning at this point, he suggested: "Following in the footsteps of nature we find that the process of education will be easy: 'If (i) it begin early, before the mind is corrupted; if (ii) the mind be duly prepared to receive it; if (iii) it proceed from the general to the particular; and if (iv) the pupil be not overburdened by too many subjects.'"[118]

Newman proposed a very different perspective on teaching, oriented as his interests dictated, to the university.

In point of view, its several professors are like ministers of various political powers at one court or conference. They represent their respective sciences and attend to the private interests of those sciences respectively; and should a dispute arise between those sciences, they are the persons to talk it over without risk.... A Liberal philosophy becomes the habit of minds thus exercised; a breadth and expansion of thought in which lives, seemingly parallel, may converge.[119]

Newman's understanding of teaching was obviously rooted in his aim of educating Catholics to take their place in the contemporary world.

Learner

Historic writers regarded human beings, learners, as complex and valuable, worth thinking about deeply. However, without the tools of modern psychology to provide structure for such thought, their views on learners were often limited, rooted as they were in intuition or cultural perception. Even so, the historic prototype sometimes enabled them to produce insights that even now seem worth considering.

Clement suggests that "To know oneself has always been, so it seems, the greatest of all lessons."[120] Interestingly, and seemingly in harmony with the historic view that learners were subordinate to teachers, Clement goes to some length to describe learners in the Christian way. "We are the children. Scripture mentions us very often and in many different ways.... For example, in the Gospel, it says: 'And the Lord, standing on the shore, said to His disciples (they were fishing): Children, do you have no fish?' Those who already had the position of disciples He now calls 'children.'"[121]

True to his espoused doctrine that God elects individuals to salvation, Augustine states: "No one rightly learns those things which pertain to life with God unless he is made by God docile to God, to whom it is said in the Psalm, 'teach me to do thy will, for thou art my God.'"[122] Augustine believed that a human being in this mortal life is a union of the spiritual and the permanent on the one hand and the material and the transient on the other. He believed this union of spirit and material held the key to understanding the educational process.[123] Perhaps relatedly, the notion of "will" is of considerable theoretical importance in Augustine. He views will as the energizing, focusing principle of the soul, uniting memory and act. "Will is an uncoerced motion of the soul directed to the attainment of an object or the prevention of its loss."[124] Quite logically, then, Augustine believed that the motives of the learner must be ascertained. He cautions the religion teacher to seek to know whether there may be some special benefit derived from the learner's journey into the church. "For faith consists not in a body bending but in a mind believing."[125] Augustine also recognized that there were meaningful differences among learners. He urged teachers seek to discern such, adjusting their teaching as indicated. "The same medicine is not to be applied to all, although to all the same love is due—Different people must necessarily affect the teacher in different ways—the teacher's talk should…affect the hearer in different ways as his frame of mind varies."[126] Benedict urges learners to be actively involved in the learning process by being obedient to the specific instructions and implications of the lesson. He theorizes: "Almost at the same moment then, as the master gives the instruction the disciple quickly puts it into practice in the fear of God; and both actions together are swiftly completed as one."[127]

Calvin's directive relative to "public scholars" in the Geneva Academy seems typical of a certain aspect of the historic prototype, that is, that maintenance of a given ("revealed") doctrinal viewpoint is critical to Christian religious education. Accordingly, the model suggests that learners are best served when they passively absorb a carefully ordered body of subject-matter content. The Academy by-law states: "Public scholars, as has been said before, shall give their name to the rector, subscribe to the confession of faith, and conduct themselves with piety and decorum."[128]

Comenius pioneered in the notion of individual difference among learners. Thus he suggested his widely known paradigm in which he identified "The mother's knee" as the infant's school; "The Vernacular-School" as the heart of primary childhood education; "The Latin-School" for the "boyhood" that today we might identify with high school; and "The University and travel" for youth making the transition into adulthood. "These different schools," he argues, "…(should adjust) the instruction to the age of the pupil and the knowledge that he already possesses."[129]

Environment

Environment as an instructional category has little place in the historic understanding of religious education. However, especially in earlier centuries, there was apparently a definite conviction that the surrounding culture negatively affected the catechetical process. The Christian community was therefore expected to guard its sacred space, maintaining an environment conducive to Christian growth. Catechumens were cautioned not even to discuss Christian mysteries, particularly the sacraments, with those who had not progressed through the appropriate stages toward baptism. Thus Cyril appeals in his introductory Lenten lecture: "If after class a catechumen (learner) asks you what the instructors have said, tell outsiders nothing. For it is a divine secret we deliver to you, even the hope of the life to come."[130]

Protection of a wholesome environment within the community may have been carried to extremes, but such was in line with the historic perception of the potentially corrosive effects of a carelessly maintained environment. Benedict's strictures on environment in *The Rule* merely illustrate the theoretical perspective of the historical prototype: "The monks are to sleep in separate beds.… The younger brothers should not have their beds next to each other, but interspersed among those of the seniors. On arising for the Work of God, they will quietly encourage each other, for the sleepy like to make excuses."[131] Again, consistent with the model he was following, Benedict comments: "The workshop where we are to toil faithfully at all these tasks is the enclosure of the monastery and stability in the community."[132]

Writers in later ages were probably as consistent as Benedict, but less graphic. Thus Gerson contends that "there can be no place (to educate children) more suitable, and more nearly above suspicion, than the Church, open to anybody."[133] In a more pedantic style than he commonly used, Comenius states: "Examples of well-ordered lives, in the persons of their parents, nurses, tutors, and school-fellows, must continually be set before children."[134] On the negative side of the same theoretical issue, he avers: "Children must be very carefully guarded from bad society, lest they be infected by it."[135]

Evaluation

Evaluation and aim are so interrelated that they are not easy to tease apart in the writings of the historic school of thought. It appears that most of these writers assume that the desired result of an inner conversion and a godly life will follow acceptance and appropriation of the revealed Christian message. Thus, Clement observes: "The first proof that one knows God, after one has put confidence in the Saviour's teaching, is that one in no way does wrong, in the conviction that this befits the knowledge of God."[136] Cyril prayerfully appeals: "God grant that all of you, your course of fasting finished, mindful of the teaching, fruitful in good works, standing blameless before the spiritual bridegroom, may obtain the remission of your sins from God, in Christ Jesus our Lord, to whom be glory for ever and ever. Amen."[137]

Looking to the conclusion of the teaching-learning process, as he understood it, Augustine suggested that "nothing further is to be done with the matter as if to teach it more at length, but perhaps it should be commended so that it becomes fixed in the heart."[138] He continues in another passage: "After the instruction you should ask him (the learner) whether he believes these things and desires to observe them. And when he answers that he does, you should of course sign him, with due ceremony, and deal with him in accordance with the custom of the church."[139] Augustine went somewhat beyond the bare vision of the historic prototype in his assessment that evaluation ultimately was a matter to be judged by the character of lived life: "That which is taught must be put into practice and is taught for that reason, the truth of what is said is acknowledged in vain and the eloquence of the discourse pleases in vain unless that which is learned is implemented in action."[140] Consistent with the historical view that God is the ultimate teacher as well as evaluator, Augustine suggests "for the profitable result of their speech they should give thanks to Him from whom they should not doubt they have received it."[141]

Luther seems a bit less specific on the matter of evaluation than one might expect, given his rather elevated goals. "It is also the duty, then, of every father of a family," he maintains, "to question his children and servants at least once a week and hear what they know or have learned of it (The Catechism) and when they do not know it, earnestly insist that they learn it."[142]

Somewhat in advance of the historic prototype's rather literal attitude toward evaluation, but quite consistent with his reputation for taking levels of maturation seriously, Comenius counsels: "By the time they are six years old, boys should have made considerable progress in religion and piety; that is to say, they should have learned the heads of the Catechism and the principles of Christianity, and should understand these and live up to them as far as their age permits."[143] More in line with the attitude toward evaluation that one might expect from the historic prototype, he maintains: "The teacher as chief inspector, should give his attention first to one scholar, then to another, more particularly with the view of testing the honesty of those whom he distrusts."[144]

SUMMARY

The prototypical model described in this chapter reflects a worldview unencumbered by twentieth-century perceptions. Even so, analysis of the works of sixteen thinkers, from Clement of Alexandria in the third century to John Henry Newman in the nineteenth, provides helpful insight into the way that informal reflection upon theoretical issues has informed religious education practice. It is obvious that these writers worked from a relatively similar worldview. This view contributed to a structuring of the prototype along lines that suggest religious education must be fundamentally concerned with communicating a divinely revealed message. With the dawn of the twentieth century, the prototype was largely replaced by a socially and educationally dimensioned model. This model was molded by a new worldview in which the energizing vision of individual salvation was exchanged for a vision of how the entire society might be reconstructed through rigorous application of scientific method. The following chapter, then, examines the work of seven influential thinkers who represent the liberal theological model. In this model the religion teacher is freed from enslavement to any revealed message and challenged to participate directly in the process of social reconstruction.

CHAPTER 3

THE CLASSICAL LIBERAL MODEL OF RELIGIOUS EDUCATION

A Theological Model

A NEW MODEL FOR A NEW CENTURY

With the dawn of a new century another model came to dominate the scene. Less than two decades after Cardinal Newman died in 1890, the historic prototype had been effectively replaced by a consciously erected, socially and educationally dimensioned, model that molded thought in the field during the first half of the twentieth century. Whereas the historic prototype emphasized individual salvation from a frame of reference with an eternal horizon, this new model was grounded in the here and now. Its energizing vision was focused upon immediate salvation through the reordering of society. The presuppositions that had mandated the framework for the older prototype were replaced with an optimistic brand of classical liberal theology, linked with a progressive attitude toward education. The resulting model prescribed monumental changes in how religious education might best be pursued. Perhaps the single most important change was that an almost complete reliance upon revealed truth was superseded by a characteristic commitment to discover, and to test, truth through rigorous application of the scientific method.

The liberal model of religious education is characterized by: (1) the position that theological constructs are open to continual change (thus human experience becomes normative for religion itself as well as for religious education theory and practice); (2) the conviction that religious education is essentially concerned with social and cultural reconstruction, not with individual salvation; (3) the view that the religion teacher's task is to create social consciousness, and to develop social living skills, by arranging situations in which learners participate directly in the social process; and (4) the espoused doctrine that Christian personality and lifestyle arise from the development of latent personal and religious capacities.[1]

Neither the doctrine of revelation nor the concept of the church play active roles in the unfolding of this model. The primary focus of attention is upon this present world and upon adjusting to living within a "worldview" from which historic perceptions of God and of His interactions with humankind have been dramatically changed.

In earlier writings, especially *An Invitation to Religious Education* (1975), I employed "social-cultural" as a descriptive term for the point of view here designated "liberal theological." A number of readers and reviewers suggested that "liberal theological" conveys the substance of the concept more accurately. I think they are right. Moreover, a theological label keeps the chapter properly parallel with the immediately following chapters that also discuss theological models. The term "liberal" does suffer from a very wide range of connotations associated with it. Accordingly, it should be understood that, in this chapter, the term "liberal" refers exclusively to the optimistic, classical liberalism that shaped the religious education scene during the earlier decades of this century.

ANTECEDANTS TO THE MODEL

Theological Reorientation

The liberal (social-cultural) model constitutes a radical departure from the historic educational endeavor of the church.

Classical, liberal thinkers generally regard the historic prototype as lamentably defective because of its rigid adherence to the "iron-clad theory" that religious education must be primarily concerned with communicating God's plan for individual salvation. Primary attention is placed upon individuals functioning within society rather than upon the content of a revealed message. Writing in the first issue of *Religious Education* (June 1906), Austen DeBlois characterized this viewpoint as seeking "not the formal but the real."[2] The "swing of things" became not metaphysical but scientific. This rather iconoclastic reorientation from the historic perspective was fueled, at least in part, by the growing impact of nineteenth-century European scholars. Ferdinand Baur, for example, advocated an essentially humanistic approach to understanding the Bible; Albrecht Ritschl insisted that Christianity was at root practical rather than theological; and Charles Darwin's influential writings connected human life directly to this world. Instead of proceeding from the historic beliefs of the church, liberal thinkers proceeded upon the assumption that religious education theory and practice "should be based on the best scientific knowledge available in regard to the nature of man and the conditions for his growth."[3] Wayne Rood has called this transference of faith from a metaphysical to a scientific object "the outstanding theological phenomenon of the twentieth century."[4]

Educational Reorientation

"It goes without saying," George Coe once remarked, "that both the processes and the aims of religious education intertwine with those of so-called secular education. The relation is more than intertwining; they are branches of the same tree, they partake of the same sap."[5] Accordingly, those antecedents to the theoretical viewpoints which came to be characteristic of progressive secular education as well as of the liberal model include the seminal thinking of such individuals as Johann Pestalozzi (1746-1827), Friedrich Froebel (1782-1852), Horace Bushnell (1802-1876), and John Dewey (1859-1952).

Pestalozzi's educational theories were rooted in the psychological movement that flowered in the nineteenth century. He believed that the individual was essentially good in much the same way that Rousseau suggested in the famous opening passage in Emile: "Out of God's hands come good things, it is by man's hands that these good things become evil."[6] Pestalozzi's argument, to the effect that love for God results from loving one's fellows, was of particular importance to the development of religious education theory. According to this Swiss innovator, effective education must follow the order of nature. He insisted that the verbalism characteristic of historic education should be replaced with a process based on relevant relationships capable of being fully comprehended by the child.[7]

Froebel also believed that humankind's core nature was good. He asserted that the divine essence must be unfolded, lifted into consciousness through education. Individuals would then be able to freely obey the divine principle resident within. Accordingly, religious education was perceived as the awakening of an already present religious element, not as a redemptive activity. As to educational practice, this "children's champion" especially valued the educative power of play. He strongly advocated teaching methods based on self-activity.[8]

Horace Bushnell directly addressed the issues that eventually shaped the religious education movement in America. In this way, some scholars think that he made his most meaningful contribution to the twentieth century. *Christian Nurture* (1861), Bushnell's best known book, is at the same time a theological and an educational classic. (The first edition of this book was published in 1847 as *Views of Christian Nurture and Subjects Adjacent Thereto.*) In answer to his own question, "What is the true idea of Christian education?" Bushnell states: "That the child is to grow up a Christian, and never know himself as being otherwise."[9] A. J. William Myers states that Bushnell's widely quoted answer "has been one of the most dynamic sentences in religious literature. The ideal embodied is the aim of all progressive religious education."[10]

Bushnell is perhaps best remembered by religious educators for having sought another than the revivalistic technique for bringing children into a knowledge of, and a relationship with, God. His approach, reminiscent of Froebel, was that religious education ought to nurture the religious bud that was already present in the child. This leading New England pastor opposed the revivalist approach by suggesting that children "do not receive religion as goods received into a warehouse." His proposal for a religious education based on the concepts of growth and nurture amounted to training children *in the way that they are expected to live.*[11]

Other tenets for which Bushnell is often remembered are that (1) the home is the proper center of religious training; (2) growth, not conquest, is the true means of extending God's kingdom; (3) teaching should suit the age of the pupil; and (4) experience rather than doctrine is the best foundation for teaching religion. Bushnell's importance does not seem based so much upon his articulation of an original theory as that he "thought the thoughts that were foundational" for the perspectives which have come to dominate so much of twentieth-century thinking.

John Dewey's philosophical doctrines and progressive proposals must be counted among the most significant of the factors which gave shape to the classical liberal model. Dewey's redefinition of knowledge and learning was totally antithetical to the historic understanding of religious education. His philosophical and educational framework became integral to progressive religious education. The historic viewpoint assumed that knowledge, and most especially religious knowledge, was an assemblage of absolute truths and certainties grasped by the mind; that learning came about through the communication (transmission) of these truths and certainties; and that religious (moral) behavior followed right learning as a matter of course. In contrast, Dewey taught that knowledge might best be thought of as modified action based on experience; that the mind should be described as a tool by which experience may be sharpened and made more meaningful; that learning may not be distinguished from the living of life's experiences (episodes) which beget knowledge (modify action); and that moral acts, which are wholly social, come before the thought.[12]

In connection with this discussion, attention must be given to the progressive education movement commonly identified with Dewey, but which should not be confused with his philosophical thought.[13] Progressive education was distinguished by its attitude toward educational practice which was in revolt against traditional, formal education. The following characteristics of the progressive education movement seem to have had a decided influence upon the development of the liberal theological model: (1) its willingness to give a considerable amount of self-directed freedom to individual learners; (2) its emphasis upon interest rather than punishment as the source of discipline; (3) its encouragement of overt, purposeful activity; (4) its focus upon growth factors in the child; (5) its classroom application of scientifically derived pedagogical principles; (6) its tailoring of instruction to different kinds and classes of children; and (7) its tendency to move beyond the classroom into the community—an attitude related to the progressive conviction that education is intrinsic to life itself, not merely a preparation for it.

Dewey's theoretical and practical notions clearly affected the development of the liberal theological model through the integration of his philosophical, moral, and educational ideas into professional training programs and literature of the religious education movement. This movement had its concretization in the Religious Education Association, but the association and the movement are usually referred to separately in the literature.[14]

THE RELIGIOUS EDUCATION ASSOCIATION

The founding of the Religious Education Association in 1903 may be taken as an event which represented a crystallizing of the forces which culminated in the evolution of the liberal theological model. William Rainey Harper, president of the University of Chicago and a "progressive spirit," was the catalyst in sponsoring this association which grew out of a 1903 meeting of prestigious American educators in Chicago. John Dewey gave one of the major addresses at the meeting: "Religious Education as Conditioned by Modern Psychology and Pedagogy." He was the leader and principle spokesperson for those who hoped that the proposed association would become mainly an agency for enriching secular education.

Another point of view, bearing on the theme of salvation by education, was enunciated by George Coe in his celebrated address, "Religious Education as a Part of General Education." Coe's key argument was that the proposed association should have religious education as its primary interest. His position won out over that of Dewey. Accordingly, the Religious Education Association was organized. Its stated aim: "To inspire the religious forces of our country with the educational ideal; to inspire the educational forces of our country with the religious ideal; and to keep before the public mind the ideal of moral and religious education and the sense of its need and value.[15]

Although Dewey drifted out of the Religious Education Association, his views continued to have a formative influence upon the theoretical positions adopted by almost all of the association's earlier leaders. It should also be noted that even though the association never took an official stance on theory and practice, a careful reading of its official journal, *Religious Education*, indicates that a preponderance of the articles appearing on its pages during at least the first thirty-five years of its existence (1906-1940) were written from the perspective of progressive education and hence of the liberal theological model of religious education.[16]

REPRESENTATIVE THEORISTS

George Albert Coe (1862-1951)

George Coe is by almost any standard of reference the most influential theorist identified with the liberal theological model of religious education. He may well have been the most widely read Protestant religious educator during the first half of the twentieth century. Coe's major book is generally acknowledged to be *A Social Theory of Religious Education*.[17] It could be argued with considerable justification that Coe defined the liberal model in its pages. His work is a persuasive exposition and application of the social and theological principles underlying this point of view. When he determined to think through the problems of Christian religious education anew, under the presuppositions of modern science, Coe accepted the prospect that historic aims and teaching practices would be found useless. He asserted (1) that the historic aim of individual salvation must be replaced by the broader, more inclusive, aim of social reconstruction; and (2) that transmissive practices must be abandoned in favor of vital participation in social interaction.

Coe's perception of religious education was obviously antithetical to the historic position that, as an instrument of the church, the teacher transmits revealed truth to the learner.

Indeed, his argument was that the teacher and learner must be involved together in the adventure of re-creating Christianity itself. Hence Coe's widely quoted (and misquoted) statement: "Religion changes in the act of teaching it."[18] Within such a recreated Christianity, postulated by Coe as a "democracy of God," the loyalty of the individual Christian would not be to one person, even to Jesus. Rather, a Christian's loyalty, and deepest commitment, would be to society, to persons.[19]

Sophia Lyon Fahs (1876-1978)

Sophia Lyon Fahs gave more than half of her long life to articulating and promoting causes closely linked to the application of liberal thought in religious education settings. She was more adventuresome in spirit than some whose seminal work architected the framework of the liberal model, but Fah's works give evidence of a mind that made a firm connection between the model from which she worked and the educational practices she advocated. Her book, *Today's Children and Yesterday's Heritage: A Philosophy of Creative Religious Development* (1952),[20] is a refreshingly clear exposition of liberal principles as applied to teaching children. Fahs' academic association was with Union Theological Seminary, New York, where she gained the reputation of requiring her students to become fully aware of the philosophical and theological implications of issues related to all phases of education. In 1959, at the amazing age of eighty-two, Sophia Lyon Fahs was "ordained to the liberal ministry" in the Unitarian denomination.

William Clayton Bower (1878-1982)

William Clayton Bower is probably the second most influential of the classical liberal theorists. His book, *The Curriculum of Religious Education* (1925),[21] became a standard of the religious education movement during the second quarter of the twentieth century. A prolific writer, Bower addressed himself to a rather wide range of reading publics which included public school teachers and administrators as well as religious educators. The deliberate introduction of scientific methodology to all levels of educational endeavor was one of Bower's special interests.[22] This interest is most noticeable in his books dealing specifically with church school matters. Bower's most important contributions to religious education theory may have grown from the attention he gave to a range of fascinating questions relating to the ways in which Christian personality might best be fostered along desirable lines. He concluded that personality develops continuously as a result of "experience," defined as "the interaction between the person and the environment." Bower theorized that, by controlling experience, the direction of personality growth may be predicted and controlled. *The Curriculum of Religious Education* directly applied Bower's theory of personality development toward a proposed program for religious education in the church. *Moral and Spiritual Values in Education* (1952)[23] extended Bower's theory into a plan for value education in public school settings.

Adelaide Teague Case (1887-1948)

Adelaide Teague Case advanced the practical dimensions of the religious education movement during the second quarter of the century, especially in her pointed application of social ethics to teaching method. Following an earlier career in the denominational library of the Episcopalian Church, she elected to become a religious educator. Case's most important literary contribution was *Liberal Christianity and Religious Education* (1924)[24] which she completed as a doctoral dissertation under her mentor, George Coe. The earlier passages of this book are unique in the clarity with which they enunciate and illustrate the liberal attitude toward religious education aims. Case is remembered for having been among the earliest women to serve on the governing board of the Religious Education Association and, when invited to the chair in religious education at the Episcopal Theological Seminary in 1941, she became the first woman to hold full professorial rank in any Episcopalian seminary.

George Herbert Betts (1868-1934)

George Herbert Betts contributed in a number of important ways to the practical fleshing out of the liberal theological model.

Betts is especially remembered in relation to his nationally recognized studies in character education while serving as director of research at Northwestern University during the last decade of his life. His most important contribution to religious education was that he extended the theses of the liberal model into the realm of method in such works as *Social Principles of Education* (1912),[25] *How to Teach Religion* (1919),[26] and *Method in Teaching Religion* (1925).[27]

Walter Scott Athearn (1874-1934)

Walter Scott Athearn exerted a notable influence on the North American religious education scene during the final two decades of his life. His model for integrating public and church education was based upon his pioneering efforts in Malden, Massachusetts. Athearn's findings, and his dreams for implementing his proposals on a national scale, were widely disseminated through his "Malden Leaflets." His comprehensive proposals were perhaps most fully developed in *A National System of Education* (1920).[28] Athearn was a severe critic of many tenets of the religious education movement and, thus, of the liberal theological model that was at its heyday during his most productive years. He does not always employ classical liberal terminology in his writings, thus his books do not clearly represent the liberal theological model at all points. Nonetheless, he optimistically set out to activate a number of key liberal principles under the banner, "A Free Church within a Free State." The once flourishing, but now foundering, "Released Time Movement" remains the major monument to Athearn's work.

Ernest John Chave (1886-1961)

Ernest Chave, author of *A Functional Approach to Religious Education* (1947),[29] was quite influential in the religious education movement near the middle of the twentieth century. His writings carried the basic principles of the liberal school of thought somewhat further along naturalistic lines than either Coe or Bower seemed willing to go. In this connection, James Smart suggests that Chave merely accepted the implications of the liberal model and that he was perhaps more consistent in carrying it through to its logical conclusion.[30] Chave totally rejected the historic formulation of the Christian faith. He argued that *Sectarianism* and *Supernaturalism* were the two greatest hindrances to effective religious education. Sectarianism resulted in a divisive loyalty to one religion. Supernaturalism, as a carryover founded upon a pre-scientific worldview, contributed to a "blurred faith in a supposedly personal God." Chave insisted that religious education cannot look to historic theological sources for its message, methods, or incentives; "it must find them in the growing present." The basic assumption upon which he proceeded to develop his vision of religious education is that religion itself arises, here and now, from the "primary adjustments of life." Chave appears to be consistent in his understanding of (1) the social aims of religious education, (2) the role of the teacher as essentially that of an arranger of the educational adventure, and (3) each learner as individually having all of the needed spiritual potential to rise through social interaction to a fully functional level of religious living.[31]

ANALYSIS OF THE LIBERAL MODEL

Aim

Social ideals exert a determining influence on the aims of religious education for classical-liberal thinkers. True-to-type theorists working from this model understand the aim of religious education to be a working construct, grounded in present social issues. This view is in stark contrast to the historic understanding of aim as "a given," derived from the facts of revelation. The historic point of view is accordingly looked upon as being incapable of generating aims that are sufficiently comprehensive to encompass the complexities of modern life. It is argued that specific aims must (1) demonstrate faith in a developmental process, (2) meaningfully account for human experience, and (3) creatively point the way to the solution of current social issues through the coordination of latent spiritual forces that would otherwise lie dormant within society. The theological rationale for this viewpoint is stated most succinctly by Coe in his influential article, "The Idea of God." He states: "The modern mind has also learned to think of God as most intimately related to the process of the world. Much of the older Christian thought represented God and the world as two separate realities, as though the world of nature were distinct from another world called the supernatural. But any such distinction as this between the natural and the divine is no longer tenable."[32] Attention to present social issues, then, is perceived through the lens of this model as equivalent to listening to the "call of God" and thus generative of appropriate aims.

Creative Aspect of Aim

Rejecting those aims which are stated in terms of handing on a divinely ordained message, this model proposes that educational processes should enter "creatively into the flow of present existence." Religious education, accordingly, ceases to be a means by which revealed doctrines and ancient standards are transmitted. It becomes, instead, a process by which these doctrines and standards are themselves revised. Thus, Chave states: "Religious education must cease to be the tool of conservatism, indoctrinating immature minds with outgrown ideas and futile customs. It must stimulate creative thought, reconstructing concepts of God, redefining spiritual objectives, and reorganizing religious programs."[33] Similarly, Fahs declares: "No longer can religious education be the simple process of instructing children in a way already decided upon as the best; no longer can it be a passing on of moral principles.... Religious growth and education in religion we must learn to conceive of as a process of questioning, of experimenting, in thought and in conduct."[34] In essential harmony with other liberal thinkers on these matters, Case explains that "liberalism is in its essential nature a progressive movement, always changing, always in flux; its conclusions are never fixed or static; it has no unalterable 'deposit of faith' to teach."[35]

The concept of continuous creation has been seized upon in support of this "creative approach" to understanding religious educational aim. It is typically insisted that historic aims have resulted in the notion that the growth of God's kingdom is merely the quantitative increase of something that is already qualitatively finished. Continuous creation, on the other hand, affords a rationale for aims targeted toward growth in a fully qualitative sense, a

> *"coming into being of something unprecedented and unpredictable...*
> *involving possibly the superseding of some ancient good." According to this*
> *school of thought, such creative aims will lead to the adoption of Christ's*
> *creative spirit and thus enable those Christians who have accepted the*
> *burdens and risks of recreating the Christian faith itself to maintain vital*
> *continuity with Christ by "following him upon his road of discovery and*
> *creation."*[36]

This approach to identifying the aims of religious education, it is argued, could become the supreme corrective for the spiritual malaise which seemingly afflicts "modern" youth. It would enable them to participate with God and their peers in the creation of a "really new" order of society. This new social order would be targeted toward universally good social experience. It would also deal creatively with the deepest personal and social values. Furthermore, it is suggested that a "continual becoming" is at once the end and the process by which both personal and social ideals, at their highest levels, may be achieved and maintained. "According to this point of view," to borrow Bower's expression, "education is vastly more and other than something that can be determined by adults and imposed from without upon passive and receptive learners, however skillful the techniques of inculcation may be. It is nothing less than the initiation of the young into a creative personal and social experience."[37]

Scope of Aim

Aim is largely encompassed by the notion of a "kingdom of God" or, as in Coe's later writings, a "democracy of God." This notion amounts to a vision of an idealized social order in which the principles "enunciated most clearly by Jesus Christ would be fully actualized." Classical, liberal thinkers reject individualized salvific goals and the historic, supernatural, interpretation of the kingdom of God as too pessimistic. Thus Coe states: "Our generation has come to see that the redemptive mission of the Christ is nothing less than that of transforming the social order itself into a brotherhood or family of God. We are not saved, each by himself, and then added to one another like marbles in a bag."[38] Similarly, Fahs asserts:

If our long-time goal is the salvation of a world community rather than merely the salvation of a few select individuals...our concept of individual responsibility is changed.... We no longer feel like racers each rushing to gain his own crown of glory.... We feel as learners, adventurers, experimenters. With God living in us, we seek together to find how to bring new values into living, how to widen our feelings of fellowship—not with the saints alone but with all kinds of people.[39]

The "democracy of God" envisioned by Coe, and other architects of this model, is perceived as a "unification that goes beyond the hooking together of ecclesiastical machines." It is to be accomplished only through the coming together of persons in the "unsectarian spirit characteristic of the sciences." Union on the basis of "faith and order," supposedly, amounts to little more than "a pooling of inefficiencies." The achievement of a synthesis of modern life through the rediscovery of moral and spiritual values is perceived as a problem for the whole democratic community, not just as a matter for the churches. The kind of religious experience (and "habit of mind") that must of necessity underlie a dynamic coming together which might eventuate in an operative "democracy of God" must be based upon a reborn religious education which has an "adequately broad" scope of aim.[40]

Social and Moral Dimensions of Aim

The democratic ideal, a conviction that individual destinies and the destiny of society are interdependent, is a notion which seems to have been inherited directly from John Dewey. In the sense that the term is commonly employed by liberal theorists, "democracy" has to do with self-realization of persons as they live out their lives in a shared social situation. Case's interpretation is helpful: "Some liberals are demanding in Jesus' name a radical transformation.... They insist that salvation of the individual and salvation of society cannot be separated, that they belong together and condition each other."[41] This viewpoint places a fundamental emphasis upon persons as persons and upon human values as superseding all other values. Moral character, accordingly, is not closely related to religious practices such as Bible reading or attendance at worship; it is perceived to be totally a matter of one's relationship to society. Such a relationship is fostered by a creatively conceived education rooted in the concrete social situation. Four fundamental considerations seem to underlie the understanding of religious education which flows from the democratic ideal: *first*, that learning is a social process (knowledge, itself, being primarily a social creation); *second*, that the Christian religion (indeed, all religion) is fundamentally social; *third*, that in religious education "immature persons are being prepared to take their places in a specialized Christian institution, a social community of like-minded persons, known as the church"; and *fourth*, that the social responsibilities of the Christian religion are by nature "functional."[42]

The most widely known statement of religious educational aims based upon the democratic ideal is surely that put forward by Coe in *A Social Theory of Religious Education*: "Granted this social idealism as the interpretation of life that now is, the aim of Christian education becomes this: *Growth of the young toward and into mature and efficient devotion to the democracy of God, and happy self realization therein.*"[43] In support, Coe gives, with implied negative criticism, certain assumptions that he believes underlie historic understandings of aim: *first*, aims which propose instruction in things which a Christian ought to know assume that religion consists essentially of a completed, authoritative revelation which must be handed on from generation to generation; *second*, aims which point to preparation for membership in the church assume that the church is the authoritative administrator of the fixed revelation; and *third*, conceptions of aim which purport to save the child's soul are based on a doctrine of redemption which calls upon the person to live separately from the world, rather than to work out one's salvation within the world.[44]

By way of contrast, the underlying assumptions of Coe's democratic aim are: (1) that no separation exists between the divine and human society because the social instincts provide the rudimentary conditions for such a divine-human democracy; (2) that devotion to a social cause is not the equivalent of crossing a line which separates the saved from the unsaved; (3) that efficiency suggests the necessity for concrete evidence of achievement which can be measured; and (4) that there must be a lessening of individualism through growing participation in the creation of an ideal society by which the learner will gain life and realize fellowship with the Father.[45]

Three specific social issues concretize the "call of God," to which Coe believes religious education must address itself: *Social welfare*, which has to do with the nonhuman environment, that is, disease; *social justice*, which touches the parts that individuals play in each other's lives; and a *world society*, which involves the integration of all humankind into a single "democratically governed brotherhood." The immediate aims of an adequately socialized education which would tend to promote fulfillment of the ultimate aims, as advanced by Coe, are: that the learner shall (1) acquire the tools of social intercourse, that is, language, number, social forms; (2) be introduced to society through the sciences, arts, literature, and most especially through participation in social life; (3) be trained for an occupation; and (4) be intelligently socialized by the shaping of his or her motives of conduct.[46]

Bower and Chave have also worked out apparently consistent statements of aim for religious education. The objectives of modern religious education as formulated by Bower are: (1) to help growing persons achieve a Christlike personality, (2) to bring society under the ideals of Christ in the progressive realization of the kingdom of God, (3) to make the resources of the Christian faith available for dealing with the issues of the day, and (4) to build a sustaining fellowship—which is the church and which will be supportive of God's causes.[47]

Chave envisioned that a new day for religious education might be achieved by incorporating an analysis of the functions of religion directly into the aims of religious educational programs. His own research resulted in the development of ten functional categories intended to be descriptive of the way religion operates in growing lives. Chave's ten categories, considerably abbreviated, are: (1) a sense of personal worth in recognition of one's being (existence) as a creative member of the universe; (2) social sensitivity—awareness of potentialities in other persons; (3) appreciation of the universe; (4) ability to discriminate among values; (5) responsibility and accountability—one cannot be a law unto one's self; (6) cooperative fellowship—ability to contribute to the transformed group life; (7)

quest for truth and realization of values—religion is a persistent quest, an effort to extend spiritual learnings and to realize human possibilities; (8) integration of life's experiences into a working philosophy of life; (9) appreciation of historical continuity— reflection upon experiences both of one's own life and of the lives of others in search of cosmic meanings and universal principles of conduct; and (10) participation in group celebrations in order to keep goals and beliefs in the focus of attention. The assumption Chave makes is that "wherever and whenever these kinds of experiences are being developed spiritual goals are being realized, whether they take place in church, home, school, playground, business, or other relationship."[48]

Betts is in essential harmony with the above perspective. The fundamental assumption upon which his understanding of aim is based is that "children can be brought to a religious character and experience through right nurture and training in religion." The end which religious education seeks is certain desired changes in the life, thought, and experience of the learner. Progress toward these ends may be tested by whether the learner does, in fact, live differently in the "here and now." Betts contends that since life itself actually sets the desired ends (aims), a proper series of questions to ask might be, "What are the demands that life makes on the individual?…What abilities must he have trained in order that he may most completely express God's plan for his life?" In answer to his own questions, Betts concludes that the aim of teaching religion may be summarized under three great general truths: (1) fruitful knowledge of religious truth can be used in daily life, (2) right attitudes of warmth and loyalty will eventuate in worthwhile actions, (3) skill in living and in the conduct of daily life is indispensable for vital religion.[49]

Content

Social-cultural theorists seem to be unanimous in their rejection of the historic notion that the content of religious education is essentially a divinely authoritative message—be it "saving truth" or "way of life"—that must be transmitted unchanged from generation to generation. Case explains: "The liberal attitude toward the Bible and toward traditional theology has released Jesus of Nazareth alike from the machinery of a prearranged scheme of salvation and from the dead hand of pious superstition. Jesus thus freed becomes the center of the liberal movement."[50] Some, such as Fahs and Bower, are in agreement that the historic understanding of the process of religious education is to some extent logical. They even go so far as to allow that a "propagandistic approach" makes the identification of content and the selection of materials a less difficult process—because learners can be given subject matter thought to have been most successful in bringing about acceptance, conversion, and loyalty to a particular position.[51]

Nonetheless, Coe charges that such content-oriented, transmissively intentioned, religious education not only does not work, "it also, of its own nature, creates evils for which it is loathe to accept responsibility."[52] Among the "evils" of content-oriented education Coe fears are (1) that it employs force, including psychic force, to outwardly achieve its aims; (2) that it brings some persons into subjection to others, even though its intentions are to promote obedience to God; and (3) that its achievements sometimes run counter to its own objectives because it does not, by rigorous analysis, keep abreast of changing conditions.[53] Fahs goes a step further, contending that beliefs held primarily "because they were once revealed" may actually become a factor in creating the opposite kinds of attitudes to those which religious leaders usually intend to inculcate.[54]

Betts pursues another line of reasoning. In his criticism of the historic position, he suggests that content-oriented teaching merely disseminates nonfunctional facts. These facts play no part in shaping life's ideals. They lie like so much "rubbish in the mind," dulling the edge of learning interest and making the achievement of more desirable goals less likely.[55] For similar reasons, Chave concludes that religious education "cannot look backward for its message, methods, or incentives but must find them in the growing present."[56] Coe enunciates a related sentiment: "If we would press toward a democracy of God, we must turn the attention of pupils to many matters that are this side of the biblical horizon."[57]

Content Is Present Living

Content encompasses all of life's possible experiences as they are enriched, interpreted, and controlled in terms of purposes in harmony with the "Christian ideal." From the social-cultural perspective, content may not be separated from teaching method. Thus, religious education becomes actual guided experience in living the Christian life. The qualities of religious thinking and responsible living are best nurtured through deliberately planned participation in life experiences as a "real part" of the world's working force. Social interaction is regarded as the "basal process" of both religious education and social reconstruction. Accordingly, these linked processes take place together.[58]

Coe elaborates upon the here-and-now focus of content which is to be found in present relations and interactions between persons. He argues that educational practices must be rooted in the incarnational notion that God makes Himself known in concrete life experiences; that they must fundamentally consist of arranging conditions in which love is experienced, exercised, and deliberately lived. He also theorizes that the intellectual and faith capacities fostered by such "real-life" experience will sustain a lifelong pattern of Christian living. Practically, then, Coe suggests that a socially grounded religious education might well include the planned involvement of learners with persons who *really love both them and others.* Involvement with loving persons should be followed by the deliberate expansion of the learner's social attachments. For example, this might be accomplished by merging family loyalties into human interests of wider cultural scope. This kind of practice in loving, provides a basis for a truly vital theory of religious instruction in which there is no longer the deadly separation of knowing from doing, of Christian doctrine from Christian experience. By thus grounding the notion of content in present social interaction, it is possible to fuse love and faith, "so that even in childhood the voice of God and the voice of human need shall be one voice."[59]

Subject-Matter Content

Social experience then, not printed facts which can be mastered, is the *true content* of religious education. "The Word made flesh," not in a historical event but in those human relations that accompany teaching, is perceived as by far the more effective factor in the process of religious education. Nonetheless, subject-matter content is a matter of considerable importance for this model. One initial assumption seems to be that there is no specifically religious subject matter, or religious knowledge, because spiritual and material reality are considered to have an interdependent relationship. It is asserted that subject matter can and should be drawn from "anything, anywhere"—from Scripture, history, church life, the world of present experience, "the early lilacs," and the "sow's pink litter." However, it is strongly maintained that the principle of social interaction must be determinative of any subject matter which is inserted into a religious education program. This is because the historic separation between *living* and *preparing to live* "must not be allowed to reenter the religious educational process via subject matter content." In addition, subject matter that is not specifically social (e.g., physical science) is to be treated as social in the sense that it is of common interest to society—and to God.[60]

Bower suggests that, if the content of religious education is understood in the manner described above, the specific content of the religious education curriculum is constituted of three elements: (1) the situation as it is being lived; (2) the past experience which the learner brings to the learning situation and which is his first resource in interpreting and dealing with new experiences; and (3) the experience of the race itself as it is communicated to individual learners—thus making it unnecessary to begin totally anew each time a different situation is faced. Bower considers the Bible to be the prime example of "racial experience."[61]

Betts maintains that two principles are to be observed in the selection of content: (1) it is to be suited to the aims that are sought and (2) it is to be adapted to the student. The "great law" to be observed in the ordering of subject matter is that it must be done psychologically. Although Betts' approach to subject matter focuses upon the learner and the learner's own individual capacities rather than upon a revealed message, it does seem to bring about a separation of content from the living of life that is not in full accord with this model.[62]

The Bible, the major source of religious education content for educators during the first nineteen centuries of the church's existence, becomes, at best, a resource. Historically, educators went to the Bible trusting to find God's thoughts and feelings concerning the human family. But, for their part, classical-liberal thinkers typically believe that the Bible is little more than a collection of records concerning human experiences. Fahs is especially clear in her statement of this point of view:

> The Bible newly interpreted, as a result of our new knowledge, is shown to be a collection of records of human experiences. It is about people. It tells us what they were like and how they believed about God and their world, and how these beliefs affected their living. In short, whereas the old Bible is thought of as divine, the new Bible is human.[63]

In similar fashion, Coe maintains that the Bible is a uniquely powerful body of social literature which will not be supplanted as a significant religious educational resource. Nonetheless, in and of itself, the Bible cannot communicate divine life. Accordingly, Coe classifies the Scriptures as one of many means for promoting and awakening that divine life that is theoretically communicated through the social process only by living itself, the Bible being a record of that social process for but one cultural group.[64]

Teacher

A key question that gets at the heart of the differences between the historic prototype and the liberal model is: "Shall religion teaching be conceived in terms of handing on a religion or shall it be conceived in terms of participation with students in the creation of a new world?" The liberal model views the latter as the only viable possibility. Underlying the rationale for this view is the conviction that living the Christian life does not differ from expertness in any other practical activity. This is especially true in that religious education is not considered to be qualitatively advanced by the reception of any "supposedly God ordained message." Accordingly, the teacher must not risk invasion of the personality by imposing "truth" upon learners. Rather, the teacher seeks to promote growth through skillfully guiding the learner's participation in "real life experiences." The goal in this process is to "emancipate" the learner for full and active membership in the "democracy of God."[65]

Coe further argues that transmissive modes of teaching children are likely to produce adults who "settle historical and scientific questions without historical or scientific study, and by the results judge whether [their] neighbors are sheep or goats."[66] On the other hand, Chave argues that teaching which consists mainly in guiding growing learners into meaningful group experience will, with greater probability, educate them for an adulthood characterized by high ideals and effective social skills.[67]

The Teacher's Qualifications

According to this model's perspective, religion teachers are qualified by necessary competencies which may be *taught to intelligent and willing persons.* Such competencies, based not upon personal piety or religiosity, but upon demonstrable skills, would relieve many of the strains which exist in church school endeavors. At least in theory, teachers could be assigned, transferred, promoted, or discharged on impersonal (but demonstrably desirable) educational grounds. In the ideal democracy of God every worker could be counted upon to acquiesce in all decisions, even those running against personal desires, providing such decisions were supported by evidence that a more efficient religious education would ensue.

"Personality" is another often mentioned qualification. Nothing, it is maintained, will take the place of a wholesome and winning personality that actually experiences and, in turn, admits others into the experience and fellowship of the Christian life. However, personality is not considered a "gift from God." The teacher's personality is caused as "everything is caused." Hence, the ideal teacher's personality is made, not born. In essence, personality can be counted among the skills which a teacher can be held responsible to learn and to exhibit.[68]

The Teacher's Training

Social interaction is at the core of social-cultural conceived teacher training. The potential teacher is not taught a "bag of tricks" such as might make one assume that he or she "really can teach religion" at some future time. Rather, the teacher in training is immediately immersed in the social process that is religious education. For this reason, Coe advances the following principles that he believes distinguish an effective program to train teachers in a local parish: *first*, that training in the motive to teach is the cornerstone of the whole enterprise—this consists of "enlisting the parental instinct as an active core" around which society may be transformed into the family of God; *second*, that the material for such a program is primarily one's interaction with particular children, and only secondarily with books; and *third*, that training the teacher does not occur in isolation from the actual work of the school—"skill is achieved by the fusion of doing and thinking."[69]

Certain obvious difficulties encountered in effectively training teachers in the time usually available in parish situations have brought some theorists to the conclusion that the most effective means of improving teaching is through "supervised practice." Supervision, as defined here, is dynamically rooted in the "social interactive process." It offers a practical way to insert a professional element into certain otherwise chaotic situations. The supervisor, however, in Chave's helpful phraseology, "is not a 'super.'" Rather he or she is a recognized coworker, appointed because of a felt need and a desired outcome. Coe, similarly, takes for granted that the fundamental idea in supervision is intimate sharing of those burdens and blames that sometimes fall heavily upon isolated individuals.[70]

The Teacher's Method

From the liberal perspective, *content* and *method* are inseparable realities. It has been suggested, if a distinction must be made, that content might be thought of as the material, the "stuff," of experience; whereas method is the way of dealing with it. Thus content and method are looked upon as being determinative of each other. One very important consequence of this way of relating content and method is that religious beliefs, attitudes, and overt behaviors are considered to be influenced more by the shape of the experience itself than by the biblical or doctrinal subject matter that is presented. Quite consistently, Chave maintains that the end point of religious education must be considered in the selection of methods employed by the teacher. When creative responses are desired, methods of transmissive indoctrination which are likely to produce "mere conformity" must be rejected in favor of democratic procedures which tend to lead to creative kinds of behavior. The teacher, then, employs social interaction as an overall method, but makes deliberate, responsible use of such other individual methods as may have shown themselves to be productive of the desired goals. One important characteristic of teaching practices based upon the liberal theological model is that the teacher functions democratically as a guide to "forthreaching" rather than "passive" learners. Obviously, this model is more concerned with the "learner's learning" than with the "teacher's teaching."[71]

The development of more dependable teaching methods by means of scientifically regulated observation and experiment has been proposed by a number of theorists, notably Coe and Bower. Coe maintains that the discovery of "laws" relating to the "measured relations of antecedence and consequence" would make it possible to reintroduce the notion of control in religious education. In Coe's mind, "control" should not be defined in a "school-masterish" sense, but in the sense that the religion teacher would be in command of a process.[72] The overall teaching process has been analyzed by Bower in terms of several related, but not necessarily sequential, learning steps: (1) clear realization of the situation; (2) analysis of the issues; (3) past experience of the learner and of the race; (4) identification of possible outcomes; (5) selection of desired outcomes; (6) experimentation and testing conclusions; and (7) reduction of desired outcomes, when achieved, to habitual behaviors.[73]

Coe gives a helpful summary of the theory underlying the social-cultural attitude toward teaching method, as well as toward the content of religious education. "Social character and efficiency are to be achieved through social experience; social experience is to be had primarily through the performance of social functions, but it may be extended through imagination in the use of well-selected and well-graded subject matter that represents the social experience of the race; school experience is most effective educationally when the pupil experiences the least break between it and the life of the larger society."[74]

Learner

The learner, as understood by the aid of modern science rather than by theological doctrines concerning human nature, may well be the determining factor in the classical-liberal model. As a product of evolution, the learner is perceived to have received both "good and bad fruits" from the experience of the race. Any doctrine of original sin which severs human relationship with God is rejected out of hand. The racial heritage is believed to leave the learner's religious capacities, rooted in the instinctual nature, intact. Accordingly, the laws by which the learner may be educated for full participation in the "democracy of God" are within the learner's own self. Such laws must be discovered scientifically through controlled observation and experiment, not through theological speculation. Thus a significant aspect of the educational task is to side with creative evolutionary forces in encouraging the "higher tendencies." Educational measures are not intended to press the learner into any divinely revealed mold. The purpose of these measures is to free the learner to creatively work out appropriate relationships with others and with God through active participation in the social process.[75]

The Nature of the Learner

A key feature of this model is the perception that the learner is a living organism, a whole being, whose primary resources for religious and social development are fully within the "self boundaries." Bower, for example, is critical of historic understandings which divide the human person into "body" and "soul," or into "natural" and "supernatural," as separate entities. He does admit that, for purposes of description and analysis, it may be convenient to think in terms of physicochemical elements, reflexes, impulses, habits, and the like. Bower maintains that all of these physical, mental, and spiritual concepts are so interdependent that it is not possible to determine their boundaries. The living person, to use his words, is a "functioning whole."[76]

Fahs castigates the viewpoint of religious leaders who assume from a position of theological dogma that children are "born in sin" and therefore have evil instincts. She argues for the contrary position, namely that learners are emotionally dynamic, motivated to struggle toward their own desires and particularly sensitive to the emotional atmosphere. Further, she asserts that, even from birth, the child is conditioned toward love rather than hostility. If this love should turn to hostility, the cause is not some inward propensity toward evil. It is rather that the child has been deprived of love. Fahs appears to base her permissively intentioned teaching methods upon a conviction that human nature is inclined toward "the good" and that it grows according to a natural developmental schedule.[77] Coe is of the opinion that children are born "bearing the image of the creator," but that they are obviously candidates for either a good or a bad character. The task of religious education is to provide encouragement and support for the better possibilities. In his rather extended discussion of the nature of the student and the implications for religious education, Coe records his view that, theoretically, the difficulties for religious education arising from the theological doctrine of depravity are largely overcome in those communions where the countervailing doctrine of baptismal regeneration is accepted.[78]

The Personality of the Learner

Religious education has a twofold function: (1) to bring about the fullest possible development of whole persons and (2) to promote social righteousness within a society of growing persons. From the perspective of the liberal model, learners and their personal development constitute the "irreducible factor" in any religious educational endeavor. The writings of Bower and Coe, clearly the two most influential theorists working from this model, evince an extensive interest in the subject of the learner's personality, especially its development through education.

Bower considers personality to be primarily a social product. Society, in turn, is considered a composition of individual persons whose collective character determines its integrity. He theorizes that the development of personality is influenced by a hierarchy of physical, reflexive, social-interactive, intellective, and valuative factors, the last two factors having particular salience. *Human intelligence* makes possible the creative, conscious, many-sided personal relations (natural, social, cosmic) which distinguish human learners from the lower animals. The *valuative factor*, interacting with the intellective factor, purportedly leads to the highest level of human behavior in which intelligent preferential choice makes possible both an organized system of values and a working philosophy of life. The task of religious education, then, "is to help self-realizing persons discover the potential values as they emerge from their experience in the course of everyday living and to test them by the insights and values of the human past, interpret them, and judge them so as to bring their experience under the discipline of a controlling purpose." Bower concludes from the above line of reasoning that personality is essentially an outgrowth of experience.[79]

For his part, Coe contends that human personality is rooted in the "depths of reality." By this he means that the human personality manifests an "interfusion" with God, having a quality which may best be described as "sacred." Coe theorizes that at an early stage of development human beings are persons more in potentiality than in fact. The human being's journey to personhood is achieved primarily through self-affirmative participation in valuational acts. Consequently, the worth of human beings as persons, based on and arising out of the underlying pervasive principle of continuous creation, is inherent in the Christian ideal. Therefore, development of a proper attitude toward the inexhaustible worth of persons might well lead to a re-created educational process which would at least aim "to awaken personality and help it to rich self-activity in a society of persons."[80] This kind of re-created education, it is maintained, would not present life's problems as solved. Conversely, it would require all persons to take their part in a risky, "mountain-ously difficult," adventure through participation with God in the re-creation of a moral order—a society of persons "bound together in lively good will."[81] Coe pithily defines religious education from this personalist perspective as "the systematic, critical examination and reconstruction of relations between persons, guided by Jesus' assumption that persons are of infinite worth, and by the hypothesis of the existence of God, the Great Value of Persons."[82]

The Learner's Responsibility to Society

The liberal model's concept of salvation lays upon religious educators the heavy burden of enabling learners to participate in the reconstruction of an ideal society. By leading the learner into the turmoil of social endeavor, and thus suffering with God, the learner hopefully loses something of individuality, but gains life. However, this activity in humanity's struggle toward a present salvation is not mere involvement in mass action; it is, rather, responsible, deliberate participation in a group. This participation, in turn, leads to an effective regard for one another in such a way that the individual is "disengaged from the mass." Thus conceived, education ultimately individualizes persons (learners), at least theoretically.[83]

Environment

Social-cultural oriented theorists fully appreciate the impact of the environment upon religious education. However, any deliberate control of environmental factors as specific variables in religious education plays little part in construction of the liberal theological model. Fahs does assert that "all life, all existence" is appropriate resource material. But it is only in a very general sense that she employs environment as a variable. The "early lilacs," "the mire of the pond-side," and the "mother at home" are indeed suggested content samples from the environment, but they are not consciously incorporated in any clear hypothesis that points to suggested outcomes.[84] Episcopal educator Case argues that liberals do value the influence of the environment on learning. She states that "to a varying degree, 'environment' is understood to include the imaginative elements present, the persons in the group, and the total 'set' of the learner, as well as the material surroundings." Accordingly, she maintains that religious education must make provision for some element of environmental control.[85]

Coe concerns himself with the religious educational effects of societal surroundings; one use, albeit a modified use, of the environmental notion. He reflects, for example, upon the "social inheritance" of the American child. This inheritance obviously includes such environmental factors as sights and sounds of the street, amusements, business and social customs, home conditions, and the influence of every "man way" that the child meets. Coe seems to pay more attention to potentially negative environmental effects, suggesting that teachers could be more aware of reasons why efforts to teach religion are so often nullified by the learner's contact with life. However, he does agree that education, in the technical sense, involves deliberately controlling social and environmental elements. He also concedes that a rigorous assessment of the effects of such control is much needed. However, Coe's treatment of environment as a meaningful variable is so broad as to be of limited practical use to the work-a-day religion teacher in a parish setting.[86] Bower maintains that if it can be accepted that personality is the result of experiences that persons have, it logically follows that the way to control the development of personality (which he regards as the central concern of religious education) is to control the quality and direction of experience. "Experience" is defined as the interaction of a growing person (a "forthreaching organism") on one hand and a stimulating, dynamic, and expanding environment (consisting of nature, society, culture, and cosmic reality) on the other. Thus, Bower recognizes environment as a significant, but largely uncontrollable, dimension in education. Because he perceives that education proceeds experimentally in a scientific fashion, one might say that environment, for Bower, is a dependent variable; experience being controllable, is an independent variable.[87]

Evaluation

The pragmatic philosophical underpinnings of social-cultural thinking insure this model's orientation toward efficiency, its setting of standards, and its development of evaluative measures. Representative theorists typically believe that since the church is directly responsible to society, it should therefore be held accountable for the results secured from its educational agencies. Religious processes and practices that survive in the church must demonstrate their right to a place in the scheme of things by surviving rigorous assessment. For this reason it is not surprising that some theorists manifest an interest in knowing the "dollar and person costs" of educational practices as tested against the results in terms of students equipped for religious, socially responsible, living. "Measure, evaluate, test—these are the watchwords of the present-day spirit, and they will inevitably be applied to the church and its methods in common with other forms of social enterprise."[88] Among the underlying reasons for careful evaluation that have been enumerated are: (1) evaluation leads to a clarified view of the elements in a religious educational situation, (2) evaluation promotes reflective thinking, (3) evaluation creates a basis for higher forms of value by which religious educators may gain insights concerning the urgent demands that are laid upon them in the modern world, and (4) evaluation gives rise to knowledge that could not otherwise be gained.[89]

Evaluation of Specific Learning Outcomes

Individual learning outcomes, especially observable qualitative changes in the learner's lived life, are the immediate focus of commonly proposed evaluative procedures. Thus Betts contends that teaching ought not be evaluated simply upon the basis of how many facts have been acquired by the learner. The real issue has more to do with how much effect has been made upon the learner's life, character, and conduct. The final test of teaching, Betts argues, is whether the learner, as a result of religious instruction, actually lives differently here and now in the home, school, church, and community.[90] Similarly, Bower asserts that Christian education is put to the test by whether or not growing persons and groups of persons have been helped by their religious educational experience both to achieve loyalty to Christ and to a Christian quality of life.[91] On this same matter Coe states:

> *For teachers of the Christian religion the universal guide and test is, Am I helping my pupils grow in the personal or ethical-love way of dealing both with themselves and with others whose lives they touch?...Am I helping them master the conditions of efficient good-will by using the methods of science with reference to all facts involved, whether facts of history, of external nature, or of the mind of man?*[92]

Supervision of Religious Education

There is a tendency to connect evaluation, especially in parish settings, with the supervisory function. Chave, for example, remarks that every phase of supervision involves some aspect of testing or measuring.[93] Coe suggests that it is a supervisory responsibility both to develop standards of efficiency and to develop tests which measure progress against these standards. Coe believes that standards of whatever sort are likely to remain somewhat hazy until appropriate tests are devised.[94]

The representative literature contains many examples of tests for measuring religious progress along a number of axes. Chave's book, *Supervision of Religious Education* (1931), for example, rather thoroughly discusses possible applications for such measurement instruments as: (1) questionnaires, (2) analytic schedules, (3) rating scales, (4) objective type tests, (5) attitude scales, and (6) conduct tests.[95]

The Scientific Method

Social-cultural theorists are unanimous in their faith that the scientific method "which has been employed with such satisfactory results in the natural, social, and educational sciences" may be fruitfully employed as a fundamental tool in religious education.[96] Bower criticizes the untested nature of historic modes of education and asserts that

> the profound movements that are sweeping through the educational work of the modern church and are effecting its complete reconstruction are, for the most part, the result of the scientific spirit. Under its influence the nature of religious experience is being charted, the materials of religious instruction are undergoing organization, a technique of method is being worked out, the conditions of teaching are being standardized, and teachers are being scientifically trained for the task of directing the development of the religious life of the young.[97]

Coe suggests that the scientific method may best be employed by adopting personal attitudes in harmony with the scientific ideal, rather than by mere slavish attention to details of scientific technique. He gives six propositions to indicate the kinds of readiness and the kinds of self-judgment that are involved in applying scientific procedures to religious educational settings: (1) the scientific method is characterized by a spirit of intellectual cooperation—the scientist acts freely as an individual, but is also sensitive to the free acts of others; (2) in scientific work there are no foreigners, social classes, or hierarchical prerogatives, because competence is the credential; (3) the scientific spirit involves eagerness to learn, not to tell someone else what is on one's mind; (4) while every sort of logical procedure is to be respected, particular reliance is placed upon observed fact (hence a penchant for measurement); (5) causal relations are sought by the scientific use of hypothesis, experiment, and statistical analysis; and (6) in the scientific method there is no orthodoxy except to scientific principles—the fellowship of scientific minds rests upon a common understanding of procedure and not upon a common conclusion.[98]

SUMMARY

The liberal theological model described in this chapter was the most influential model of religious education for the first four decades of the century. It caught the spirit of the times and profoundly affected the life of the church. However, a transition to another model began in the years immediately following World War I. This transition accelerated in the 1930s with the Great Depression and with events foreshadowing World War II. These sad events of history undermined the optimistic tenets of the liberal model. At the same time, energized by the writings of Karl Barth and Reinhold Niebuhr, a new interest in theology was being generated. During the 1940s it was evident that the religious education scene was changing. By 1950, with the publication of Randolph Crump Miller's *The Clue to Christian Education*, the scene had changed. In the following chapter, I have employed "mainline theological" as a descriptor for the model that arose out of these mid-century churnings. Writers from this theologically dynamic point of view seem united (1) in their agreement that individual human beings do need some kind of spiritual redemption, and (2) in their conviction that the Christian church is the proper locus for an adequate religious education.

CHAPTER 4

THE MID-CENTURY MAINLINE MODEL OF RELIGIOUS EDUCATION:

A Theological Model

TRANSITION TO A THEOLOGICALLY DYNAMIC MODEL

The mid-century mainline model features a heightened attention to a dynamic theology that originated in the decades immediately following World War I. Whereas the attention of the liberal model is rather narrowly centered upon social interaction, the attention of the mainline model is broadened so as to include a "God who works." Educational antecedents to the mainline model, at least in its earlier expressions, remain closely linked with those of the liberal model. Thus the thought of Bushnell along with, for example, that of Dewey, Froebel, and contemporary researchers informs the educational theory of this model. Theologically, however, the mainline model represents a distinct shift from a classical, liberal stance toward a range of newer perspectives.

This shift might well be described as a transition from a "this-worldly" to a decidedly "God-and-church" orientation. The transition to this "new way of thinking" began in the 1920s, accelerated during the Depression of the 1930s, and came into focus by about 1940. It was during this period that the optimistic programs launched under the tenets of the liberal model lost their momentum and their optimism. One precipitating factor in this change was the straitened economic environment brought on by the Great Depression. In turn, this forced a retrenchment in most programs. Throughout the period of retrenchment, roughly the decade of the 1930s, powerful currents were generated by the theological impact of such works as Karl Barth's *Der Rommerbrie* (1919),[1] and Reinhold Niebuhr's *Moral Man and Immoral Society* (1932).[2] Together with works of similar import, these influenced a number of thinkers to engage in a serious reassessment of the theoretical foundations of the classical liberal model that had been put in place by Coe, Bower, Fahs, and others identified with the so-called Religious Education Movement. The focal point of this reassessment seems to have been the optimistic "doctrine of man" which had been a principal underpinning of the theories that molded the liberal model during the earlier decades of the twentieth century.[3]

By the 1940s, it was evident that the effects of this reassessment had generated sufficient strength to influence the climate of the religious education scene in America. Harrison Elliott was among the first to present a clear analysis of the changing situation. His *Can Religious Education be Christian?* (1940) stated the issues confronting the field at the beginning of the decade: "There has been an increasing tendency in Protestant churches to return to the historical formulations of the Christian religion and to repudiate the adjustments which had been made under the influence of modern scientific and social developments."[4] Elliott personally rejected the tendency to return to what he considered to be an inadequate, neo-orthodox, version of Christianity and the authoritarian approach to religious education which he believed would grow out of it. He strongly supported a continuation of a thoroughly liberal position with its emphasis upon human responsibility to pursue solutions for the problems of the world.[5]

H. Shelton Smith's *Faith and Nurture* (1941) expressed a point of view diametrically opposed to that of Elliott. Smith's influential book appears to have played a significant part in opening the way for a consciously revamped model of religious education. Smith argued that the emerging patterns of investigation, such as he found in Reinhold Niebuhr, so undermined the liberal model that the question must be asked: "Shall Protestant nurture realign its theological foundations with the newer currents of Christian thought, or shall it resist those currents and merely reaffirm its faith in traditional liberalism?"[6] Although Smith's sentiments quite obviously favored this realignment with the "newer theological" (neo-orthodox) currents, *Faith and Nurture* was largely devoted to "unsparing criticism" of the theoretical bases of religious education as represented in the school of thought associated with Coe and Bower. Smith thus left the work of "realignment" to others.[7]

A landmark, of sorts, in the new orientation proposed by Smith resulted in the establishment of a committee of the International Council of Religious Education in 1944. Among other responsibilities, this committee was charged with the specific task of examining "the need of a considered statement as to the place of theological and other concepts in Christian education." The major report of this committee, edited by Paul Vieth, was published in 1947 as *The Church and Christian Education*.[8] Even though it did not bring about a consensus, this work did incorporate elements that are described by James Smart as being "far removed from the optimistic liberalism of Coe or Chave."[9] Sara Little identifies Vieth's report as the beginning of a clearly discernible theological emphasis in religious education which is distinctive enough to be termed a movement.[10]

After its rise in the post World War I decades, the mid-century mainline model took shape and became extremely influential during the two decades from about 1950 to 1970. Since 1970, diverging expressions of this rather flexible model have continued to exercise an important role in the ongoing development of the profession, especially among so-called establishment religious educators.

CRITERIA

The mid-century mainline model is defined by these criteria: (1) Normative educational decisions are based on judgments informed by a wide range of twentieth-century theological expressions including, though not limited to, those commonly labeled neo-orthodox, process, and liberation. (2) The broad aim is to establish individuals in a right relationship with God and then to educate them for socially responsible, intelligent, and adult Christian (religious) living. (3) The teacher's task is regarded as one of entering into a communal relationship with learners for the express purpose of guiding them in their growth within themselves, toward God, and toward others. (4) The learner's spiritual life is most effectively fostered within the revelatory fellowship of the church (religious community).

These theorists and writers seem essentially united in (1) their renunciation of the optimistic brand of theology that undergirded the classical liberal model; (2) their reservations concerning what they regard as an inadequate expression of theology implicit in "transmissive" education; (3) their agreement that individual human beings do need some kind of spiritual redemption; (4) their position that the church, not merely society, is the proper locus of religious life and education; (5) their agreement that human freedom is necessary for authenticity in fleshing out the Christian life; and (6) at least in earlier writings, their preference for the term "Christian education" rather than "religious education." This latter is perhaps not a substantive distinction, but it is important to record since the change in phraseology was extremely meaningful during the formative phases of the model.

REPRESENTATIVE THEORISTS

Randolph Crump Miller (b. 1910)

Randolph Crump Miller, longtime editor of the journal *Religious Education*, emerged as the most influential of those whose efforts eventuated in a refocused theological emphasis during the 1950s and 1960s. Throughout his numerous writings, Miller states and restates the proposition that "Christian theology is the primary source of Christian educational theory and procedure." His most fundamental contribution to the early development of the mainline model, with its renewed theological vitality, was probably his *The Clue to Christian Education* (1950).[11] This book was written in direct response to the issues raised by the Harrison Elliott and

Shelton Smith dialogue. It brought back into the religious education scene "a portrait of a deity who makes all things new."[12] A rather widely quoted summary of the mainline model, as well as of Miller's viewpoint, is:

> The clue to Christian education is the rediscovery of a relevant theology which will bridge the gap between content and method, providing the background and perspective of Christian truth by which the best methods and content will be used as tools to bring the learners into the right relationship with the living God who is revealed to us in Jesus Christ, using the guidance of parents and the fellowship of life in the church as the environment in which Christian nurture will take place.[13]

Miller's edited work, *Empirical Theology: A Handbook* (1992)[14] continues his long record of creative contributions to the profession at the intersection of his lifelong interests, namely theology and Christian education.

Lewis Joseph Sherrill (1892-1957)

Lewis Sherrill attained a high reputation as professor of religious education at Union Theological Seminary, New York. However, he may well be best remembered for his widely read history, *The Rise of Christian Education* (1944).[15] For the purposes of this study, Sherrill's major contribution is *The Gift of Power* (1955).[16] *The Gift of Power* was intentionally a contribution to that theorizing which Sherrill perceived to be "emerging as a result of the plight of modern man, and the new currents of religious and psychological thought concerning it."[17] Sherrill professes to be in search of a genre of Christian education in which the core process is a revelatory encounter between God as Self and man as self. He believes that the relevance of such an educational process is that it will meet the individual's existing spiritual and psychological needs, as well as call forth his or her capacities as a person. The locus of this kind of education is the religious community (church) in which God and learners are brought together in an intricate, dynamic web of relationships. Sherrill nicely summed up his position in commenting that Christian education "is the attempt, ordinarily by members of the Christian community, to participate in and to guide the changes which take place in persons in their relationships with

God, with the church, with other persons, with the physical world, and with oneself."[18]

Sara Little (b. 1919)

Sara Little's widely known book, *The Role of the Bible in Contemporary Christian Education* (1961),[19] seems itself to have played a role in identifying the structural elements and providing a perspective on the model that was already beginning to take shape in the work of Miller, Sherrill, Smart, and others. Little has been a consistent contributor to the ongoing shaping and reshaping of religious education theory, mostly within the parameters of the mainline paradigm. In some of her later work she engages in important adventuring, stretching the boundaries of the model by considering the implications of advancing theological under-standings in relation to her special interest in teaching. Little's *To Set One's Heart: Belief and Teaching in the Church* (1983)[20] makes an especially helpful contribution by proposing concrete applications of the mainline model's implications for the ministry of teaching.

James D. Smart (1906-1982)

The church is possibly the key element in James Smart's attempt to develop a viable, ecumenically Christian, solution to the theoretical and practical problems of religious education. He argues that religious education, in the Christian sense, can only be understood against the background of the New Testament concepts of "God" and "church." Since the church is "the fellowship of those persons to whom God is making himself known," Smart theorizes that it is the proper focal point of all Christian educational activity. His extensive writings address a number of biblical and theological matters, but Smart's most influential books on religious educational theory are *The Teaching Ministry of the Church* (1954)[21] and *The Creed in Christian Teaching* (1962).[22] Smart effectively applied the results of his investigations to upgrading the curricular offerings of his own Presbyterian communion. His more scholarly writings, especially *Teaching Ministry of the Church*, exerted a positive influence in support of the professional community of religious educators. It gave solid, academically responsible, support to the linkage of educational ministries with the broader mission of the church.

Iris V. Cully (b. 1914)

Iris Cully has advanced the field in a number of notable ways through her teaching and writing. Some of her books cogently implement the perspective of the mainline model with respect to specific practical matters such as worship, Bible teaching, and Sunday School renewal. Other books, for example, *The Dynamics of Christian Education* (1958),[23] *Change, Conflict, and Self-Determination: Next Steps in Religious Education* (1972),[24] and *Education for Spiritual Growth* (1984)[25] contribute more immediately to the body of literature that addresses the broader outcomes of Christian religious education in the light of theory-practice relationships. In clear contrast with the liberal viewpoint with which she compares her own understanding, Cully's writings incorporate the Bible, the church, and a "God who works" as meaningful theoretical elements.[26] As is true of certain other mainline theorists, Cully's later works give evidence of her continuing effort to remain abreast of changing patterns of theological thought and to incisively incorporate these into her own, ever developing version of the mainline model.

D. Campbell Wyckoff (b. 1918)

D. Campbell Wyckoff's carefully crafted writings have added considerably to the dialogue on theory and practice. Having "grown up in a liberal atmosphere, shot through with the imperatives of the social gospel," in his theologically formative years Wyckoff came under the influence of the wave of thought energized by Karl Barth and Reinhold Niebuhr. At that point, his thinking became "more conservative and biblical without losing its educational focus or its concern for social responsibility.[27] Thus Wyckoff became something of a personal example of the shift in thought that affected religious education theory during the middle years of the twentieth century. A number of Wyckoffs writings illustrate the mainline model, but *The Task of Christian Education* (1954)[28] and *The Gospel and Christian Education* (1959)[29] have special relevance. These two books provide a persuasive statement of model and, perhaps even more importantly, they pinpoint its more important theory-practice connections.

Howard Grimes (b. 1915)

During his long career as professor of Christian education at Southern Methodist University, Howard Grimes contributed a number of books that added meaningfully to the development of religious education as a profession. His *The Church Redemptive* (1958) is among the clearer statements arguing for the primary features of the mainline model. Consistent with the model, in Grimes' words *The Church Redemptive* is "a confession of faith in the importance of the Church in the day-to-day existence of the Christian."[30] Grimes studied at Union Theological Seminary under Harrison Elliott during the period that the liberal model was undergoing the aforementioned reassessment at the hands of Shelton Smith and others. He exhibits an especially clear grasp of the issues that separate the liberal and mainline models. Grimes considered the matter at hand and, in what he terms a "rebellion against the twentieth-century liberalism," embraced this "new kind of thinking." Among the theological issues typical of those that seem to have energized mainline theorists, Grimes lists (1) his continuing interests in those aspects of human nature that require redemption, (2) his inquiry into the nature of the relationship between revelation and the Bible, and (3) his investigation of ways in which process theology can effectively enhance the practice of religious education.[31]

C. Ellis Nelson (b. 1916)

C. Ellis Nelson, for some years chair of the Department of Religious Education at Union Theological Seminary (New York) and later President of Louisville Presbyterian Seminary, invested a significant portion of his considerable creativity in writings that are by-and-large supportive of the mainline model. From time to time, he pursued research projects addressing a longtime interest in the development of conscience. However, his most significant contributions that shaped the field are probably *Where Faith Begins* (1967)[32] and *How Faith Matures* (1989).[33] At least a minor classic in the field, *Where Faith Begins* examines the thesis that faith is communicated as persons of faith interact with others. A key issue, for Nelson, is to identify ways in which this socialization process can be made more intentional and thus more effective. *How Faith Matures* gives attention to the transformational power of religious experience. It seeks to identify ways in which such a transforming encounter with the living God can be facilitated in the life of the congregation.

John H. Westerhoff III (b. 1933)

In spite of the fact that his rather widely read books tend to be "conversations" rather than objective treatments of theory, some passages in John Westerhoff's writings may well be the purest examples of the mainline model in operation.[34] Westerhoff's writings add little to the model's structure. Rather, he seems to explore options within the model and then, with a certain verve, applies these results of his armchair investigations to meaningful educational settings in church life. Westerhoff credits his teachers at Harvard with helping him arrive at three convictions, each of which fits quite neatly into the mainline model: (1) that there is no learning unless someone is passionately searching; (2) that all anyone else can do is offer their life in all its brokenness and incompleteness as a resource for someone else's learning; and (3) that any truth which is discovered breaks in from a source that transcends both the seeker and the sharer.[35] In a number of passages Westerhoff underscores his conscious commitment to essential elements of the mainline model. Consider, for example, his statement in *Will Our Children Have Faith?* (1976): "Indeed, the church cannot proceed to develop an educational ministry without a clear, acknowledged theological foundation. A unity of theology and education is a necessity, not a luxury."[36] Westerhoff's creative applications of the model continue in "Fashioning Christians in Our Day," a chapter in *Schooling Christians: "Holy Experiments" in American Education* (1992).[37]

J. Gordon Chamberlin (b. 1914)

Chamberlain's perceptive observation of the religious education scene in *Freedom and Faith* (1965) offers a useful set of categories for analyzing, planning, and implementing educational concepts in the local church. His categories include examinations of the: (1) context in which church education is carried on, (2) the relation between the fields of education and theology, (3) objectives of the educational enterprise, and (4) processes of education.[38] Chamberlin's books reflect helpfully upon the mainline model's attitude toward aims in the light of a continually changing environment.

Rachel Henderlite (1905-1991)

Rachel Henderlite's *The Holy Spirit in Christian Education* (1964),[39] enunciates a number of the mainline model's key constructs in relation to the active working of the Holy Spirit within the world, as well as within the community of faith. Henderlite's book is often quoted in mainline literature, apparently because it goes further than most to develop a theory of learning, and ministry, that is consistent with the model. Although her writings sometimes employ biblical terms in ways that are almost reminiscent of the historical prototype, Henderlite's actual proposals, and her arguments for them, have a definite mid-twentieth century mainline flavor.

Gabriel Moran (b. 1935)

For more than three decades Gabriel Moran has invested his interest in language and his speculative energies toward describing and cultivating better ways of accomplishing the educational tasks incumbent upon the religious community. Although the categories in which Moran works are commonly cast in religious rather than theological idioms, a number of his earlier writings employ concepts that seem in substantial accord with the mainline model. Moran continuously subjects his own vision of religious education to scrutiny from various disciplines, including philosophy and theology, but especially linguistics. One result is that his later writings typically do not harmonize with earlier ones. For his part, Moran accepts the judgment that his writings may "seem at times to have completely reversed positions." His explanation is that his writings are stages on the way toward a "larger, continuing project of understanding."[40] It seems fair to suggest, then, that Moran's later writings more than stretch the boundaries of the mainline model, especially in its earlier expressions which insisted upon employing "Christian education" as a key descriptor. Moran's vision for ecumenical education, then, is so all-encompassing that his *Religious Body* (1974) is quite appropriately subtitled *Design for a New Reformation*.[41] Pursuant to his linguistically influenced efforts to describe a "religious education" that is inclusive of religions other than Christianity (e.g., Buddhism), Moran offers his more mature reflections in *Religious Education as a Second Language* (1989).[42]

More in line with the issues normally discussed among mainline thinkers, Moran's earlier writings often address the topic of revelation, defined as "a personal communion of knowledge, an interrelationship of God and the individual within a believing community."[43] As is true of most mainline thinkers, Moran regards the process of religious education as a revelationally active process in which the teacher's role "is to set students on the road toward self understanding by helping them use their intelligences creatively, originally, and constructively."[44] Accordingly, even from his earlier understanding, religious education is not a process of indoctrination by which children are prepared to be good members of a particular religious communion; rather it is a preparation for adult participation in life as it flows into the future.[45] Moran is a Roman Catholic, but his liberal outlook and his commitment to ecumenical education have contributed to making his writings uniquely acceptable to a wide range of perspectives.[46]

Maria Harris (b. 1934)

Maria Harris' writings also do not fit the mainline model at all points. For example, she does not place the writings of liberal thinkers in a negative light and she recommends certain teaching strategies that presage the social-science model. Still, her books such as *Fashion Me a People* (1989)[47] and *Teaching & Religious Imagination* (1987)[48] go far to explore religious education strategies that appear to have some roots in the mainline model. As a Roman Catholic laywoman, Harris' enthusiastic ecumenical stance seems to provide a certain freedom for her to test the ramifications of the model's implied strategies.

ANALYSIS OF THE MAINLINE MODEL

Aim

Responsible theological interpretation of relevant information gleaned from the Bible, the church's life, the culture, and the human situation is crucial to the development of mainline aims. Such aims typically reflect an attempt to give due recognition to cultural change while continuing in the spirit of the biblical tradition. Cully insightfully contrasts the liberal view in which "Man became the center of the educational process" with the revived theological view. "The church too," she argues, "has a center around which life revolves. This center is God. 'Theology,' the very title by which its science is called, denotes that fact."[49] In a similar vein, Miller suggests that aims must be grounded in a theology which recognizes God as the center and goal of its educational process.[50]

The concept of "revelation" likewise plays an important role in the process of generating aim. Revelation, from this perspective though, should be distinguished from the concept in which revelation is perceived as a more-or-less static "given." In this case, revelation has an ongoing quality that is directly connected with human experience, particularly in the life of the church.[51] Sherrill states the matter nicely: "When man encounters the Self-revealing God he is confronted…by a Person who offers himself to us in love and judgment, and calls upon us to give ourselves a living sacrifice in response. It is a matter of personal communion. If this is the core of revelation, so it must be the core of Christian education."[52]

Harris introduces another dimension as a help in understanding the underlying dynamics of aim. She suggests that education in the church must be perceived as "fashioning and refashioning" our being as God's people by continually moving in the direction of "creating and living more and more adequately as religious beings in the world."[53] Westerhoff's image seems quite compatible with Harris' when he argues, with acknowledged indebtedness to Tillich, that the church's educational task is to introduce each new generation into the life and ministry of the faith community. "To be a Christian," Westerhoff argues, "is to be in fellowship with the historic community of faith called the church…

and share that experience through their corporate activity in the world."[54]

Focus of Aim

In contrast both with historic aims which focus upon the transmission of a salvific message and with liberal aims which focus upon the development of an idealized social order, mainline aims are typically focused in the church, particularly in its corporate life. Thus, Smart affirms that the purposes of religious education from the Christian perspective cannot be understood apart from a clear understanding of the church which came into being as a consequence of God's breaking into our world in Jesus Christ.[55] With similar import, Miller states: "The main task is to teach the truth about God, with all the implications arising from God's nature and activity, in such a way that the learner will accept Jesus Christ as Lord and Savior, will become a member of the Body of Christ, and will live in the Christian way."[56] Within the scope of aims centered in the church, mainline thinkers have concerned themselves with a number of specific objectives, namely: planting faith, personal growth, intellectual growth, biblical understanding, and training for effective participation in the life of the church.

Planting the seeds of faith in the lives of those who look to the church for instruction in life is considered a key aim by a number of mainline theorists. Nelson, for example, makes it a basic assumption that "faith in the God of the Bible is the basic reality we want to share."[57] Grimes images this "faith planting" as encompassing much more than providing biblical and theological information, character formation, or even than conversion. He argues that the purpose of Christian education is to "lead persons into a living encounter with the God and Father of our Lord Jesus Christ, and to illuminate and enlighten the meaning of this encounter for all of life."[58] Little perceives this "faith planting" as the establishment of a "belief system" that might well be described as the "idea of truth and how it functions in our lives." This vital orientation to truth, in turn, provides a frame of reference for understanding and decision-making that will enable an individual to be in possession of a source of power for implementing genuinely Christian life-ways.[59]

Personal growth and development within the church's fellowship is regarded as a key dimension of aim. The educational process, it is theorized, should aim both to lead individuals into a living encounter with God and to provide spiritual support for them as they grow toward wholeness through living out the meaning of this encounter. Thus, Miller asserts that a major purpose of religious education is to make the learner whole through the establishment of secure relationships among persons within a dynamic Christian community in which there is also a continuing encounter with God and an organic connection with the environment.[60]

The *intellectual growth* of individual Christians is looked upon as a valid aim, albeit often neglected. It is taken for granted that the proper business of religious education is not merely the divine task of saving students, but also included is "the human task of freeing men for life in the Spirit by awakening intelligence and freedom."[61] Chamberlin phrases this attitude toward aim nicely, suggesting that Christian education has sometimes been employed simply as a tool to "press virtue into young sinners" instead of pressing toward the also well-founded objective of educating Christians.[62]

One principal function of the educational work of the church is to introduce learners to the Bible. This biblical introduction, it is acknowledged, must go well beyond mere transmission of information about the Bible or the rote memorization of biblical passages. It must promote an *understanding of the Bible* in terms of its relevant contemporary message. The Bible, then, is considered to be worth knowing in and of itself because it is the primary written witness to revelation. Furthermore, the Bible is the basic source of Christian theology and its principles provide potential solutions to many human problems. In addition, it has been theorized that a knowledge of the Bible will "prepare the way for men to receive God and to respond to him in the present."[63]

The education and training of persons within the church to be the church is another often mentioned consideration in determining aim. This education for the "life in Christ" is said to involve a remaking, renewing, and transforming process that not only sets it off from other forms of education, it makes it "specifically Christian." The ultimate aim is that the living Christ will take hold of all of life through the witness and functional ministry of an educated and committed church. Sherrill declares that this kind of transforming education, which is not fully possible outside of the Christian community, takes place naturally within the fellowship of the church. Here God confronts persons in the continuing redemptive disclosure of Himself.[64] In a similar spirit, but using different imagery, Smart maintains:

> *Christian education exists because the life that came into the world in Jesus Christ demands a human channel of communication that it may reach an ever widening circle of men, women, and children, and become their life. The aim of Christian teaching is to widen and deepen that human channel, to help forward the growth and enrichment of the human fellowship, through which Jesus Christ moves ever afresh into the life of the world to redeem mankind.[65]*

Scope of Aim

The scope of aim is broadened by a sensitivity to varying cultural conditions and by the high view placed upon individual freedom. Mainline consciousness of the need for flexibility in an ecumenical environment also contributes to a certain willingness to state aims in rather nonspecific and often nonbehavioral terms. Overly definite aims "as might be appropriate for an era in which it is rather certain that learners will stay with a particular tradition and continue to view life from that tradition's perspective" are not considered appropriate in an "everchanging contemporary society." Wyckoff captures the mood of the model by proposing that aim might well be stated: *"that we may become persons who see things as they are and who come to grips with life."*[66] On the basis that it seeks to nurture a Holy Spirit guided and transformed life, Wyckoff argues that those factors which most clearly differentiate Christian education from other forms of education may be most effectively fostered through this reality of "seeing things as they are." Of course this "seeing" must be accompanied by "coming to grips with life" in the "context of this reality."[67] Chamberlin demonstrates a similar concern for stating aims in the context of worldview and environmental change. He proposes the concept of "no static ends" as a means of eventually attaining "the educated person who has engaged in a self-conscious reexamination of his views on the meaning of existence, who has been confronted by a competent interpretation of the Christian faith, and who accepts his responsibility for the many decisions of his life in the light of his decision."[68]

Sherrill seeks to avoid the peril of establishing aims that are so specific that religious educators are drawn into the "unhappy business" of predetermining desirable behaviors. He insists that one means of avoiding this peril is to keep the learner's presently existing self at the center of the educational process. Sherrill believes that the principal educational changes occur during the encounter which takes place within a learner's personal depths in confrontation with the self-revealing God. The learner's Christian life, then, is not merely a living out of predetermined rules that have been attached in some, possibly manipulatory, fashion to the periphery of the self; instead, it is the living response to a God who offers himself in love, as well as in judgment.[69]

Moran gives helpful expression to the concept of scope in determining aim. He proposes that aim must include freedom for individual learners, arguing that freedom can no longer be a side issue because of the rising consciousness which has become a fact of modern life. To include the deliberate giving of freedom within the scope of aim gives a necessary recognition to the potential for a more conscious kind of Christianity. In this way Christianity will truly offer "the incentive to open understanding and freedom to the boundless reality of personal value and communal love."[70]

Henderlite broadens the discussion of scope somewhat beyond the typical mainline horizon. She anticipates the outcome of Christian education to include "fellowship of redeemed men and women who are filled with the Spirit of God and driven out into the service of Christ in the world." Christian education must, in her mind, include education for mission beyond the mere local setting. Lacking such a missional dimension, Christian education is not "Christian education."[71]

Social and Moral Dimensions of Aim

Although aim tends to be focused in the church and in the nurture of the learner's personal Christian life, mainline theorists are careful to incorporate social and moral dimensions in their model. Such dimensions are considered incumbent upon the church and upon Christians. Thus, Miller contends that the very relevance of the Christian faith depends upon the living response of the Christian to faith in Jesus Christ. In the first place, this living response involves discovering the actual implications of the faith and then, in the second place, to live them out through participation in social change or in some other ministry of the church to the world.[72] In similar fashion Wyckoff suggests that, beyond the aim of nurturing the Christian life, there is the aim of a life to be lived and a character to be built. He finds three separate aspects to this dimension of aim, namely that Christian education may (1) be effective in helping persons build lives of integrity, (2) help persons live lives that are socially responsible, and (3) enable persons to live lives in full recognition of God.[73] Christian education cannot claim to have achieved its ultimate aims until Christians have effected such changes in society whereby the very processes of the larger community contribute to, rather than hinder, the process of religious and Christian growth. "A Church," to use Wyckoff's words, "may well state its Christian education aims in terms of such outcomes as these in the lives of its pupils: intelligent belief, Christian commitment, Christian character, churchmanship, and participation in the redemption of the community."[74]

Mainline thinkers sometimes advocate a pedagogy centered upon the personal revelation of God in the risen Christ on the basis that this might lead to the resolution of most of the moral and social questions upon which so much time is wasted in "fruitless teaching activity." Christian morality, from this perspective, needs to be presented as a creative response on the part of human beings to the, often difficult, situations in which we find ourselves. The moral anchor, then, would not be a list of do's and don'ts. Rather it would reside in one's individual understanding of the life, death, and resurrection of Jesus—and especially of His continual working in the church (and world) today. From this viewpoint, every genuinely loving act is revelatory of God through Christ and the Spirit. The social vision underlying model, in sum, is that Christian education would lead to a truly adult level of responsible Christian living. The teacher's role in an education based upon this kind of understanding guides the learner in discovering resident potentialities and promotes growth in the direction of becoming a free and responsible, unique and creative, person.

The church's mission and ministry to the world has a central place in Smart's historically generated conception of the social and moral dimensions of aim. The larger purposes of religious education must be continuous with the line of development that was marked out in the New Testament. The narrower goal must be coextensive with that of Jesus and the apostles. This goal would demand that religion teaching aim at no less than (1) to enable God to work in the hearts of learners making of them committed disciples; (2) to produce both understanding and personal faith adequate for maintenance of a vital Christian witness in the midst of an unbelieving world; (3) to enable God to bring into being a church marked by His presence and committed to the service of Jesus Christ "as an earthly body through which he may continue his redemption of the world"; and (4) to enable learners to grow into full life and active faith in the church, thus sharing its mission.[75]

Content

The mainline notion of "content" is not easy to encapsulate in a brief statement. An attempt is usually made to steer a carefully considered course between the view that asserts subject matter can and should be drawn from "anything, anywhere" and the view that understands content almost exclusively as a product of a revealed communication that must be passed on by direct communication. Harris offers a helpful, dynamic understanding of content based upon her construct of "indirect communication" that catches the spirit of the mainline theological model in a striking way. She suggests that it may be useful to consider content as "essentially elusive, ambiguous, and in the realm of mystery—that about which we can never know everything." For her, content will always bear the marks of mystery, of the apophatic, of paradox. Content then becomes the bearer of revelation.[76]

Content Corresponds with Present Experience

Mainline writers commonly seek to define content in such a way that it is neither disconnected from the historic Christian message nor meaningless in terms of present experience. The Christian message and present experience are sometimes said to "correspond." Such correspondence of subject matter content and present experience is a critical element in the model. Grimes describes the standpoint for this perspective, "The heart of the content…will be creative encounter between man and man and man and God. This takes place in community."[77] Westerhoff suggests that faith itself is communicated within the community, which implies a change in emphasis from "content" (what we teach) to "process" (how we teach).[78]

The notion, correspondence, is conceptualized in a number of ways. Miller, for example, theorizes that a twofold relationship between God and the learner is at the center of the curriculum. This means that the curriculum must at the same time be God-centered and experience-centered. Theology, "truth-about-God-in-relation-to-man,"[79] has both critical and explanatory functions; and, it "must be prior to the curriculum." Nonetheless, "the task of Christian education is not to teach theology, but to use theology as the basic tool for bringing learners into the right relationship with God in the fellowship of the Church."[80] Within the guidelines delineated by an "informed theology," Miller agrees with those who assert that materials for teaching are probably best developed directly out of the experience of the teacher and the learner together. He insists that both past and presently happening experiences offer a solid base for bringing systematized knowledge from the past to bear upon the concerns of the present. In this way there is developed a rationale for employing biblical materials in a life-oriented religious education program in which the learner is hypothesized to be "enabled to live meaningfully now and in the future." This kind of experientially based, theologically sound, curriculum will bridge the gap between content and method, truth and life, doctrine and experience. It will also allow religion teachers to "teach not so much things as the meaning of things."[81]

Wyckoff advances three principles which he believes may be of help to the religion teacher in dealing with the relationship between subject-matter content and experience. He submits, in the first place, that human experience is continuous for every individual; in the second place, that personality develops through experience; and, in the third place, that experience may be guided and enriched. These three principles constitute the groundwork for a unified concept of the process in which "subject matter and experience, content and experience " are combined. Theoretically, the teacher would employ his or her own experience and that of the learner, together with the rich truths of the Christian faith, toward the experience of God as a central reality. For most writers, this education "for life in Christ" would include "a thoroughgoing analysis of and commitment to the Christian faith as doctrine, as teaching, as a definitive formulation of what the life in Christ is."[82]

Thinkers such as Sherrill and Grimes ascribe considerable importance to the notion of fellowship or community. Together with others, they maintain that the content of Christian education is constituted in major part by those inner changes in persons that grow out of interactions within the Christian community. Sherrill is particularly concerned with the relationship between education and revelation. He distinguishes between *content of learning* (those changes that take place within the person as a result of participating in a dynamic, revelationally active educational process) and *materials of learning* (matter presented to the learner as a means of bringing about changes). Sherrill's most intense interest is concentrated upon matters related to the "deeper" levels of communication that take place within the Christian community, the scene where God redemptively reveals himself and where individuals influence one another in the responses they make to God. The Christian education growing out of this deep communication (which, it is said, can only take place to its fullest extent within the Christian community) does not lead to the accumulation of information as such, "but to the actual experience of the Person and the events with which the information deals."[83] Grimes pinpoints the heart of content as the creative encounter that takes place in community. This means that, in order to convey its message of love and concern, the church must become a community, a model, of love and concern.[84]

Moran is convinced that teachers should be much more interested in helping learners know God than they are in transmitting information about God. Consequently, he suggests that debate concerning matters of content and method is often so simplistic as to be practically meaningless. The more important theoretical questions might be addressed in the context of considering the circumstances under which any human being can help another person come to know God. Moran's conviction is that experience, present experience, constitutes the pivotal point of successful teaching practices.[85]

Subject Matter

Although experience is a major component for theorizing about content, there is nearly unanimous agreement among Protestants that subject matter relating specifically to the Christian faith must be integrated into the educational process. Commonly mentioned sources include the Bible, Christian theology, church history, and stories of the church today. These specifically Christian sources of subject matter are, obviously, in addition to those sources which extend as far as the experience of the race. Most such writers seem likely to agree with Miller's argument that subject matter ought to be employed selectively for the purpose of "opening up the channels of God's grace so that men may respond in faith to the Gospel."[86] Theological judgments are usually considered determinative in the selection of subject matter in a given situation. However, individual differences such as interests, capacities, and needs are recognized as mandating some form of subject matter grading.[87]

The Bible is considered to be the single most important source of subject matter, though it ordinarily is perceived to be a record of revelation rather than a revelation in and of itself. Mainline writers, however, typically reject the notion that religious education is best effected by the direct transmission of biblical content. Smart, for example, castigates religious education which stops short when biblical information has been handed on, although he agrees that biblical facts can be helpful and do need to be assimilated by learners. He maintains that the central purpose in teaching the Bible is that God may speak through it into the lives of learners as they are being taught—now. The religion teacher's handling of the Bible, then, should be with the expectation that God will make His word come alive with the power in which it was originally spoken.[88]

Henderlite agrees that there are certain problems in trying to steer between the twin perils of transmissive education on the one hand and liberal education on the other. Still she argues that it is incumbent upon the Christian educator to teach the "data of our faith in the hope that they will become the data for another's faith as the Spirit moves his heart to hear Christ and respond." She rather strongly contends that the Bible is the basic content, the basic subject matter, of Christian education; a content which requires the educator to provide an opportunity for the learner's decision and response.[89]

Sherrill theorizes that the Bible, as a record of God's disclosure of Himself, may fruitfully be used to prepare learners to respond to God in the present. Accordingly, biblical subject matter is introduced into the experience of the learner as a means of precipitating a personal encounter with, and a personal response to, God. One subsidiary purpose for using biblical materials in religious education is that God's people today may thus become familiar with the story of God's people in the Bible. Sherrill thinks that the histories, narratives, and life stories contained in the Bible are especially suitable for this purpose.[90]

Miller is similarly committed to the view that the Bible is a primary source of the Christian faith and thus has a rightful place at the center of the educational process. While holding that the Bible is the basic authority for theology, he believes that a responsible theology is the proper guide to the meaning of the Bible. Within the guidelines determined by a "responsible theology," then, Miller argues that biblical concepts are an appropriate and necessary element in teaching the Christian faith. In Miller's major work on this theme, *Biblical Theology and Christian Education* (1956), he develops his biblical theology in terms of the drama of redemption.[91] Grimes agrees that the Bible will commonly be the source of subject matter. True to the model, he argues that, when taken seriously as the record of God's search for humanity and our response, the Bible becomes the content laden "vehicle of God's revelation to us today."[92] In his way of probing at the intersection of theory and practice, Westerhoff asks, if these things are so, "where, then, do we begin church education?" He suggests, in harmony with his espoused position, that the answer is to begin "not with isolated individuals or an isolated document, the Bible, but with the issues and events of life and history, the arena where God acts and is known."[93] Westerhoff continues his argument by suggesting that, as our Christian faith is at its core a story, just so do we enter the story as a part of the community in which God is present as historic actor.[94]

In his earlier writings, Moran appears to agree with those who believe that the Bible should have a role in the process of teaching religion, but he argues that teaching biblical content must not be confused with the larger process. Although he denies that the Bible is in any sense a collection of static, revealed truths, Moran concedes that biblical words may play a part in the revelatory relationship of God and man since "the revelatory process could not help but have a verbal element." Moran suggests that the Bible may in fact enable us to recognize revelation as it happens in the free existence of persons within the present community of Christians. While not advocating a program of teaching Bible content, as such, he agrees that the Scriptures are indispensable in teaching about Jesus Christ, "who is the revelatory communion of God and man."[95]

Teacher

One key assumption of the mainline model is that God participates with us in the revelationally active process of Christian education. A second, closely related, assumption is that responsibility for religious education, from the human side, rests with the whole church. Accordingly, the religion teacher functions (1) in subordination to the Holy Spirit (the Great Teacher who teaches over and above humanly contrived methods) and (2) as a representative of the church (whose members are called upon to support the teaching process by their lives and witness). From this perspective, then, the teacher is neither the transmitter of an unchanging message nor the hopeful creator of an idealized social order. Rather, the teacher is both promotor and participant in a process through which God is revealing himself today.

The Religion Teacher's Qualifications

"Intelligently active participation in the Christian community" is the initial qualification for teaching religion. "Active participation" includes the notion that a prospective teacher must be willing to become "personally involved in thinking through theological problems. The ideal candidate, according to Wyckoff, is a continually growing person who is becoming more competent in (1) biblical understanding, (2) the Christian faith, and (3) active Christian service, fellowship, and worship.[96] Little makes a spirited case for her view that the most important qualification is that the teacher be a caring individual who knows how to learn. Such an individual is likely to be of the greatest benefit to others.[97] A number of writers share the conviction that a prerequisite for Christian teaching is an enthusiasm born of a contagious commitment to the Christian faith and a loving concern for students. It is generally assumed that one who meets the above general requirements can develop into a competent teacher through participating in available programs for developing skills and spiritual sensitivities.[98]

The ideal characteristics of the teacher from a perspective that seems quite in harmony with the mainline model are very helpfully summarized by Reuel Howe. *First,* the teacher will seek to incarnate the Holy Spirit rather than merely to convey subject matter. *Second,* the teacher, while valuing the learner's freedom as an individual, will offer the gift of relationship in support of the learner's search for the realities of the Christian faith. *Third,* the teacher will trust both the Holy Spirit and the learner in the educational process. *Fourth,* the teacher will be neither anxious about methods nor too strongly committed to any individual method, but will creatively use whatever methods meet the demands of a particular situation. *Fifth,* the teacher will be committed to the belief that revelation occurs in person-to-person relationships and will speak as a person to the person of the learner expecting that revelation will call forth a response.[99]

Teaching and Revelation

A fundament of the mainline model is that revelation occurs in the teaching act. Harris may well be the one who is most faithful to the model at this point. In one sense, *Teaching and Religious Imagination* directly addresses this issue. The kind of religious knowledge that is most needed in the church is not gained by handing on a specified subject matter or by telling someone who does not "know" what the teacher "knows." Rather, "one who would foster revelation must take on a wide range of roles in the house of religious imagination: contemplative (explorer of darkness and silence), ascetic (professing rigor and detachment), creator (reforming with ontological tenderness), sacrament (alert to the presence of mystery)." These indirect methods generate the congruence so highly valued by the model and they retain the quality of intention that must be at the heart of all teaching.[100]

The Religion Teacher's Training

There remains general agreement among mainline writers that among the highest priorities must be the development of a well-defined theoretical base upon which to build the kind of large-scale program which could accomplish the training of an adequate number of competent teachers. Those training programs proposed under the rather broadly defined tenets of this model, at least in its earlier literature, exhibit a clearly theological orientation. They are typically targeted toward (1) the teacher's intellectual and spiritual growth, (2) the teacher's acquisition of appropriate educational skills, and (3) the teacher's development of spiritual and interpersonal sensitivities.

Smart, among others, strongly supports the view that the training of religion teachers should have a primarily, perhaps exclusively, theological orientation. He charges that teacher training in church school settings has been notably weak in preparing teachers to deal with theological questions even though it has sometimes been able to give them effective methodological skills. He maintains that individuals preparing to teach require the same biblical, theological, and historical grounding as those preparing to preach. Theological error in teaching, he avers, is quite as damaging as theological error in preaching. On the other hand, since the purpose of teaching is not merely to pour knowledge into learners, Smart favors some studies which would enable the teacher to guide students in their growth as Christian persons.[101] Other writers are convinced that theological inquiry must be at the heart of any training program which will have the capacity to supply truly competent religion teachers. As prospective teachers inquire into presently significant religious and secular issues, they can be brought to see beyond the distracting religious questions of the past to the main issue, namely, that God confronts us revelationally in the present. Such a training program, it is theorized, should result in the training of a teacher who through reading, reflection, discussion, and self-generated theologizing will have gained a high level of intellectual confidence. Such will enable the teacher to give up any unhealthy reliance upon religious educational content which supposedly descends from above. Rather, the teacher will discover both content and teaching methods in communion with learners as they, together, participate in God's present revelatory activity.[102]

From a somewhat different perspective, Wyckoff puts forward the notion that, in addition to skills and methods, teacher training should emphasize the qualities of the teacher's personal life. "Teacher training will seek to develop teaching skills that will give ever more effective expression to our mutual search for the Christian truth and way of life. It will stress training in the life of the spirit—not just, 'What do I do with these children?' but, 'How may I become the kind of person who can do the kind of job that needs to be done?'"[103] In addition, Wyckoff strongly advocates "on-the-job" training for new teachers, provided that there is access to competent supervisory aid.[104]

The Religion Teacher's Method

Revelation, defined in terms of a here-and-now occurrence within the Christian community, is a key element in theorizing about teaching method. As previously discussed, it is believed that God through the Holy Spirit is revelationally present and actively involved in the teaching process. Method is accordingly looked upon as a potentially dynamic vehicle of Christian revelation. The kind of knowledge to be fostered does not easily lend itself to direct utterance; it is more likely to be conveyed through indirect methods such as parables, indirection, silence, and community. Interaction within the family, in addition to "Christian fellowship, may also be seen as a method to be emulated in the search for the reality of Christian faith."[105]

The overarching teaching method which flows quite naturally from the underlying theories of the mainline model is, in sum and substance, to be the church of Jesus Christ as resonating with the

Holy Spirit. Thus Wyckoff submits that the heart of method in teaching the Christian religion is full participation in the life of the church by living the Christian life under "experienced guidance." Each class in the church school "is the church of the living Christ."[106] Therefore, the clue to method is for the church to involve everyone of its children, youth, and adults in the responsibilities of maintaining a creative relationship with its living Lord.[107] With similar import, Smart claims that the work of the teacher is rooted in the ministry of the church in the same way that the work of the preacher is rooted in the ministry of the church. In his view, a full recognition of the "essential nature" of the teaching function might well lead to a resolution of the uncertainties which sometimes surround the teacher and undermine the teaching ministry within the church. Responsibility for teaching, though, does not rest solely upon the teacher; it rests upon the whole church. In the larger view of the church's teaching ministry it is ultimately God who teaches. "Therefore," Smart states, "the vital function of the church and church school is not to explain all human experience, but to bring together, in a living way, the person who is confronted with the mystery of the meaning of the world and the Christian revelation of God which alone is the key to the mystery."[108]

Miller likewise identifies the church as the functional center of Christian education method. He reasons that if a congregation is a vital community of the Holy Spirit, all that happens in the religion classes will be vitally affected. Specifically, these classes will be transformed into centers of true fellowship, each bearing the marks of a "Christian group." Miller's understanding of the process whereby a class becomes a Christian group may be summarized. First, the Christian group begins with persons where they are, the teacher assuming initial responsibility for activities. Second, the Christian group starts with God, even though group members may differ in their ability to verbalize their faith. Third, the Christian group interaction begins as the living Lord becomes a part of the encounter which takes place where two or three are gathered in his name—things may well happen within this interaction process which would not normally happen because God in Christ moves through the Holy Spirit in a mysterious way to heal wounds, break down barriers, and sustain fellowship. Finally, the Christian group is ultimately created by the Holy Spirit as he establishes relationships in which God's revelation can be shared. To be sure, there are no "sure-fire" methods to create this kind of spirit. Also, there are some dangers; pressure for group conformity, for example. However, Miller believes that the potential values outweigh the dangers because it is God who acts through the group "to provide spiritual growth which is a gift of grace."[109]

With much the same emphasis on method as other theorists, Sherrill suggests that religious education takes place primarily within the Christian community, specifically through the process of interaction between persons. His concern is that methods must be conducive to enabling human selves to enter the high destiny for which they were created. The core purpose of any method is to facilitate effective, spiritually uplifting, two-way communication between selves. If any particular method proves to be effective in accomplishing this "spiritually uplifting" communication, Sherrill thinks it may be an appropriate method to use in Christian education. However, by way of caution, he notes that methods which prove fruitful in certain situations and with certain selves may prove unfruitful in other situations and with other selves. Hence no one method can lay claim to being the method for Christian education.[110]

Moran's approach to method is influenced by his conviction that religious education "is a personal communion of knowledge, an interrelationship of God and the individual within a believing community." Teaching method, accordingly, does not begin with a body of curricular subject matter; it begins with persons. Subject matter has its place in the religion teaching process primarily as a means of aiding the expression and understanding of God's revelation of himself in human life. This is most fruitfully accomplished by methods that fully involve the learner in active theologizing. It is axiomatic. that methods are employed to help learners discover their own possibilities rather than to attempt to mold them into a predetermined pattern. Moran's theory of teaching method also recognizes that, pursuant to the task of freeing persons for an intelligent life in the Spirit, there is a vital need for serious intellectual *work* in the educational process. At bottom, little confidence is placed in any specific method. In a very significant passage Moran remarks that it is not for us to control either God's Spirit or the learner's response. What the religion teacher does, in the final analysis, "is to show what a Christian life is by living one."[111]

Learner

Although mainline theorists are well aware of the established facts and laws of learning, they tend to rely quite exclusively upon theological considerations in theorizing about the learner. A thorough understanding of humankind (anthropology) is deemed basic to any valid theory of religious education. Miller, for example, declares that it is not enough for teachers merely to be acquainted with the learner's psychological characteristics and learning patterns. They must go the next step in considering the implications of these "characteristics" from the standpoint of Christian theology.[112] Smart, with apparently similar intent, states: "A program that operates with something less than a Christian understanding of persons is likely to produce something less than or other than Christian persons."[113] Nelson wrestles with the theological implications of the fact that learners are so much the products of the culture in which they were reared.[114] On the other hand, it should not be inferred that mainline theorists purposely neglect the study of teaching/learning or of psychology. Indeed, Moran puts the matter pointedly by remarking that it is possible to speak badly of God because reflection upon human experience has been superficial.[115]

The Learner Is Both a Child of God and a Sinner

From the perspective of the mainline model, a key "truth" about the human person is that he or she is both a child of God and at the same time, in some sense, a sinner in need of redemption.[116] Theoretically, this rather paradoxical view means that the learner in a religious educational setting is not limited to being merely the recipient of a salvific message, as in a transmissive model. Neither does the learner have, by virtue of being a member of the human family, the inner personal resources to work out one's own salvation, as in the liberal model. From this perspective, then, the learner is perceived to be an active participant with God, and also with other persons including the teacher, in that revelational relationship which is envisioned as the core of the religious education process. Miller claims that this twofold relationship between God and the learner might well be considered the center of the curriculum. That is, provided this relationship flows out of theology—"the-truth-about-God-in-relation-to-man."[117] Essentially the same attitude toward the learner is observed in Sherrill. "Christian education," he states, "is the attempt, ordinarily by members of the Christian community, to participate in and guide the changes which take place in persons in their relationships with God, with the church, with other persons, with the physical world, and with oneself."[118] The revelation which occurs in this kind of relationship is both individually redemptive and contributory to a sustaining fellowship which is ongoingly revelational.[119]

Westerhoff observes the sinfulness of humankind from a slightly different perspective, but well within the mainline model. Sin, he suggests, is particularly revealed in our willingness to withdraw from life's struggles. Institutionally bounded programs of nurture are not by their nature able to bring the withdrawn person to maturity in faith. What is needed is conversion which, by its nature, is never an isolated event. Christian education that might reverse the withdrawnness of persons and draw them back into vital relationships with the community of faith must be oriented to conversion. This does not occur through mere belief in an institutional affirmation, but by the kind of conversion that leads Christ's disciples to active commitment in the world.[120]

The Learner Is a Person

Perhaps the cardinal principal in this model is that the educational process should eventuate in a kind of learning that will be clearly evidenced by the growth and development of the learner as a person. "Learning," according to Grimes, involves "the total spectrum of influences that make a person what he is." Accordingly it is a considerably broader enterprise than church educators have sometimes believed. [121]

Certain distinguishing marks of personhood are often mentioned in the literature. *First*, a consciousness of individual identity. *Second*, a capacity for relatedness and fellowship both with God and with other persons. *Third*, a capacity for making intelligent, free choices. *Fourth*, a capacity to bear responsibility. *Finally*, a capacity to respond to others—to love.[122] Scientifically derived learning theories such as "conditioning," "trial and error," and "learning by insight" are largely excluded from the model since they are regarded as being inadequate to explain or predict religious learnings and, especially, because they do not sufficiently encompass the notion of personality. The prevailing view is that practices generated by these theories tend to treat the learner as a manipulable "object" rather than as a potentially growing, self-conscious, intelligent, free, and responsible "person."[123] While it cannot be said that mainline theorists share a fully common view on matters relating to the learner's personality, it does appear that most agree that learning which contributes significantly to the religious growth of persons is accomplished in large measure through interaction between persons in community. Such interaction is necessarily attended by the, as yet undefined and perhaps undefinable, working of the Holy Spirit within the relational context of a Christian community which recognizes the freedom of persons to be themselves. A significant number of theorists, having reflected upon the complexities of the human personality, seem quite willing to concede that religious learning is fundamentally a mystery.[124]

The Learner Is to Become a Knowledgeable, Responsible Christian

A major intent of mainline religious education is that the learner will be enabled to become a knowledgeable, responsible, adult Christian. To this end, Moran remarks that "schools are places for serious intellectual work" where learners may begin upon the "road toward understanding" as they are taught to use their intelligence in creative, original, and constructive ways.[125] Beyond the church school, then, the learner ought not merely exist as a good and harmless Christian who has been delivered from those ruinous evils that bring unhappiness to individuals and families. Rather, the learner's ultimate task is to participate actively, intelligently, and maturely in God's service through helping other persons, giving, in this way, a living witness to the reality of God's love.[126]

Ideally, the learner comes from the secular world into the fellowship of the church and is redemptively exposed to the love of God. Within this community of Christians, the learner is provided with access to that knowledge which will enable him or her to understand the Christian faith and provide a solid foundation for eventually living an adult life as a responsible Christian. Ultimately, the learner will come to know that the meaning found in the church must be freely carried back into the world through loyal and courageous Christian living and Christian service.[127]

Environment

It appears that the Holy Spirit is the determinative environmental factor relative to mainline Christian education. This does not mean that other factors are considered irrelevant. Home, school, and associates are obviously important influences. So are other physical and social factors. Miller puts the viewpoint succinctly when he states that the scientifically demonstrated organic relationship between persons and their environment is transcended by the theologically discovered truth that "central in the Christian's environment is the living God...the frame of reference for Christian living is he in whom we live and move and have our being."[128] Wyckoff also considers the existence of God to be the most real aspect of the environment, especially insofar as Christian education is concerned. However, he recognizes that a balanced program of Christian education must give due recognition to the human aspect as well as to the divine aspect of the environment. [129]

The environment, then, is a significant, supernaturally dimensioned element which remains largely in the background of the theoretical model. Therefore, it does not enter prominently into the deliberative planning of specific Christian education practice. Accordingly, mainline theorists do not normally look with favor upon deliberate control of the environment as a valid practice. "We do not," Wyckoff remarks, "become Christians, as it were, brick on brick through some automatic system of controlled conditioning."[130] Nonetheless, most theorists regard the Christian community, including Christian homes, as being responsible to create environmental conditions whereby the Spirit of God may work most fruitfully in the learner's life. Smart takes for granted that the environment within the church, and within church-related homes, is a critical factor which either helps or hinders the church from accomplishing its appointed educational function.[131] Sherrill also remarks upon the effects of the immediate environment (the people children know, the things they hear, the events they observe) upon religious learning. Accordingly, the scene of genuine "Christian" education is within the environment provided by the koinonia (fellowship) of the Christian community. Koinonia, by virtue of its own nature, includes God (the Holy Spirit) as a participant. The Holy Spirit exists as truly within the home as within the church.[132] Miller summarizes this model's view.

Christian education is the process of growing up within the life of the Christian church, and it goes on all the time. The atmosphere in which grace flourishes is the environment of Christian education. With all of our plans and standards and techniques and insights, it is God who does the educating. We are the channels of his grace, doing the planting and the watering, and the increase is a gift of God.[133]

Grimes calls the church to be involved in shaping the larger atmosphere of the environment by being faithful to its original mission of being the body of Christ in the world, by witnessing to the gospel, and by nurturing those who have responded to the call of Christ. He understands the process to be one of reaching out and drawing persons into the community of faith, an environment conditioned by persons whose lives have been, and are being, transformed by the gospel.[134] Westerhoff succinctly underscores a key element in the mainline model: "Faith can be inspired within a community of faith, but it cannot be given by one person to another."[135]

As is true of others from this school of thought, Miller includes the Christian home within the scope of his remarks on environment. After all, the atmosphere in the home "reaches the child as naturally as the air he breathes."[136] Grimes expands on Miller's point by suggesting that the environment around the child can and will have both "desirable" and "undesirable" effects upon the child's reactions. The clear implication is that the church must attend to the environment in the homes in its faith community as a key element in its plans for the religious education of its children.[137]

Harris goes a step further in charging religious educators with the task of actually structuring the environment. Making her argument largely in the words of Mary Tully, her teacher at Union Theological Seminary, Harris argues that the teacher's main job is to set up the environment" in such a way that the learner's interaction with the environment actually facilitates learning. This kind of environmental manipulation may seem "a lot of drudgery," but from Harris' observation, it pays off. Crucial to Harris' argument is the underlying theory that a properly arranged environment, of itself, educates.[138]

Evaluation

Evaluation of learning outcomes, especially on a day-to-day basis, is not an integral element in the mainline model of religious education. It is theorized that a premature attempt to measure progress might well disturb the educational progress and actually prevent religious growth. The attitude toward assessment of religious growth and learning seems to be that such assessment serves better when it is periodic and occasional. One reason why at least short-term assessment does not seem to be valued more highly is that, as previously mentioned, aim is conceived in a relatively broad, whole-life dimensioned, manner. This tendency to shy away from definitely stated (operationally defined) aims precludes the use of aim as a meaningful standard for evaluation—at least at the classroom level.[139] Henderlite accents the mainline theory at this point by arguing that, as Christian educators take into account the work of the Holy Spirit, the outcome can be guaranteed. The church, she states, "has only to know its true nature as the servant people of God and the temple of his Spirit. Then it is able to know what it must do and what it cannot."[140]

Some thinkers and theorists have advocated employing sophisticated and well-founded scientific procedures for accumulating and processing information as a basis for evaluating Christian religious education programs and, indeed, measuring individual progress.[141] However, as Miller acknowledges, a specifically theological assessment is more in harmony with the principles underlying the mainline model. Therefore he offers his judgment that, in the final analysis, when the data from such sources as tests, scorecards, and observations have been collected, these data must be evaluated by comparing them with theological standards. The real question, for him, is whether the things that are happening in individual lives as a result of the education program are consistent with the Christian truth.[142] Smart likewise assigns the ultimate assessment task to theology. "The function of theology" he states, "is to be constantly exercising a critique upon doctrines and practices that exist within the church, holding them against the criterion of what God has shown us in his Word...and so enabling us to see what ought to be and what ought not to be."[143]

It should be mentioned that there seems to be a yearning for better ways of assessing the direction and extent of change in the lives of learners. On this issue, Westerhoff suggests, "Life is a great possibility, realizable through hope and organized, planned human activity. A birth of new vitality and relevance in religious education can break forth.... At stake are tomorrow's children."[144]

SUMMARY

The mainline model discussed in this chapter was at its zenith from the 1950s into the 1970s. Its broad aim is to foster a right relationship with God through a communal relationship in the church. Theoretically, a dynamic, revelatory activity accompanies the teaching process as learners are guided in their growth (1) toward God, (2) toward others, and (3) within themselves. This model has a strong appeal to thoughtful adults with its attention to social responsibility and its advocacy of an intelligent, informed approach to Christian (religious) living. The reader should be apprised that the transition to the next chapter is not as linear as the movement between the earlier chapters where there is a more direct historical connection. This is so because the roots of the evangelical/kerygmatic model are intimately linked with the prototype where both aim and content are primarily concerned with transmission of a revealed message. Faithful transmission of this message, accordingly, is considered to be the primary teaching task.

CHAPTER 5

THE EVANGELICAL/KERYGMATIC MODEL OF RELIGIOUS EDUCATION

A Theological Model

REVIVAL OF A PROCLAMATORY PERSPECTIVE

Augustine's previously considered *de Catechizandis Rudibus*[1] provides a convenient starting point for a brief review of the theological and educational antecedents to twentieth-century versions of the evangelical/kerygmatic model. In this ancient book, Augustine offers a series of suggestions on how to attain more salutary results from one's teaching. *De Catechizandis Rudibus* accordingly touches upon a number of significant theoretical matters: the capacity of language to convey truth, the appropriate roles of teacher and learner, and the possible impact of the affective environment. Even so, the thrust of this historic treatise clearly focuses upon subject-matter content. Augustine locates content almost entirely in the Bible. He outlines several possibilities for arranging biblical materials so that efficient instruction in the Christian faith can be accomplished according to the learner's needs.

Augustine's expressed theory is typical of the implicit theory upon which the catechumenate was based. Following that long-lived institution's demise in the sixth and seventh centuries, the church was largely without a conscious, overarching theory and practice of education until the Reformation in the sixteenth century when, as early as 1529, Luther began publishing catechisms. Within a very short time Roman Catholic leaders responded by publishing their own. Naturally these catechisms expressed divergent viewpoints on extremely important matters. Still, both Catholic and Lutheran versions had obvious roots in the historic prototype. Furthermore, there is considerable evidence that both Lutheran and Catholic thinking on education was strongly influenced by Augustine's theories, especially those found in *De Catechizandis Rudibus*. By the middle of the sixteenth century, catechism books had become a prominent part of the scene. These were almost always intended to define and defend particular perspectives on the Christian faith. The common theory controlling their substance was that knowing the right answers was the best way to define and defend one's espoused version of the faith.[2]

By the beginning of the nineteenth century, education in the church had begun to reflect the influence of the Enlightenment with its concentration upon reason as humanity's highest power. The rationalistic tendencies of the period actually served to cement practices already in place. Methodologically, this contributed to a static, line-by-line, explanation of religion lessons on the part of teachers. Complementarily, learners were often required to engage in a rather rigid form of rote memorization. Further, by mid-century in America, the Sunday School movement was in full bloom. Here the Bible had replaced the catechism books spawned by the Reformation. During much of the nineteenth century, then, while Catholic and Lutheran children were busy memorizing the lessons of the catechism, children in Sunday Schools were busy memorizing the Bible. In either case, when a child could repeat what was true and right, he or she would surely believe the truth and do the right thing as the Holy Spirit worked within through the lessons learned—or so the prevailing theory went.

EVANGELICAL VERSION

The dawn of the twentieth century witnessed a series of signi ficant changes in the rather singular point of view which had domi nated both Protestant and Catholic education up to, and through, much of the nineteenth century. Within Protestantism, the evangelical[3] cause which had supported and guided the Sunday School through its nineteenth-century heyday was rendered increasingly rudderless by the emergence of changing religious and educational views. These new views incorporated a liberal theology together with progressive educational theories. In turn, this gave rise to a perspective on religious education that was certainly out of harmony with evangelical thinking, committed as it was to the notion that communication of a divinely ordained message is the most essential factor in religious education.[4]

The Protestant version of the historic perspective on Christian education, dormant during the earlier decades of the twentieth century, experienced a reawakening in America during the 1930s and 1940s. In 1931, under the leadership of Clarence H. Benson, an energetic, interdenominational association to promote teacher training was organized. Eventually named the Evangelical Teacher Training Association (ETTA), its curriculum exhibited a primary emphasis upon the Bible as the key to a revitalized program of church education. The ETTA became an important source of renewal for a sizable segment of the Sunday School movement.[5]

Perhaps more theologically significant, a further awakening of the evangelical educational enterprise came about through the founding of the National Association of Evangelicals (NAE) in 1942. The NAE, with its broader academic base, provided additional encouragement to traditional, yet reflective, thinking. The continuing commitment of this organization has been to the orthodox doctrines of historic Protestantism, "doctrines that it finds in the Bible, received as the Book given throughout by inspiration." The educational leanings of evangelicals continued to be expressed throughout the 1940s in a desire for a renewal of the Sunday School along the lines of its earlier, evangelically oriented, form. These sentiments eventuated in the establishment of the National Sunday School Association through the NAE's Church School Commission in 1946.

A more-or-less official statement on matters of educational policy was made by Frank Gaebelein in *Christian Education in a*

Democracy (1951). Gaebelein's summary statement seems to rather fully characterize the evangelical position on educational theory and practice.

> *It is with this evangelical faith, not simply as another system of theology but as a unifying factor of Christian education, that this book is concerned. In a sense it is a summons to a position that is old and at the same time new. There are times when the only way to go forward is to go back.... And so, while our call to education is a call back to the Bible and Christ, it is at the same time a summons to go forward in Him.*[6]

The National Association of Evangelicals provides a center of theological and educational identity for evangelical Protestant thinkers. Evangelicals commonly approach educational matters from a perspective clearly in harmony with the historic prototype. A number of refrains appear again and again in their writings: (1) the Bible provides the norm for Christian education, (2) communicating the gospel message is the central purpose, (3) the teacher is supernaturally assisted by the Holy Spirit, and (4) acceptance of the gospel is necessary for individual salvation.

At the theoretical and professional levels, issues related to the improvement of evangelical Christian education are regularly addressed in the *Christian Education Journal*, published by Trinity Evangelical Divinity School, Deerfield, Illinois. The journal is something of an evangelical counterpart to *Religious Education*: "designed to promote growth and advancement in the field of Christian education by stimulating scholarly study in Bible and related fields; providing a forum for the expression of facts, ideas, and opinions on Christian education topics; promoting the understanding and application of research."[7]

KERYGMATIC (ROMAN CATHOLIC) VERSION

On the other side of the Atlantic, toward the end of the nineteenth century, the impact of the emerging science of psychology was beginning to be felt in educational circles. The writings of Johann Herbart, a pioneer in the application of psychological principles to educational method, were of particular importance. Herbartian thought was quite compatible with the historic point of view. It profoundly influenced the character of twentieth-century religious education in the Roman Catholic Church, especially through the, then called, "modern catechetical renewal." This renewal began about 1900 in Munich, Germany. Heinrich Steiglitz, the early leader of the movement, developed a method of teaching religion which reflected an application of psychological principles as they were then understood. The Munich Method, as Steiglitz's proposals came to be known, made explicit use of the principles advanced by Herbart. These principles were rooted in the assumption that *knowledge of content* is automatically transferred into feeling, willing, and doing.[8]

The Munich Method and the theory upon which it was based exerted an expanding influence over European religion teaching during the early years of the twentieth century. Although with ever waning force, the catechetical movement associated in the beginning with the Munich catechists under Steiglitz's leadership continues to influence a number of thinkers in America. In a celebrated speech at the Eichstätt Conference on Catechetics (1960), Valerian Cardinal Gracias distinguished three stages that are descriptive of the way in which the movement has maintained its influence by responding to changing times and situations: (1) the psychological stage, (2) the theological stage, and (3) the institutional stage.[9]

The *psychological stage* was occupied during the earlier years of the twentieth century mainly with the previously mentioned problems of applying the then current psychological theories to religion teaching. The *theological stage* of the renewal began in 1936 with the publication of *Die Frohbotschaft und unsere Glaubens-verkundigung* by the Jesuit liturgist Josef Jungmann.[10] Jungmann longed for an infusion of the joyfulness of which he had seen glimpses in his liturgical studies of the early church. He called for a return to the supernatural element in religious education by insisting upon attention to content. Jungmann perceived content as principally the proclamation, or heralding, of a message—of which Christ must be the "core or center." Because of this emphasis upon the heralding of a message (the *kerygma*) this stage of the catechetical renewal has sometimes been called the "kerygmatic movement." Theorists identified with this movement also commonly employ an approach which is quite consistent with the historic prototype. Their writings include many historic themes: (1) a theology grounded in the Bible and church tradition must be the basis for all religious education, (2) transmission of the saving, Christian message is the primary task, (3) the teacher is the Holy Spirit-commissioned herald of the message, and (4) complete reception of the authoritative message will eventuate in Christian living.

The *institutional stage* had its concretization in the post World War II development of such international organizations as *Centre international d'etudes de la formation religieuse* (International Center for Studies in Religious Education *"Lumen Vitae"*) in Brussels and The East Asian Pastoral Institute in Manila. Thinkers associated with this movement have frequently worked in and through these institutions to refine the theoretical underpinnings of Catholic religious education. The international journal, *Lumen Vitae*,[11] published by the *Centre*, has been an important means of disseminating theoretical and practical notions characteristic of the kerygmatic movement—and thus of the Roman Catholic version of this proclamatory model of religious education.

CRITERIA

The evangelical/kerygmatic model of religious education is identified by the following criteria. *First*, theological views derived from data thought to be received by authoritative revelation are normative for theory and practice. The Bible is the source of authoritative revelation for Protestants. Roman Catholics include church tradition which, with the Bible, is interpreted by the magisterium. *Second*, both aim and content are fundamentally concerned with the transmission of a unique message derived from the facts of revelation. *Third*, the primary teaching task is to fully and faithfully transmit the message to learners. *Fourth*, learners will then live out the implications of the message with respect to Christian living and eternal destiny.

In some ways, this model is the twentieth-century revival of the historic prototype described in chapter 2. One obvious difference is that, as heirs of the twentieth-century explosion of knowledge, representative theorists are in a position to incorporate substantially more sophistication into their proposed strategies for educational leadership and teaching practice. Further, at least as described in this chapter, this model reflects a point of view which overtly includes the supernatural as a key theoretical construct. Admittedly, the term "supernatural" has a number of conflicting nuances. Thus, in discussions of this nature, it is helpful to keep in mind Ernst Niermann's observation, to the effect that supernatural trends are most evident among Protestants concerned with preserving the supernatural character of biblical revelation and among Catholics desiring a guaranteed, authoritative, divine revelation.[12]

REPRESENTATIVE THEORISTS

The analysis of the evangelical/kerygmatic model in this chapter is based upon an examination of pertinent books selected primarily from the writings of Protestants associated with the evangelical movement and from among Roman Catholics involved with the kerygmatic movement. Thinkers from these two Christian contexts have engaged in possibly the most true-to-type theorizing along the lines of this theologically oriented, proclamatory model. To be sure, it must be understood that the similarity of language used by both Protestant and Catholic theorists occasionally masks extremely important theological nuances and outright differences in viewpoint. Nonetheless, even if it is granted that very significant theological differences exist, these theorists do appear to work from a common, proclamationist model.[13]

REPRESENTATIVE EVANGELICALS

Frank E. Gaebelein (1907-1983)

Frank Gaebelein may well be the most important spokesperson in the mid-twentieth century revival of the historic perspective on Christian education among American evangelicals. No small part of his importance is due to the range, credibility, and timing of his major work on educational theory, *Christian Education in a Democracy* (1951).[14] Although the genesis of this book was a charge to an NAE committee, it appears to represent Gaebelein's personal position. The bases of his highly orthodox and theologically organized outlook are biblical doctrines. Gaebelein considers the communication of biblical truths by teachers who are able to lead learners to an understanding and wholehearted acceptance of these truths to constitute the very heart of Christian education. He places a high priority on the verbal teaching of the Scriptures and upon the pulpit as the functional center of Christian education.

Lois E. LeBar (b. 1907)

Lois LeBar must be considered among the major contributors to the mid-century renewal of the historic perspective. Her long tenure at Wheaton College (Illinois) gave her a powerful platform to influence the burgeoning evangelical Sunday School movement. LeBar judges all matters of theory and practice upon the evidence of their fidelity to biblical and theological standards. She holds that valid educational concepts are discernable by theorists who will look to the Creator of truth ("who has made the learner, his teacher, his content, and his environment") rather than to secular sources for information relative to Christian education. LeBar is acutely sensitive to the potential vagaries of some classical methods such as the lecture. She seems to have been more aware of the teaching-learning process than were her evangelical contemporaries during the period of her greatest influence, the 1950s and 1960s. In LeBar's view, the structure of the curriculum and of teaching method are both derived from the Bible. She also places considerable emphasis upon the theory that the Holy Spirit, working through the teacher, actually accomplishes the aims of religious education. LeBar's best known and most enduring book, *Education That Is Christian* (1958),[15] presents a consistent evangelical, proclamationist position throughout.

Clarence H. Benson (1879-1954)

Clarence Benson, mentioned earlier in connection with his role in energizing the mid-century resurgence of the evangelical Sunday School through his leadership of the Evangelical Teacher Training Association, contributed a number of influential books that found wide use in both academic and local-church, teacher-training settings. His works give evidence of a wholehearted commitment to the evangelical model. Benson was among the earlier writers of this school of thought to adapt the findings of child and adolescent psychology to teaching in the Sunday School. *Introduction to Child Study* (1942)[16] and The Christian Teacher (1950)[17] are representative of his more theoretical works. Benson's *A Popular History of Christian Education* (1943)[18] provides unique insight into the way in which one important leader perceived the evangelical Sunday School against the backdrop of the broader currents affecting the life of the church.

Charles Burton Eavey (1889-1974)

C.B. Eavey played an important role in underscoring many of the issues addressed by Benson. His association with Wheaton College (Illinois), coupled with a certain sophistication, added an essential dimension to evangelical thinking. Eavey's *History of Christian Education* (1964)[19] shortly became a standard evangelical text that influenced several generations of students. His *Principles* of *Teaching for Christian Teachers*[20] survived more than twenty printings. Though thoroughly evangelical in sentiment and thrust, this latter book employs a number of useful constructs derived from the social sciences.

Harold Carlton Mason (1888-1964)

Harold Mason contributed a small body of writings that are especially clear in their representation of the transmissive aspect of the evangelical model. Mason states: "Jesus said: 'I am the Way, the Truth and the Life.' This is an authoritative statement to be taught to children as final truth. There is more to Christian education than self-expression and activity from the Evangelical point of view. In Christian education there is a body of knowledge to be transmitted, an ancient book to be perpetuated." Mason's best known book, *Abiding Values in Christian Education* (1955), is a rather carefully considered popularization of this proclamationist mode of thought.[21]

Herbert W. Byrne (b. 1917)

Herbert Byrne's writings found extensive use in evangelical institutions of higher learning during the 1960s and well into the 1980s. His *A Christian Approach to Education: Educational Theory and Application* (1977)[22] is a straight-out argument for an evangelical model of Christian education. *Christian Education for the Local Church: An Evangelical and Functional Approach* (1963)[23] was printed more than twenty times before it was retired from Zondervan's booklist in 1985. This last book is indeed a catalog of the evangelical version of this theologically conceived model. It covers such matters as foundational and organizational issues, supervisory tasks, and teaching methods.

Kenneth O. Gangel (b. 1935)

During the 1970s Kenneth O. Gangel rose to prominence as an articulate and theologically consistent shaper of the evangelical perspective. He argues that a biblically rooted philosophy is the only adequate starting point from which to begin theorizing about Christian education practice. Although Gangel's writings seem fully in line with the evangelical model, he is considerably advanced in the way that he connects his understanding of teaching, organization, and leadership methods with social-science theory. Naturally, Gangel is careful to orchestrate the employment of social-science methods so that they serve traditional, theologically determined goals. Gangel's 1981 book, *Building Leaders for Church Education,*[24] is an important contribution to evangelical Christian education and to literature expressive of the model. While less theoretical in nature, his *Christian Education: Its History & Philosophy*, coauthored with Warren Benson, is especially helpful in establishing historical, philosophical, and theological benchmarks for evangelical Christian educators. Of particular importance to this study, this latter work goes far to make the connection between the "historic prototype" and the "evangelical model" clear.[25]

Roy B. Zuck (b. 1932)

Roy Zuck has been a thoughtful contributor to the literature of the Christian education scene for more than three decades. Zuck's writings are addressed to a number of specific needs common to evangelical education and ministry interests. Among his books that give evidence of his faithful adherence to the structural outlines of the evangelical model is *The Holy Spirit in Your Teaching* (1963). This important book consistently defines the descriptive categories *aim, content,* and *teacher* in ways that are clearly supportive of the evangelical model. Furthermore, to make his position yet more clear, Zuck is careful to show where his understanding of the biblical foundations of the evangelical model stand apart from those of models influenced by progressive education as well as by classical-liberalism and/or by neo-orthodoxy.[26]

James DeForrest Murch (1892-1972)

James DeForrest Murch is representative of the range of scholars whose books contributed in important ways to the development of the model during the mid-nineteenth century. Murch, ordained in the Disciples of Christ but identified with the conservative side of the Restoration Movement, had a significant influence on the shape of the proclamation model near the middle of the twentieth century. His extremely wide range of interests included history, philosophy, and helps for the work-a-day Sunday School teacher. Murch's widely circulated text, *Christian Education in the Local Church: History-Principles-Practice* (1943/1958)[27] is a good example of his considered integration of theology, history, theory, and practice.

Lawrence O. (Larry) Richards (b. 1931)

Larry Richards has been a creative and wide-ranging contributor to the Christian education scene for nearly three decades. Richards writes from an unquestionably evangelical perspective, though he does not always employ typical idioms or terminology. His most definitive work is *A Theology of Christian Education* (1975), republished in 1988 as *Christian Education: Seeking to Become Like Jesus Christ.*[28] Highly readable, this valuable book has enjoyed wide use as a text in introductory Christian education courses. Richards is critical of formal education that requires learners to remain passive. He is an enthusiastic advocate of nonformal, whole-person, discipleship-targeted education that requires learners to be active participants in a whole-life process. In *A Theology of Christian Education,* Richards gave promise of engaging in an informed evangelical interaction with the social sciences. One could wish this promise might have been fulfilled to a greater degree in his later writings.

Donald M. Joy (b. 1928)

Donald Joy's *Meaningful Learning in the Church* (1969) caught attention by raising an issue neglected not alone among evangelicals, but by many in the field. "By showing little awareness of *how* persons learn," Joy suggests that an introspective religious education philosophy manages to miss the point of its essential task.[29] Joy has invested his professional life seeking to help Christian educators come closer to the point, by finding and publishing better answers to such questions as: How does meaningful religious (and moral) learning occur? How can it be facilitated? How can it be integrated with an evangelical version of theology? And, how can one finish life's journey, still growing as a child of God? Joy's theological and philosophical commitments are in harmony with evangelical thought. Albeit in different ways, Larry Richards and Donald Joy have challenged Christian educators to be about the Master's business by utilizing the findings of the social sciences in support of the momentous task at hand. Among Joy's works in which he wrestles with integrating an evangelical faith with the findings of the contemporary sciences are his edited work *Moral Development Foundations* (1983)[30] and *Bonding: Relationships in the Image of God* (1985).[31]

Findley B. Edge (b. 1916)

A Southern Baptist and longtime professor of religious education at Southern Baptist Seminary, Louisville, Findley Edge is the author of *Teaching for Results* (1956).[32] Still in print, Edge's most important theoretical work in religious education theory stretches the boundaries of the model defined in this chapter. Nonetheless, its irenic spirit coupled with useful applications of biblical as well as social-science-based information have made it a practical resource for helping succeeding generations of evangelically oriented teachers become aware of better methods for reaching meaningful goals. Among Edge's important contributions are his focus on the teaching-learning process, his attention to the learner as well as to biblical content, and his concern for bringing the notion of *transfer of learning* ("carry-over") into play as a meaningful, theoretical element.

Robert W. Pazmiño (b. 1948)

Robert Pazmiño introduces himself as an "ecumenical evangelical" who writes from the perspective of a bicultural Hispanic North American. *His Foundational Issues in Christian Education* (1988) is offered as an introductory textbook to the study of Christian education at the college and seminary level. Pazmiño portrays Christian education as "preparidigmatic," or, in other terms, not yet an academic discipline. He seeks to raise the kinds of questions that will lead to the development of theories and practices suitable for "the new wineskins" of a developing discipline. *Foundational Issues in Christian Education* affirms the authority of the Bible as the groundwork for a version of Christian education that is responsive to the Christian heritage, to changing cultural variables, and to proven educational principles.[33] Pazmiño's sequel, *Principles and Practices of Christian Education* (1992), presents and explicates a broad vision rooted in the principle of "conversion," but incorporating such dynamic (connecting) dimensions as Kerygma (proclamation), Koinonia (community), Diakonia (service), Profeteia (advocacy), and Leiturgia (worship).[34]

REPRESENTATIVE ROMAN CATHOLIC THEORISTS

Josef Andreas Jungmann (1889-1975)

The theoretical stance and leadership thrust of such well-known European born thinkers as Josef Jungmann, Johannes Hofinger, and Marcel van Caster seems to be well within the parameters of the model described in this chapter. Their thought has also been influential in shaping the American scene. Jungmann's *Die Frohbotshaft und unsere Glaubensverkundigung* (1936)[35] was instrumental in bringing about a renewed interest in the communication of a biblically based message. However, his theoretical notions are much more fully developed in *Handing on the Faith* (1962).[36] Even the title of this latter book is indicative of its theologically oriented, proclamatory posture. Jungmann is insistent that the task of teaching religion involves the transference of doctrinal content by the joyous announcement of the kerygma in much the same way that the apostles preached the gospel in the early church. Hence, the kerygmatic designation of the movement that follows upon Jungmann's work.

Johannes Hofinger (1905-1984)

Hofinger, author of numerous works on educational themes, has advanced his position most completely in *The Art of Teaching Christian Doctrine* (1962).[37] Theology is plainly preceptive in his theory of religion teaching. Proclamation of the Gospel message is central to his understanding of teaching practice. Hofinger states, "Christ, the great Gift of the Father's love and our Way to the Father is Himself the central theme of our message." A critical element in Hofinger's perspective is that the totality of the Christian message, with its many dogmas and doctrines, must be fully proclaimed. He argues that it would be a "catechetical crime" to transmit to learners only a fragment of the "organic divine message." Theoretically, then, correct and complete communication of the message would result in an appropriate religious lifestyle on the part of the learner.

Marcel van Caster

Marcel van Caster has contributed in important ways to shaping certain facets of the kerygmatic perspective. Van Caster's principal theoretical work is *The Structure of Catechetics* (1965).[38] Its companion, *Themes of Catechesis* (1966),[39] is more practical in emphasis. Van Caster's theory is based on doctrines derived from the Bible, but he also professes to be faithful to tradition as well as to the interpretation of the magisterium. Van Caster's aim is faithful transmission of the "word of God" in such a way that it eventuates first in "faith as knowledge" and then as "living faith." To be sure, he is sometimes critical of "traditional transmissive," as well as of "activist" modes of religion teaching. Still in all, van Caster's synthesis of "proclamation" and "interpretation" of the " word of God" differs little from the proclamation model as defined in this chapter. Nonetheless, it seems fair to suggest that in some of his writings there is evidence of movement in the direction of a rather sophisticated, experiential model that employs some findings of the social sciences; especially in his four chapters in *Experiential Catechetics* (1969).[40]

Other Catholic Theorists

A number of internationally oriented Catholic thinkers contributed widely read books generally supportive of the kerygmatic model, especially during the 1960s. Three whose writings played a role in establishing benchmarks for the analysis presented in this chapter are G. Emmett Carter, primary author of *The Modern Challenge to Religious Education* (1961);[41] Josef Goldbrunner, editor of *New Catechetical Methods* (1965);[42] and Alphonso Nebreda, author of *Kerygma In Crisis?* (1965).[43] In addition, a number of American Catholic religious educators write in support of theologically structured views, albeit with insights informed by greater awareness of the American scene. Included are such thinkers as Alfred McBride (b. 1928), author of *Catechetics: A Theology of Proclamation* (1966);[44] Michael Warren (b. 1935), editor of *Sourcebook for Modern Catechetics* (1983);[45] and Berard Marthaler (b. 1927), author of *Catechetics in Context: Notes and Commentary on the General Catechetical Directory Issued by the Sacred Congregation for the Clergy* (1973).[46] These writers deserve careful reading by anyone seeking a well-rounded perspective on Catholic religious education theory during the third quarter of the twentieth century.

ANALYSIS OF THE EVANGELICAL/KERYGMATIC MODEL

It may be well to keep in mind that the evangelical/kerygmatic proponents probably have greater investment in the specific theological underpinnings of their viewpoints than do proponents of other models. Thus an important factor that colors this model is that it represents an effort to recover and maintain the spirit, the uniqueness, and especially the dynamic of the early Christian church. Jungmann observed more than half a century ago that teaching the Christian faith involves far more than merely demanding a dutiful belief expressed by keeping the commandments and using the means of grace. Rather, through a supernaturally infused pattern of teaching, he sought to reproduce that joyful quality which he found in the faith of the early church. He describes this faith as having a quality that caused the gospel to be spread by means of empowered "informal missionaries" who, when occasion demanded, could give their lives for the faith.[47] Zuck underscores a related theme by pinpointing three theological fundaments that highlight key distinctives of the model: "(1) the centrality of God's written revelation, (2) the necessity of regeneration, and (3) the ministry of the Holy Spirit."[48]

Aim

Quite understandably, then, theological considerations exert a determining influence on aim. Aim is not a working construct to be changed as experience or culture dictates; it is ultimately determined by divine purposes. Gaebelein declares that while the goals of Christian education concern man and society, "the creative source of these goals is not within man and society. Rather it is implicit in a philosophy which is derived neither from a sociological context nor from the pragmatic method but from revealed truth."[49] Van Caster dogmatically asserts that religious education's real purpose is "to communicate the word of God with a view to spreading the faith."[50] Such statements illustrate the propensity for these writers to understand aim in such a way that it may be realized only through the communication of a divine message. Aim, thus perceived, requires that it be grounded in divine purposes. Hofinger succinctly summarizes the matter with his judgment that the aim of teaching religion is "to convey the Christian message."[51]

Transmissive Aspect of Aim

Transmission of the Christian message comprises a key element for both evangelical and kerygmatic writers. Thus, Mason frankly states that the aim of religious education "involves transmissive teaching so much frowned upon by those whose views of democracy extend to freeing the child of any doctrinaire or imposed values as absolute.... In Christian education there is a body of knowledge to be transmitted."[52] Apparently with much the same concern in mind, Jungmann reminds Catholic religion teachers not to lose sight of the fact that teaching religion means transferring the content of Christian doctrine to learners.[53] In agreement with the above theorists, Zuck argues even more strongly: "Christian education concerns itself with Bible content because through it persons are brought into direct, personal contact with the living God. For this reason, Christian education is transmissive. Christian teachers have a Book to teach, God's divine Word to communicate, a written revelation to make known."[54]

Supernatural Element in Aim
Inclusion of a supernatural dimension in the communication of the Christian message can be a crucial element in describing this model. Accordingly, evangelicals quite often contrast *secular education*, perceived as concerned only with life on the natural level, with *Christian education*. Christian education, as they define it, regards the human being as more than a creature of this world. In recognition, the teaching process deliberately aims to "bring in" the supernatural dimension. Christian religious education, accordingly, should facilitate a direct, experiential, present, and continuing encounter between the learner and God through the communication of a divine message.[55] In support of this viewpoint, Gaebelein argues that it is the divine prerogative of the Sunday School to lead learners toward a vital experience with Christ and then to train them to live in harmony with God.[56] Byrne states that the assumptions of the model include the "conviction that the supernatural world is just as real as the natural world. God does exist there and has chosen to bridge the gap between the two worlds by a process of Self-revelation. Such revelation is transcendent; it comes from God Himself."[57] With similar import, Eavey suggests that the primary task of the teacher is "to teach the Bible, pray that the Holy Spirit will make its truths alive and active in those taught, and allow himself [the teacher] to be used by the Holy Spirit in guiding, helping and encouraging his pupils."[58]

Following the lead of Jungmann's 1936 call for a revival of the "truly supernatural" by means of the joyous heralding of the "Good News proclaimed by Christ," Catholic writers quite often emphasize the supernatural element in their theorizing about aim. In support, van Caster states that religious education must aim "to help bring about an encounter with the Lord."[59] Goldbrunner proposes that religion teaching ought to impart not only an understanding about God, but it should also impart an "experience of God."[60] Hofinger suggests that even as the religion teacher is engaging in a number of teaching activities, priority must be given to a single goal which is to help the learner "open wide his heart to the activity of the Holy Spirit."[61] In *Handing on the Faith*, Jungmann declares that the teacher must "introduce the children to the supernatural world of faith in such a way that the momentous thoughts that are embraced by it become those ideals by which they can orient themselves and by which they can be guided on life's highway, and that these ideals evolve into powerful virtues which will propel them along the ways of Christian living."[62]

Knowledge of the Faith and of Christian Living
Imparting information is ordinarily considered a necessary aim, though not the ultimate goal, of religious education. The character and quality of the learner's life is the larger end toward which knowledge and understanding are contributory. This goal of lived religion is, in turn, intimately related to contact with the supernatural. This model, then, assumes that Christian living is rooted in one's reception of the Christian message and in the resultant work of the Holy Spirit through that message. In a passage purporting to define aim for Catholic religious education, Hofinger asserts, "We not only have to give our students a thorough knowledge of their faith, but we must form true Christians, who truly live their Christianity. Religious knowledge in itself is not the real goal of our teaching, it is only a means. The goal of religious instruction is religious living."[63] A similar perspective is expressed by Eavey in a monologue which details aims and objectives for evangelicals: "All that is done in Christian education has the one final aim of bringing those taught to perfection in godly life and character."[64] Edge, in turn, argues that Bible knowledge is important, but not at the expense of obscuring the matter of Christian living. He suggests that teachers keep in mind two dangers when working toward these aims: (1) The danger of learning only verbalized concepts and (2) the danger that an emotional catharsis be taken for learning.[65]

What these thinkers mean by "religious living" and "a godly life" is helpfully elaborated upon by Benson and Jungmann. Benson proposes that the spiritual growth of the learner should ideally result in a life in which there is (1) a place for worship and a continuing sense of fellowship with God, (2) right living through the development of Christian habits, and (3) a place of service to both man and God.[66] Jungmann likewise advances a comprehensive goal: "Christian culture will show signs of new life and become truly vigorous only when men bear the kingdom of God so enthusiastically within themselves that they will not have to await a command to carry it with them to their places of work, their recreation, their social life and their solitude."[67]

Concern for personal reception of the Christian message and for personal responsibility in living the Christian life has resulted in a heightened interest in the individual learner. This interest in the individual is illustrated in the literature by the use of singular terms such as "the child," "the student," or "the one who comes to be catechized." However, the initial assumptions of the model have sometimes caused individual differences in particular learners to be overlooked. Such differences have often been disregarded in the development of aims, especially those relating to religious living. Historically, within the Sunday School, for example, Christian living has been taken to be the natural by-product of a knowledge of the Bible and of a conversion experience. Sunday School teachers have sometimes labored under the impression, all too easily deduced from the model, that if they teach the outer facts of the Bible the Holy Spirit will accomplish the necessary work of bringing about the desired goals in the lives of individual learners. "Such teachers," LeBar observes, "didn't consider it necessary for them to study human nature or to know the developmental stages through which pupils passed."[68] Nonetheless, this propensity for stating aims in terms of the reception of a unique message seems to make it difficult to be consistent in recognizing individual differences, in spite of a professed interest in individual persons.

Scope of Aim

The scope of aim ranges from right living in this present world to full participation in the eternal dimension of God's kingdom. Evangelicals typically take a literal approach to this duality of aim. They understand human beings as creatures of two worlds, related to the supernatural as well as to the natural realm, both of which must be included. "Secular education" and a wide range of it religious education" are both perceived as being excessively preoccupied with proximate, natural goals. Purportedly, true Christian education does not neglect this world; in addition, it also looks toward ultimate, eternal, supernatural goals—the personal knowledge of God and redemption through Christ.[69] Gaebelein recognizes that this concentration upon ultimate goals raises the risk that the development of persons in society may be overlooked. However, in a manner characteristic of evangelicals, he maintains that true morality rests first of all upon love of God and, following this, upon love of others.[70]

Kerygmatic writers sometimes suggest that aim should include both a present and an eternal dimension, but they do not normally force a separation upon these dimensions. For them, fulfillment of the entire scope of religious education occurs naturally through full participation in the liturgical life and witness of the Catholic Church.

The Role of Conversion

Edge verbalizes a concept which seems quite implicit in almost all evangelical thinking, namely that a conversion experience is necessary for true growth as a Christian. "We believe," he writes, "that a conversion experience—a personal experience in which the individual accepts Jesus as Saviour and Lord—is the means by which an individual enters the Christian life and is the only adequate foundation and sufficient motivation for Christian growth." Conversion, Edge explains, may be helpfully considered as having at least five specific results. Thus the converted person receives (1) a new nature, (2) new appetites, (3) new behavioral goals, (4) new power to follow the demands of the Christian life, and (5) new motivation for actually living the Christian life. Of course, Edge adds, conversion does not assure reaching all of the goals one might wish, but it is the first step on the way to doing so.[71] Zuck takes some pains to integrate a rather typical evangelical interpretation of the role of the Holy Spirit into the flow of possible events which might lead to conversion and to vital Christian living. He states:

> *Christian teaching is necessary to present to the pupil knowledge which, transmuted by the operation of the Holy Spirit, becomes truth for the spirit which, accepted and acted upon by faith in Christ, transforms the pupil*

into a child of God. Further teaching is necessary to nourish the new life to the end that the Holy Spirit may perfect the pupil in well-rounded, completely-developed personality after the image of the Infinite Personality.[72]

Catholics employ the term "conversion" to describe a wider range of religious experiences than evangelicals usually have in mind. For them it includes not only a direct impartation of new life, but also suggests those moments of clarity, or refocusing, that necessarily redirect a Christian's lifeways. However, Catholic theorists do attribute a role to baptism, as an entrance into the Christian life, that plays much the same part that evangelicals attribute to the notion of conversion.[73]

Christian Maturity as an Element in Aim

The notion of Christian maturity, variously phrased, is customarily mentioned as a primary aim. As a matter of fact, Wilhoit suggests that "Christian Maturity" might well be considered the central purpose of Christian education.[74] Murch understands the primary educational function of the church to have as its "sublime object *fitting men to live in perfect harmony with the will* of God."[75] "To state it simply, yet biblically," Gangel asserts, "*the overwhelming and all-encompassing objective of the church is total Christian maturity for all of its members.* Total Christian maturity includes an individual and collective life of biblical worship, biblical fellowship, and biblical evangelism, all of which are stimulated through properly functioning programs of biblical church education."[76]

Use of Aim in Evaluation

Insofar as it is a standard for determining the direction and extent of learner progress, aim has received scant attention. Two apparently related reasons for this neglect are (1) that aims rooted in divine purposes are difficult to translate into meaningful phenomena which are subject to measurement and (2) that stated aims often lack here-and-now specificity. Benson does postulate that aim makes measurement possible by providing a basis for determining how well religion teaching is progressing. However, no matter how desirable, it would be interesting to learn how Benson would propose to measure progress toward the aim he proposes: "to shape the immortal destiny of a soul according to the Word of God."[77]

Content

From the evangelical/kerygmatic perspective, content is an authoritative, biblically and theologically founded message to be given to learners by teachers who are a witness to it. In this perspective the Bible is the major source of content, and Christ is its central theme.

Method-Content

Teaching method and subject-matter content are sometimes dichotomized. Indeed, teaching method is often looked upon as subservient to the message (or content) of religious education. Benson, for example, asserts: "Christian teaching realizes its responsibility for the proclamation of the gospel message, and therefore does not permit the message to be eclipsed by the method."[78] Similarly, Hofinger insists: "Rightly understood, methods of teaching are servants. They assist the teacher in making his teaching understood as accurately and as easily as possible. But methods must never be allowed to tyrannize over the meaning of what is taught."[79]

Biblical and Doctrinal Basis of Authoritative Content

The perceived authoritative character of content is evident in the writings of both evangelicals and kerygmatics. Evangelicals typically draw subject-matter content directly from the Bible, and they deduce the authority of the message from it as well. Kerygmatic writers also derive subject-matter content mainly from the Bible, but they include the magisterium as a source of authority for the message.

From the evangelical perspective, then, Christian education in the local church is built upon the revelation of Jesus Christ in the Old and New Testament Scriptures. Consequently, evangelicals argue strongly for the use of the term *Christian education* because of what they consider to be its distinctive content. Gaebelein trenchantly articulates this position: "Let it be said at once that the word 'Christian' is something more than a pious synonym for 'religious.' There are many religions; there is only one Christianity. The faith of the apostles and their successors through the ages is not just one among a number of world religions; instead, it is nothing less than the revelation of God to a lost world."[80] As to content, this perspective is typically committed to the position that there is only one authentic and infallible source, the Bible. Thus, Eavey pointedly affirms that the Bible is the textbook for Christian teaching.[81] Byrne agrees, "More and more," he states, "Christian educators are beginning to realize that to be truly Christian, the curriculum must be Bible integrated in theory and practice." In Byrne's view this means that the Bible "provides the criteria by which all other subject matter is judged."[82]

The Bible as Content

Evangelical educator Zuck believes that to accept the authority of the Bible is the distinctive mark that identifies true Christianity. It is "the only basis of an adequate curriculum in true Christian education. Education that bypasses the central finality of God's Word is not evangelical Christian education."[83] Still, it would hardly be correct to draw the conclusion that evangelical theorists encourage no use of nonbiblical materials. As a matter of fact, most do suggest the use of other materials such as hymns, history, and social problems. Nonetheless, they strongly insist on a biblical core of subject-matter content and on a biblically based interpretation of such other materials as are used. The message of the gospel must, for their part, be preserved intact by a concentration upon biblical truth in the process of Christian education.

From the kerygmatic perspective, the content of religious education is a revealed message of salvation which is not discoverable by humans. This message, received by divine revelation, must be transmitted with authority under mandate from God. This mandate is given to religion teachers through the bishop in behalf of the divine person, Jesus Christ, himself the focal point of the message.[84] Kerygmatic writers place much more emphasis upon the church as a source of authority for content than do evangelicals. Therefore, it is not surprising that van Caster should state that "God has provided certain guarantees within his Church.

All religious instruction is imparted in accordance with the magisterium."[85] Van Caster further maintains that if the religion teacher teaches faithfully what the Catholic Church teaches, the content will be something so vital that it will demand the adherence of the whole person.[86] Still, Jungmann suggests that, relative to content, the notion of authority has to be adapted to new times. He notes that the complete and total submissiveness of an earlier Catholicism which entrusted itself to the motherly direction of the Catholic Church is no longer intact. Jungmann holds that religion teaching cannot content itself with merely handing on hereditary formulas; rather, religion teaching must lead toward an "interior grasp" of the content of faith itself. The content of religious education must be identified with the "all embracing, salvific plan of God." Accordingly, the authority of this message lies in the proclamation of the facts concerning God's salvific intervention in history, the kerygma.[87]

The writings of the above Catholic theorists indicate that they rely almost as heavily upon the Bible for subject-matter content as do evangelical Protestants. This biblical source of spirit and language is especially evident in the following summary of the Christian message by the Jesuit religious educator, Johannes Hofinger.

> *THIS IS THE MESSAGE WE PROCLAIM: In His infinite goodness, the Father in heaven has called us to be united with Him in life and joy, sharing His divine riches: through Christ His Son—Him He gave as ransom for us sinners, and into His likeness He desires that we be conformed, so that, born anew of water and of the Holy Spirit, and thus made partakers of the divine nature, we may be children of God. And because we are God's children, He has sent the Spirit of His Son into our hearts: thus being the temple of God, we are to live the life of God's children, following the example of Christ, our first born brother, so that we may gain the kingdom of God and His glory, as heirs of God, joint heirs with Christ.[88]*

Christ the Central Theme

The centrality of Jesus Christ is taken to be the distinguishing element in the Christian religion. In turn, Christ is considered to be the theme, the underlying principle, the heart of the content of that education which enables learners to live as Christians.

Above all, learners must be introduced to the transcendent Christ. Without a vital contact with Him, no effective education is possible. Accordingly, Gaebelein argues that "the pupil must be guided toward a crisis in his education that involves his repentance, his unwithholding acceptance of Christ as his personal Lord and Savior, his obedience, and his infilling by the Holy Spirit."[89] Such an experience with Christ, theoretically, will produce a regenerated person and lay the foundation for a Christian life by enabling the learner to conform to God's will and grow toward Christian adulthood. LeBar proposes a paradigm in which both the living Word (Christ) and the written Word (the Bible) are at the center of a truly Christian curriculum.[90] Teaching religion according to this paradigm amounts to allowing the Bible, as empowered by the Holy Spirit, to change learners according to God's standards. Tests of effective teaching are made by measuring growth and progress along the lines of the following goals: (1) to lead individual learners to Christ; (2) to build them up in Christ; and (3) to send them out for Christ.[91] Reflecting on the educational implications of these matters, Eavey concludes: "This amounts to saying that Christian teaching is concerned primarily and fundamentally not with the dispensing of a body of truth but with the impartation of a Life, even the life of a crucified, risen and living Saviour."[92]

According to the Catholic version of the model, the central mystery to be proclaimed is the message of the riches that are in Christ. This "Mystery of Christ" is a fundamental theme and unifying principle.[93] Focus on the person of the Savior is perceived as contributing to a life-giving understanding of the distinctive content of the Christian message. Jungmann, for example, states that "the Mystical Christ sets forth most clearly the luminous center from which the whole of faith grows together into clear unity, since it is from the radiance of Christ that God's merciful plan, as well as its concrete realization, is rendered intelligible."[94] The duty of the religion teacher, then, is to proclaim the sacred message as clearly and meaningfully as possible, so that Christ shines forth as "the luminous core, who illumines every question, every doctrine, every commandment."[95]

Transmission of Content

The faithful transmission, or impartation, of an intact salvific message is the heart of effective education. This message is a matter of divine revelation and must be proclaimed as the word of God. Theology is considered fundamental to the determination of the specific content which must be transmitted. Jungmann believes that it is becoming increasingly evident that the most important and most authentic manifestation of God's Word is not its scientific elaboration but the transmission of that Word through teaching.[96] Benson avers that since the aim is to shape the immortal destiny of the soul according to the Word of God, the content of Scripture must be imparted before its principles are applied.[97] Mason maintains that the Christian message which centers in Christ must be taught as final truth and that this involves the transmission of a body of content.[98] Jungmann's judgment is that teaching religion necessitates transferring doctrinal content in fulfillment of learner needs, needs which are basically spiritual in nature.[99]

The major currents of thought among theorists writing from the proclamation perspective continue to support the notion that transmission of the unique Christian message will result in desired cognitive, affective, and overt behaviors of learners. However, some thinkers are challenging the viability of the way that the model has relied almost exclusively upon verbal and cognitive formulations of the Christian message. Van Caster, for instance, remarks upon the language problems inherent in transmitting religious truth through words alone.[100] LeBar laments that through the years Sunday School teachers have relied almost exclusively upon verbal communication of facts. This communication has been assessed in most Sunday Schools only by the ability of the learner to repeat this outer knowledge verbally rather than by other evaluative measures which might have touched upon lifestyle or attitudes. She remarks somewhat acerbically, that evangelicals have often been content to point toward the morally failing person and say, "He knows better than that; why does he do it?"[101] Edge raises an issue that adds a certain dimension to understanding the transmissive aspect of the model. He suggests that even though Jesus' message had the power to bring about right relations between humankind, it left room for freedom. Individuals have the right to think and choose. Edge further argues that such freedom is a necessity if religion is to be experiential. "Although authoritarian [transmissive] education may force conformity on the part of the individual, external authority can never force belief or experiential religion upon a person."[102]

Arrangement of Content

Arrangement of subject-matter content to maximize the likelihood of clearly transmitting the Christian message is a prime concern. Perhaps the most common characteristic of proclamationist teaching plans is a concentration upon the biblical narrative as the framework for ordering content. Within this framework, the economy of salvation centered in an understanding of the person and work of Christ provides a unifying theme. Even the actual outline arrangement is thought by some to be a theological rather than an educational matter. Still, it would be misleading to imply that all other factors affecting organization of content are ignored. However, these factors are generally looked upon merely as aids to a better theological solution for the focal problem of effecting faithful transmission of the message. Hofinger offers a typical rationale for this concern: "We heralds have no right to be careless with these riches given us, nor to transmit to our charges only certain fragments of the whole message."[103] Similarly, Benson argues that the Sunday School simply cannot fulfill the requirements of the task committed to it unless the peculiar content of the Gospel message is arranged in a consecutive, comprehensive, and complete plan."[104] Marsden comments upon the propensity of this school of thought to see biblical truth as basically "things to be sorted out and arranged." In a sense, as Marsden intimates, "this is the fundamentalist mind's way of applying scientific order."[105]

Teacher

The Teacher's Religious Qualifications

As the agent who transmits the Christian message, the religion teacher is the central instrument in the religious educational endeavor. Hence, religion teachers must be selected with great care from among those prospects who first of all have the necessary religious and personal qualifications to fit them for this distinctive task. Both evangelical and kerygmatic writers specify that the religion teacher must be a member of "the faith," as "the faith" is defined by the particular writer. Thus, Byrne maintains that "the first and prime requisite for the Christian teacher is that he must be a *Christian*. He must manifest Christlikeness. Hereby it becomes possible for him to witness to God's truth while at the same time give a demonstration of the goal of Christian education which is Christlikeness."[106] Gaebelein contends that the qualification of "newness of life through faith in the savior" is so essential for teaching in a Christian educational setting that it must never be waived.[107] Eavey maintains that only the teacher who has been "made a new creature in Christ" is able to nurture others in the Christian faith. He poses a series of nine questions to aid in assessing the extent to which teachers aspiring to teach in an evangelical Sunday School might be evaluated. Does the prospective teacher give evidence of (1) being a child of God? (2) growing as a Christian? (3) being cognizant of the nature of the sacred task in view? (4) being mindful of a sense of obligation to God? (5) being a practitioner of the art of prayer? (6) maintaining a consistent Christian life? (7) possessing a "real heart interest" in individual learners? (8) readiness to meet the needs of pupils? and (9) always allowing the supreme place to the Holy Spirit in preparation?[108] It probably should be mentioned that evangelicals generally make little distinction, so far as religion teaching is concerned, between ordained and lay teachers. In view of the stupendous nature of the task, they commonly argue that ministers, professionally trained educators, and lay volunteers must work side by side in the teaching ministry of the local church.[109]

From a Catholic perspective, Carter suggests that the life-giving truth of Christ reaches learners only through the ministrations of the Catholic teacher who is an instrument of God and of the Catholic Church.[110] Some Catholic theorists believe that, whenever possible, only priests should teach in religious educational situations. Jungmann, for example, states: "Granted equal pedagogical ability the priest catechist will always be more highly esteemed than other catechists."[111] When necessary, the use of other teachers, including lay teachers, is encouraged, with the provision that they stress the role and authority of the ordained priest and that they manifest a "genuine Catholic subordination and harmonious collaboration with him."[112]

The Teacher's Personal Qualifications

In addition to the initial, specifically religious qualifications, proclamationists have suggested a broad range of complementary personal requisites for the teacher. Authentic Christian character is normally considered to be the first personal requisite. The teacher must live in witness to the message that is proclaimed. LeBar argues that it will do little good to refine teaching procedures if the teacher's life does not correspond to the message that is delivered.[113] Other proclamationists make personality the prime factor contributing to successful teaching. Thus, Jungmann quotes Michael Phiegler with approval: "The religion teacher will succeed in teaching to that extent to which he himself has advanced as a personality."[114] A commission or call is almost always assumed to be a necessary requisite. Gaebelein believes that without a call no other capacities will make a Christian teacher worthy of the name.[115] From the Catholic perspective, when a religion teacher is commissioned by ecclesiastical superiors, he or she is sent out to teach by Christ himself.[116] Both Protestants and Catholics theorize that a holy zeal for the kingdom of God is a requirement for teaching religion effectively.[117]

Fidelity to the message is another requisite held necessary. Hofinger says that fidelity to the message is the most important virtue of the herald of Christ's message, a virtue which causes one to proclaim the message exactly, carefully, and diligently.[118] Still other requisites mentioned by traditional theorists are: *a sense of prayer*, without which the teacher will accomplish nothing by way of communicating faith to others;[119] *unselfishness*, perfect accomplishment of Christ's commission is said to leave no time for interest for oneself;[120] and *"brains,"* because mediocre efforts on the part of teachers imply that Christianity stands for second best.[121]

The Teacher's Training

The theoretical issues involved in training religion teachers are perceived in much the same way by evangelicals and kerygmatic theorists. Both insist that the most necessary competencies of religion teachers are rooted in and nurtured by the previously discussed religious and personal characteristics. Nevertheless, there is strong support among them for some sort of a program to prepare prospective teachers, especially to update the teaching skills of teachers in service.

Proposed training programs are highly reflective of the traditional spotlight upon communication of a divinely revealed salvific message as the major responsibility of religious education. Accordingly, such programs usually concentrate upon *faithful understanding of the message* as the most essential element in any training program. To this end, evangelicals typically advocate Bible studies while kerygmatics recommend doctrinal studies as the heart of the program. All other elements in teacher training programs theoretically contribute to the capacity of the teacher to transmit the content of the message to the learner.

Evangelicals usually have the teaching staff of the Sunday School in mind when they speak of training teachers. In this instance the teachers are almost always lay volunteers. Reisinger insists that teachers in Sunday Schools typically (1) lack formal training; (2) have little knowledge of the Sunday School textbook, the Bible; (3) may be quite unaware of effective teaching methods; and (4) are often indifferent in their attitude. Most evangelical teachers, he suggests, confess that God and the Bible are important, but what they believe (and say) may be entirely different from what they teach. Consequently, by observing the nonverbal communication of teachers, students may in fact learn that the sacred truths spoken in Sunday School are really not as important as the secular truths taught by superior teachers in public school.[122] Benson maintains that issues such as those mentioned by Reisinger are best solved by thorough training that anticipates and prevents such problem arising from incompetent teaching.[123] Benson further believes that success in teaching can be assured to all who will be guided by the recognized principles of pedagogy. He is also careful to intimate that these principles do not conflict with the work of the Holy Spirit.[124] Zuck regards teaching as one of the ongoing, spiritual gifts necessary for the edifying of the church. It involves capacity to instruct in and apply the doctrines of God's truth.[125]

In a key chapter, "Studying the Bible and the Pupil," Edge argues that it is important for the teacher to be growing in biblical knowledge and understanding. But, he adds, the teacher must continue learning about learners, and especially those learners in the teacher's class.[126] Byrne argues for a reasonable academic training appropriate for the level at which one will teach, adding: "Above all, such training should be integrated and correlated with the Christian Theistic World View. Here the spiritual and theological truths of our faith will take precedence and be the means of interpretation and evaluation of all other fields of knowledge."[127]

The format of teacher-training programs most often put forward by evangelicals includes: (1) *the study of the Bible* and related subjects such as doctrine, historical geography, and antiquities; (2) *the study of the learner and psychology*; and (3) *training in techniques and methods of teaching*. Some consider mastery of the Bible to be the most essential foundation for teaching, not only because it is the textbook but because it is also thought to be the best source of information about the pupil and about teaching method.[128]

Kerygmatic theorists commonly concern themselves with (1) the training of priests, (2) the training of persons intending to serve in religious orders, and (3) the training of lay religion teachers. Each of these categories presents somewhat different theoretical problems. Jungmann argues, for example, that every priest and religious possesses the basic talents required for teaching religion.[129] By and large, traditional Catholic training programs emphasize three areas: *first*, the content of the divinely revealed message through the appropriate study of Christian doctrine, the Holy Bible, the liturgy, and other contributory topics (religious, and most especially priests, are presumed to fulfill this and the following requirement in their normal studies); *second*, the personal development of religion teachers through stress upon spiritual formation, character training, and social behavior in order that they may be "good witnesses to Christ"; and *third*, the acquisition of skills and methods deemed appropriate to the sacred task of teaching religion (which task, though perceived to be ultimately a matter of divine grace, must make use of human resources, i.e., methods).[130]

The Teacher's Method

Traditional theorists typically consider teaching method to be a means to an end (i.e., the faithful communication of the Christian message to learners). There is little commitment to a particular method since one method is reputed to be quite as good as another so long as it helps convey the Christian message to learners. The teaching method advanced by Herbart during the nineteenth century, however, has profoundly influenced twentieth-century teaching practices in both Protestant and Catholic religious educational settings. The Herbartian method (popularly formulated in five so-called "formal steps": preparation, presentation, association, generalization, and application) affected the methodological thinking of a number of evangelical theorists. Then, too, as previously discussed, its concepts were used in the development of the Munich Method of religion teaching. Oriented as it was toward the communication of ideas in a clear and complete way, the Herbartian method appealed to theorists concerned with the orderly transmission of a divinely ordained message as the best means whereby both desired behaviors and the salvation of students might be effected.

Possibly because of their more European orientation, kerygmatic writers seem to make more use of methodological concepts directly related to Herbartian theory than do evangelicals. The overarching teaching method, as distinguished from teaching techniques, advocated by most writers is derived directly from the Munich Method. Jungmann's discussion of teaching method in *Handing on the Faith* indicates his conviction that this method, which he calls the "text-developing method," is the most reliable one for teaching religion because of its capacity to convey subject-matter content. Jungmann believes it is the preeminent teaching method, the method used by Christ himself. He objects to the exclusive identification of the text-developing method with Herbart's notions. "Vitalization" of the text-developing, or Munich Method (the five steps of which are preparation, presentation, explanation, summary, and application) may be accomplished, according to Jungmann, through the judicious use of "the activity principle" and "the personal experience principle."[131] Hofinger, who insists that method exists primarily to serve the teacher in communicating "the message," similarly sets forth an overall teaching method which closely resembles the Munich Method with its Herbartian framework. He distinguishes three stages of learning (perception, assimilation, and response) as a "basic law" to which correspond three stages, or steps, in the process of teaching (presentation, explanation, and application). Hofinger believes that this method is "based on God's way of winning men" rather than upon mere psychological theories.[132]

The teaching method most often advanced by kerygmatic theorists unfolds through the narration of salvation history. According to their view, the biblical narrative provides the theologically and psychologically soundest, as well as the simplest and most effective means of initiation into the Christian religion. It should also be remembered that the religion teacher's life is considered by Catholic traditional theorists to be generative of the teaching method which is outwardly employed. Thus van Caster can remark, "We must be excused for insisting on this, but in our opinion, the spirit of the teaching is far more important than the technique. More than skill, it is the mentality of the teacher which influences his pupils. It is his mentality based on his deep knowledge of the Christian faith which forms conscious Christians."[133]

A striking aspect of evangelical thought is the eclectic manner in which methods are proposed for use by religion teachers. Some writers assume that since neither learners nor lesson content can be taught in the same way, the teacher should be taught basic competencies in a number of methods (better termed "techniques") such as storytelling, recitation, discussion, lecture, and the like. Another often expressed opinion is that teachers of young children should have a flair for the dramatic and be adept storytellers while teachers of adults should be able to use discussion and lecture as the preferred methods. No single teaching method seems to have been adopted as a model by evangelicals in the same way that the Munich Method has been adopted by certain Catholic theorists. Gaebelein observes that there is much work yet to be done in integrating the teaching methodologies employed in schools operating within the evangelical tradition.[134] LeBar charges that many Sunday School teachers use a method, to be blamed on an "earlier Herbartian influence," that can only be described as "poor lay preaching."[135] Mason regards it as unfortunate that the commitment to "transmissive teaching" (of which he approves) has led to a dependency on "stereotyped verbal teaching methods." He believes that "transmissive teaching" is capable of adopting many methods and techniques to its purposes.[136]

LeBar has proposed a comprehensive teaching method consistent with the proclamation model. She surmises that a chief reason for the lack of life and vitality in much evangelical teaching is that methods derived from a number of "man-made systems" have been used. The "distinctive" content of Christian revelation, she contends, calls for "distinctive" treatment. Consequently, a better approach to teaching method would be to discover "God's system" and to develop teaching methods from it. LeBar's *Education That Is Christian* amounts to a search for "God's system through the analysis of teaching methods used by biblical personalities, especially Jesus, the Teacher come from God." Since Jesus did not use stereotyped methods, LeBar concludes that the "scriptural method" is not a stereotyped method. She develops a curriculum plan for teaching religion in which the Word of God, both living (Christ) and written (the Bible), is at the center. The appropriate teaching method for this curriculum makes use of such concepts as pupil needs, life situations, personal experiences, and (most especially) the Holy Spirit. Indeed this "scriptural method" supposedly eventuates in the human teacher working harmoniously with the Divine teacher, the Holy Spirit. In summary of her approach to teaching method, LeBar states:

> The problem is to find God's ways of working, and work with Him, not to try to wheedle God into blessing our schemes. Since Christian teaching may be defined as discovering God's ways of working and working with Him we need to learn by Scripture and by experience all God wants us to know of the ways of the Spirit. Not that we should try to unscrew the inscrutable, but these things which God has revealed belong to us and to our children (Deut. 29:29).[137]

For the sake of making his point, Edge simplifies his discussion of teaching methods to two approaches: (1) the approach that suggests Christian character is developed automatically if one knows what the Bible teaches; and (2) the approach that suggests Christian character is developed by leading the learner to make choices and engage in experiences that are Christian. In Edge's view the second approach does not deny the underlying need to know the Bible. He suggests that these two methodological approaches can be supportive of one another, although they lead, in actual application, to the employment of vastly different teaching techniques, namely, the lecture and, what Edge terms "a circle of interaction."[138] Byrne reflects a more typical evangelical understanding than Edge in his discussion of method. He argues that "the Christian view of method is based on supernatural interpretation. With God central in the universe, the Creator and Source of all truth, all method must also center in Him.... This whole process is a matter of the teacher cooperating with the Holy Spirit to accomplish this glorious end."[139] Eavey summarizes the matter: "The central problem of method, then, is how to guide the pupil so that he learns well," keeping in mind the truism, "in teaching we should talk less and teach more."[140]

Evangelicals, as do kerygmatics, often argue that over and above any teaching method, the teacher's personal life and Christian witness is foundational to success in teaching. "The person himself," according to LeBar, "is the key to spiritual ministry: we are our own chief method."[141]

Learner

The learner is regarded as the recipient of an authoritative, divinely ordained, eternally saving message. Learner variables (how learning occurs, developmental differences, and the like) are of theoretical interest essentially because of the possibility that such information may enable the message to be more effectively communicated to the learner. This attitude is succinctly stated by Donald Joy: "Humans are specially endowed creatures with a capacity to know and to learn. If they are to be well served by the church, we must be attentive to the ways of knowing and to the emerging strategies of learning so as to help human beings grasp the vision of themselves and their world which is the distinctive property of the Christian faith."[142] From a more typical perspective, Jungmann writes: "As catechists, we must as a consequence present Christian doctrine in such a way that it is grasped by the child. To this end we must take into account their psychological differences, especially those peculiarities of disposition, which are relevant to their religious training."[143]

Possibly the characteristic most crucial to the proclamation model is that the learner is assumed to participate in the supernatural as well as the natural order. The core educational process is considered to be a supernatural one. Evangelicals accordingly look upon the learner as God's creation, made in his image, but with the image distorted through sin and in need of supernatural renewal.[144] Gangel clearly describes the evangelical viewpoint.

> *Since the aim of church education is to nurture those who are in Christ, it obviously follows that drawing men to the Savior must precede the nurturing process. The regenerate person receives a new nature, but the Adamic nature is not obliterated. In dealing with it, church education continually relies upon the Word of God as the sanctifying agent which carries on a cleansing process in the life of the Christian.[145]*

Zuck adds:

> *Pupils who understand the will of God are those who are filled with the Holy Spirit (Eph. 5:17, 18). Thus it may be concluded that the filling of the Spirit increases the capacity of pupils to learn more quickly and adequately.... The ability to learn spiritual truths increases in proportion to yieldedness to the Spirit of God. Prayer, spiritual preparation, and an obedient heart are also essential to genuine learning.[146]*

Eavey regards the learner as a spiritual being, one who shares God's image, "a purposeful energy system, who functions through a body and through a mind. As a living person, he acts and, because he acts, he learns.[147]

Catholic writers understand the baptized learner as not merely a natural being, but also as a creature who belongs to the supernatural order through sanctifying grace; the largely unconscious supernatural life of the learner needs to be developed and brought to consciousness by religious education.[148] For these Protestants and Catholics alike, it is through transmission of the Christian message that the supernatural core process of religious education is effected, at least theoretically.

Protestant theorists usually agree that the learner deserves to be considered more seriously in theorizing about the education process. After all, as one writer puts it, even church-related schools are not ends in themselves since they exist for the sake of the pupils in whose life the goals of education are to be realized.[149] Another writer avers that learners really ought to have a more significant place in the theoretical process because it is they who "must have dealings with the Lord."[150] However, even though they do give some consideration to the learner and to the teaching-learning process, evangelicals appear to place too little reliance upon these factors in their actual theorizing. Thus LeBar writes: "The important thing is what is happening inside the pupil.... We teachers can influence these inner factors only by manipulating the outer...Modern man cannot hope to improve upon the concept of teaching that the Lord God Himself has given in John 16:13. Because the Holy Spirit is the only Teacher who is able to work both inside and outside the pupil."[151] Gaebelein pinpoints the philosophical reasons why evangelicals distrust pedagogical practices based upon studies of learning psychology: "Since man is in reality a creature of two worlds and possesses spiritual capacity and eternal destiny, the present provides no adequate basis for his education."[152]

Catholic thinkers likewise express a theological and philosophical perspective which moves them to regard the learner in a religious education setting as mainly the receiver of a message. Given this perspective, the theoretical problem for both evangelical Protestant and kerygmatic Catholic writers is to ascertain and express how the divinely ordained message might best be fully and faithfully communicated to the learner.

Environment

As a usable construct in day-to-day practice, environment is largely ignored. Despite the fact that they acknowledge certain environmental effects, proclamationists appear to be committed to a viewpoint which ultimately attributes behavior (overt or otherwise) to intellectual and other inner, "spiritual," factors. Thus, one writer suggests that learners themselves determine their behaviors, notwithstanding their continual interaction with the environment.[153] In a similar vein, another argues that a clear mental possession of the details of the Christian faith should provide a bulwark against a hostile environment.[154]

Among proclamation theorists, particularly Catholics, recognition is given to the home, the school, and the parish church as environmental components which contribute positively to effective education. However, these components are considered more or less adjuncts to the "real" (i.e., content-oriented) religious educational process and are not integrated into theory and practice in any dynamic way. In fact, the establishment of Christian schools may be looked upon as an attempt to ameliorate rather than actually to use environmental effects because the environment is generally perceived to be unfriendly to Christian values. Such a mentality militates against inclusion of environmental variables in day-to-day religion teaching because of the perceived possible contamination, or dilution, of the Christian message.

The modified, overall environment of the typical Christian school, then, supposedly affords learners the opportunity to tighten their grasp upon the Christian message so that, as a result, they will be enabled to "live the Christian life" when they "go out into the world." Gaebelein argues that it may be put down as a cardinal biblical principle that the Christian is not at home in the world, that there is always tension between the Christian and the environment (i.e., world) which can never provide an adequate basis for one's education.[155] Jungmann similarly contends that Catholics ought to resist the influence of the hostile world by creating another kind of world within the school and its religious life.[156]

Writing from his background as a psychologist, Eavey is more sympathetic to environmental effects than are most of the writers from this school of thought. "Environment," he states, "influences learning. It is from the environment that problems arise. The environment helps or hinders solution through what it furnishes or does not furnish toward solution. It also gives learning a certain amount of direction through what it does or does not supply."[157]

Eavey presages a key dimension of the social-science model by raising the possibility that environment might be employed as a useful teaching strategy. "The first essential in teaching," he states, "is control and direction of the environment so that pupils have experiences related definitely to the ultimate purpose of teaching... an effective teacher does not teach—in the ordinary sense of the word. What he does is to organize the environment and set the stage so that the pupil learns."[158]

Evaluation

Evaluation of learning outcomes whether of knowledge, attitude, belief, or overt behavior, plays a relatively small part in the proclamation model of religious education. One apparent reason is demonstrable effects of the Christian message are not necessarily expected to follow immediately upon its reception. A careful reading of the literature reveals a common attitude to be that "the truth of God, faithfully taught, often works by delayed action."[159] Hence, the teacher and the content of the lesson, rather than the learner and learning outcomes, are the foci of evaluation from the viewpoint of this model.[160]

It is true, however, that some evangelical writers have given a certain amount of thought to the place of evaluation. Byrne, for example, offers a rather complete encapsulation of the evangelical attitude toward evaluation: "The Christian educator recognizes the value of tests and measurements but in the final analysis the interests of the student himself are paramount. Teachers, therefore, should supplement test results with personal judgments" recognizing that life itself provides an education.[161] Gangel developed a useful list of questions to ask in evaluating the total educational program of the local church. The questions posed are addressed to: (1) organizational structure, (2) curriculum and instruction, (3) records of outreach, (4) personnel and recruitment and training, (5) evaluation of church-home relations, and (6) facilities and equipment. This practical and extensive list, with helpful comments, is adaptable to a number of settings.[162] Perhaps the most comprehensive treatment of the ways that a considered process of evaluation might add to the Christian education enterprise is that by Eavey. He suggests that the purpose of evaluation is actually to promote learning. Evaluation, from his perspective, relates to objectives, involves the learner, relates to behavior, advances learning, and is continuous. Furthermore, evaluation cannot be separated from the teaching-learning process. Eavey does regard Christian learning as of a somewhat different genre than other forms of learning in that Christian learning is perceived as more complex. It is complex because, in his view, it assesses such outcomes as the experience of learner with Christ, knowledge of Bible contents, understanding of the implications of Christian truth, and the extent that the learner comprehends the meaning and practice of the Christian life-walk.[163] Edge reflects upon the need for evaluation for the teacher to get some reading on changes that are actually taking place, remembering that life tests one's teaching, others test one's teaching, and God tests one's teaching.[164]

SUMMARY

In a number of ways the evangelical/kerygmatic model is a twentieth-century revival of the prototype described in chapter 2. Accordingly, it represents an effort to recover and maintain the spiritual dynamic of the early church. In spite of obvious differences, it seems apparent that both Protestant and Catholic thinkers working from this proclamationist model are committed to a point of view from which theological considerations are preceptive. An authoritative revelation is normative for both theory and practice. In the discussion of the social-science model that follows in chapter 6, it is helpful to keep in mind that James Michael Lee is highly critical of the way in which theology functions in the theological models. His argument is that the social sciences (not theology) offer a proper language for theorizing about the process of teaching and learning.

CHAPTER 6

THE SOCIAL-SCIENCE MODEL
OF RELIGIOUS EDUCATION:
Religious Instruction

THE GENESIS OF THE SOCIAL-SCIENCE MODEL

The social-science model is marked by a scientific mentality that is made evident by: (1) its commitment to empirical rather than to armchair methodology; (2) its orientation toward objective, quantitative treatment of data; (3) its emphasis upon understanding and predicting religious behavior on the basis of laws derived from empirically observed and verified phenomena; (4) its concentration on hypothesis-making and testing as a means for identifying and developing teaching practices by which desired religious behaviors may be reliably facilitated; and (5) its strong theory-practice linkage. The social-science model, then, is clearly distinguished from the models discussed in earlier chapters in that it considers the findings of the social sciences as normative for instructional decisions.[1]

The social-science model of *religious instruction*[2] is developed in a systematic way in the writings of James Michael Lee, a Roman Catholic layman and teaching-learning specialist. Several of Lee's earlier books and articles evince a definite social-science viewpoint toward matters concerning religious instruction.[3] An early statement of the model was put forward in a series of three articles which appeared in the fall of 1969 in *Today's Catholic Teacher*.[4] In this series, Lee argues that religious instruction is more fruitfully conceptualized as a mode of social science than as a mode of theological science.

In 1970 the first presentation of a distinctly social-science model of religious instruction to appear in book form was made in several chapters of *Toward a Future for Religious Education*. The central thrust of Lee's argument is that *"the religion teacher fundamentally is a professional specialist in the modification of student behavior as it affects his religious life."*[5] This thesis has far-ranging implications. In the first place, it suggests that the religion teacher must be competent to identify the specified learning outcomes which are desired and to successfully implement the pedagogical processes by which these learnings are most likely to be attained. In the second place, it affords a rationale for viewing the religious instruction act as being value free because the teaching process by its very nature facilitates behavioral modification about as readily in the direction of one system of religious values as another.

Following his foundational proposals, Lee began to erect what is possibly the first consciously comprehensive model of religious instruction ever proposed. The framework of this model is most clearly set forth in Lee's trilogy: *The Shape of Religious Instruction* (1971) which provides the basic rationale for the social-science model; *The Flow of Religious Instruction* (1973) which surveys, assesses, and interprets a wide range of research data pertaining to the teaching/learning process; and *The Content of Religious Instruction* (1985) which deals with the substantive content of Christian religious education. He regards this trilogy as advancing a comprehensive model (system) which is rooted in the actual dynamics of the teaching/learning act; but which, in contrast to the model identified with George Coe and William Clayton Bower, does not downgrade theological content. Lee maintains that such a thoroughgoing, comprehensive model is necessary in order (1) that diverse instructional practices may be made coherent and (2) that they may be related in both their methodological dimension and their content dimension.

While the structural outlines of the social-science model are carefully developed in Lee's books, especially the trilogy, he provides important depth and color in a number of chapter-length writings.[6] Perhaps the most important of these, for the purpose of this study, is "The Authentic Source of Religious Instruction."[7] In this nearly 100-page chapter, Lee explains the logic undergirding his development of the social-science model as a macrotheory of religious instruction. A repeated refrain is that no theological conceptualization can provide as adequate a macrotheory for the enterprise of religious instruction as may be developed out of a social-science milieu. Lee believes the evidence is conclusive that, thus conceived, religious instruction, as a mediated reality, is not subject to theology. Rather, it is a separate and independent field, operating on an ontic level of reality.

Since every ontic reality has its own ground and its own medium, the proper ground and medium of religious instruction is social science. Lee argues strongly that social science is the proper ground of religious instruction precisely because its essential nature is to facilitate desired religious outcomes. Further, he argues that social science is the proper medium of religious instruction because all of its activity functions essentially along facilitational lines. Accordingly, the fundamental operational dynamic of religious instruction is substantially different from theology and its norms are not derived from theology. Even so, in this chapter as elsewhere in his writings, Lee presents theology as essential to the religious instructional task. Theology obviously plays a key role as a recurring dimension in the substantive content, and it introduces norms that are indispensable for focusing and enriching religious instructional activity.

In this regard, it is important to keep in mind that it is not possible to follow Lee's argument unless one is aware of his presupposition, "based upon empirical evidence," that religious learning does not differ from any other form of learning. Religious instruction, then, in Lee's terms: "uses the same theories, laws, concepts, and procedures which apply to all general instruction precisely because it is an indispensable and inextricable aspect of general instruction."[8] Accordingly, the language of religious instruction is essentially different from the language of theology. Lee states: "Because religious instruction is a mediated reality and enjoys ontic autonomy from theology, its proper language must be that of religious instruction and not that of theology."[9] By working from an underlying social-science mode and in a language appropriate to the mediated reality of religious instruction, Lee believes that it is possible to satisfactorily resolve the problem of method-content duality that has long undermined the effectiveness of Christian religious education.[10]

Of particular significance to religious education as a field, or as a would-be field, is the fact that Lee appears to be the first major theorist to treat both Protestant and Catholic religious education (and theorists) alike, in an integrated way. In this chapter, then, the analysis and description of the social-science model is based upon Lee's works, especially his trilogy, each volume of which is deliberately subtitled *A Social Science Approach*. Obviously, Lee's is not the only model that might be constructed from a social-science perspective. However, the care with which he has worked, together with the range of his thought, justifies using his writings as the essential data for this chapter.

CRITERIA

The social-science model of religious education (instruction) is delineated by the following criteria. *First*, normative roles relative to decisions concerning theory and practice are assigned to an existential fusion on the one hand of both religious and theological conceptualizations in harmony with the prevailing viewpoints of individual churches or denominations, and to empirically validated facts and laws pertaining to the teaching-learning act on the other. Theological and biblical content is accepted and inserted as pedagogically appropriate. *Second*, religious instruction is defined as the facilitation of specified, behaviorally defined, religiously targeted behaviors. *Third*, the teacher's function is to deliberatively structure all of the demonstrably relevant pedagogical variables in such a way that the learner's behavior will be modified along desirable lines. *Fourth*, the learner's religious behavior (lifestyle, affective, cognitive) is learned in essentially the same way as any other human behavior.

ANALYSIS OF THE SOCIAL SCIENCE MODEL

Aim

From the perspective of the social-science model, aim is most fruitful when it is determined specifically for each particular teaching situation by the religion teacher in active collaboration with parents, learner(s), and persons representing the larger church community. When determined in this way, aim is influenced by a number of variables, such as: (1) family life, which has been demonstrated to be the most powerful and pervasive variable affecting religious learning; (2) the learner, who is after all the proper focus of instructional endeavor; (3) the ongoing ministry of the church "as commissioned by Jesus Christ"; and (4) the teacher's scientifically based knowledge of the possibilities for religious teaching and learning.[11]

Scope and Focus

Lee agrees with the majority of Christian religious educators who hold that the ultimate aim of instruction is that *every learner should live a life characterized by love and service to both God and humankind in this present world and attain happiness with God in the world to come.* He contends, though, that this generally accepted aim is so broad in scope as to offer little practical assistance in the actual teaching of religion. Lee argues that it is the *primary proximate aim* which exerts a determining influence upon the selection of religious instructional practices. In several places in his writings Lee describes what he believes are the three major positions relative to the primary proximate aim of religious instruction, namely, the intellectualist, the moralist, and the integralist.[12]

The *intellectualist position* holds that the primary proximate aim of religious instruction is the intellectual development of the learner in matters pertaining to religion. Religious instruction is essentially targeted toward knowledge of Christian doctrine and toward an understanding of Christian values (in line with the prevailing viewpoint of a particular church or denomination). Lee maintains that the intellectualist position overvalues knowledge in assuming that if the religion teacher can somehow give knowledge to learners they will thereby become virtuous as a matter of course. "Real Christians," he asserts, are not those who know or even, at a notional level, believe—the right things. Rather they are those who live the kind of life exemplified by Christ.

The *moralist position* assumes that the primary proximate aim of religious instruction is to make the learner in some way more virtuous by bringing him or her closer to Christ. Moralists typically conclude that religious knowledge is a worthy aim only insofar as this knowledge will be productive of virtue. According to Lee, the moralist position creates an unwarranted chasm between knowledge and action. This position is said to lead to a lifestyle so defective in intellectual quality as to be neither fully Christian nor fully human.

The *integralist* position, which Lee contends is the position most appropriate for defining holistic religious instructional aim, regards the primary proximate aim as "the fusion in one's personal experience of Christianly *understanding, action,* and *love* coequally."[13] He elaborates upon the three constituent elements of this position as follows: *understanding* in the full sense of the term is not attained by vicarious means such as study or being told, rather, it is gained through knowledge plus experience; *action* must be understood as a performance which may be either an internal or an external carrying out of a thought, desire, or emotion; *love* brings about the synthesis of understanding and action as one person becomes concerned with the needs of another. Lee believes that a commitment to the integralist position will eventuate in the focusing of aim upon the enablement of Christian living as the primary goal of religious instruction. This focus upon Christian living as the primary goal radically affects instructional practice in that the integralist "will typically opt for a primarily environmental strategy, emphasizing product-process, cognitive-affective, verbal-nonverbal, action-oriented practices as they intersect in a prepared, educationally-oriented, total environment."[14]

Behavioral Aspect of Aim

Christian living, then, is a central theme in theorizing about religious instruction. Christian living, though, is a broader concept than either Christian belief or Christian love. It subsumes both natural and supernatural virtues and incorporates them into the self-system of the individual and into the *behavioral pattern* of the here and now. Lee suggests that the five dimensions of religiosity identified by Charles Glock illustrate what he means by Christian living. Glock's five dimensions are: (1) the ideological dimension—religious belief, (2) the ritualistic dimension—religious practice, (3) the experiential dimension—religious feeling, (4) the intellectual dimension—religious knowledge, and (5) the consequential dimension—religious effects.[15]

It quite logically follows that the aim and emphasis of instruction should be upon the total cluster of behaviors which constitute Christian living in its entirety. Accordingly, Lee puts forth four cardinal goals of the religious instructional process: *first,* the modification of cognitive behavior so that the learner will develop a command of religious knowledge and understandings by which he or she will be able to intelligently synthesize faith; *second,* the modification of the learner's affective behavior so that there is an acquired capacity to form Christian values and attitudes as religiously related realities are confronted in the course of one's life; *third,* the modification of the learner's product behavior so that he or she has command of existential, theological, and other relevant subject matter; and *fourth,* the modification of process behavior so that the learner can ongoingly think, feel, and act in a continuingly relevant Christian way.[16]

From the viewpoint of the social-science model, religious behaviors are learned in much the same way as all other human behaviors are learned (learning being defined, in its simplest expression, as a change or modification in behavior). A key tenet is that religious instruction *"consists in facilitating the modification of the learner's behaviors along desired religious lines."*[17] Facilitation, as Lee uses the term, implies that aims must be envisioned and framed in behavioral terms (i.e., stated as behavioral objectives) and that the assessment of the degree to which the learner's behavior is changed be made in terms of performance.

This framing of aims in terms of performance objectives is accomplished through *operationalizing*. When applied to religious instruction, operationalizing refers to the clear and definite statement of a specified performance from which religious learning can be inferred. Accordingly, the teacher who has operationalized appropriate aims for a specific lesson will be able to identify both what is expected of learners at the conclusion of the lesson and how well they are able to perform the expected behavior. Quantitative procedures therefore play a crucial role both in the establishment of religious instructional aims and in the assessment of the degree to which these aims are realized as a result of the practices which are employed.[18]

Because of the problems inherently associated with measuring Christian living in meaningful quantitative terms, Lee has suggested that the most important next step for the field of religious education might well be the development of a taxonomy of appropriate instructional objectives. (A "taxonomy" is a hierarchically ordered classification of principles and laws. Here the term refers more specifically to "an overall classification system of those behaviors specifically recognized as religious.")[19] Such a taxonomy would classify the full range of behaviors both comprehensively and hierarchically. It would be based upon empirically verified facts and laws of learning, and it would incorporate these facts and laws into a purely descriptive set of behaviorally defined statements of religious instructional objectives. According to Lee, this proposed taxonomy would serve a number of vital purposes. *First*, it would supply a readily available, ordered, sequential, and hierarchical classification of demonstrably attainable religious learning outcomes. *Second*, it would define criteria for religious learnings and thus make them "operational." *Third*, it would establish a validated base for evaluating religious learning outcomes. *Finally*, it would facilitate more effective teaching of religion by reducing the number of vaguely stated objectives.[20]

The social-science model, then, to use Lee's phraseology, "is concerned with goals in religious instruction not merely as product ends to be attained, but rather as a set of dynamic learning activities which of themselves lead to the attainment of the desired product and process outcomes."[21] This emphasis upon performance flows from the nature of religious instruction when it is identified as a branch of the social sciences. Lee believes that the relative lack of attention usually given to operationalizing aims is a natural outgrowth of the view that theology, and theology alone, is normative for religious instruction.

Lee is careful to remind his readers that behavioral modification in religious instruction is not synonymous with psychological behaviorism after the model of B.F. Skinner or of John Broadus Watson. The term "behavioral modification," as employed in the literature of the social-science model, refers to the attempt by the religion teacher to enable the learner to change specific human behaviors and, indeed, one's entire lifestyle to correspond with the agreed upon aims which are deliberatively formulated to be in harmony with the Christian stance toward life. However, the laws by which these behavioral changes occur are looked upon as falling within the field of learning psychology.[22]

Content

The proper content of religious instruction is identified as being neither more nor less than the *religious instruction act itself*. Because the religious instruction act is a *religious* instruction act, rather than a *theological* instruction act, the substantive content is said to be *religion*. (In order to follow the thrust of Lee's argument, it is necessary to grasp his logic at this point.) Thus he states: "*Religion is …the substantive content; instructional practice is the structural content. The substantive content plus the structural content as they are existentially formed and fused in the religious instruction act itself comprise the proper content of religious instruction.*"[23]

Delineation of the proper content of religious instruction is especially important from the viewpoint of the social-science model because the entire instructional program is rooted in the desired outcomes which learners are to acquire. In addition, it is highly important to note that since substantive content and structural content do not subsist in any real fashion other than in the religious instruction act itself, there exists a fundamental distinction between religious instruction and other forms of instruction. This distinction is critical. Accordingly, Lee's views on substantive content will be treated in this section whereas his views on structural content (i.e., teaching) treated in the immediately succeeding section, "The Teacher."

Substantive Content

From the perspective of the social-science model, the substantive content of religious instruction is religion—a lived experience, not just a conceptualization. In addition to the concept of religion as substantive content, Lee notes that, historically, at least three other notions have been concretized. In the first place, *theology* has been advanced as the substantive content of religious instruction. Among other trenchant criticisms which he makes of this view, Lee suggests that the empirical evidence indicates that *theology*, in and of itself, does not necessarily give rise to religious lifestyle behavior which is the goal of religious instruction. In the second place, a number of theorists (e.g., Coe and Fahs) have posited the notion that the substantive content of religious education is "all of life itself." A principle shortcoming of this view, according to Lee, is that it carries an immanentist theology to an absurdity. He regards the third notion, namely that religious instructional content is so *"supernatural"* that it cannot be taught, as an unproductive one. If this third view is true, teaching itself is useless. If it is false, it is *prima facie* without any merit whatever.[24]

The experiential quality of the substantive content of religious instruction is underscored by perceiving it as a cluster of interacting contents, each of which may be viewed as a content within its own right. Individually, each separate content demonstrably yields a different form or mode of learning outcome. The sum total of all these outcomes, added to the outcomes which flow from instructional practice as the structural content, is said to form the overall content of religious instruction. These distinctive contents which together form this "cluster" or "bundle" of substantive content include: *product* content, *process* content, *cognitive* content, *affective* content, *verbal* content, *nonverbal* content, *unconscious* content, and *lifestyle* content.[25]

Product content refers to that content which is typically regarded as the outcome (product) of a cognitive operation. It is particularized, static, and usually "tangible." *Process* content, in contrast to product content, is generalized, dynamic, and usually "intangible" in the sense that it is motion rather than in a fixed state. "A vital feature of process content," to use Lee's expression, "is its developmental nature and thrust." *Process* and *product*, as contents, are not easy to tease apart in any satisfactory manner because they are conceptual rather than existential realities. Like any other instructional act, a religious instruction act is a compound of product and process content fused together. This fusion is not according to the mode of the product, but "according to *l'existentiel* of the act into which they are subsumed." From another perspective, Lee reminds his readers that content cannot be identified totally with product since both product and process are kinds of contents—as well as kinds of messages. Many religion teachers seem to assume that product and process content are identical; whereas from the social-science viewpoint, process content appears to be a considerably more important learning outcome than product content. This is so, Lee argues, because product content is particularized and transfers readily only to identical situations; whereas process content, being of a more general nature, is more readily transferable. Since religion is a process characterized by think*ing*, lov*ing*, and liv*ing*, Lee is convinced that a major breakthrough in effective religion teaching waits upon the full recognition that process is a crucial content in its own right.[26]

Cognitive content refers to intellectual content of which there are at least three levels: knowledge, understanding, and wisdom. With respect to cognitive content of religious instruction, knowledge is the learning of the basic elements of Christianity; understanding is the learning of why these elements are important; and wisdom calls for a relating of this knowledge and understanding to the ultimate principles of existence. Lee notes that it is obviously indispensable for religion to have a cognitive component "since man is a rational being." *Affective* content, in contrast to cognitive content, refers to feelings, attitudes, and values. Lee holds it to be apparent that religion teaching ought to include both cognitive and affective contents. On balance, though, more attention should be given to affective content than to cognitive content because religious behaviors have been empirically demonstrated to be more closely related to affect than to cognition. The research evidence cited by Lee indicates that the affective content in a religion lesson will be enriched by the creation of a warm and accepting atmosphere in which the religion teacher loves and prizes each learner for the person that he or she is.[27]

Verbal content is a symbolic kind of content which tends to mirror objective reality to learners instead of providing them with a firsthand encounter with reality itself. Although it is very helpful for some aspects of religion teaching, verbal content tends to be ambiguous and abstract. Furthermore, it is typically cognitive rather than affective in nature. *Nonverbal* content includes all forms of communication which do not use words. Examples of nonverbal content include (1) the religion teacher's voice, (2) body language, and (3) facial expressions. Nonverbal content is a powerful content which may well be the most authentic and genuine of all forms of religious communication. With respect to this distinction between verbal and nonverbal content, Lee suggests that the quality of religion teaching in most settings would be enhanced (1) by consciously using verbal content to reflect upon and to analyze concrete, firsthand experience rather than by allowing it to serve as a substitute for experience; and (2) by concentrating upon the deliberate use of nonverbal content in religion lessons. This argument is strongly supported by the fact that nonverbal communication has been shown to be an extremely effective means of augmenting affective content.[28]

Unconscious content is important because it has a powerful impact upon the color and texture of what an individual learns, especially at the affective level. Lee suggests that the deliberative utilization of unconscious data, such as dreams and fantasies, in the unfolding of the instructional act would have a profoundly beneficial effect upon the religious education enterprise.[29]

Finally, Lee asserts that in many ways *lifestyle* content is the most important of the nine contents which comprise the substantive content of religious instruction. It seems obvious that, unless there is a definite Christian lifestyle outcome flowing from the instructional process, the other contents are quite meaningless. According to data derived from the social sciences, lifestyle content is best taught in a learning situation which is structured in such a way that learners learn by living. Among the practical suggestions which Lee repeatedly makes is that the religion class should be thought of as a "laboratory for Christian living." This means that learners should learn to live in a Christian manner by engaging in Christian behaviors rather than by just talking about them. He states at the outset of *The Shape of Religious Instruction* that "Christian living is at once the means toward and the goal of religious instruction and indeed of all of religious education."[30]

By thus envisioning the substantive content of religious instruction as an interactive cluster of experientially valanced contents, Lee believes that the false dichotomy of "content-centeredness" versus "experience-centeredness" which has plagued the field of religious education for decades can be disposed of once and for all. Attempting to teach a lesson based entirely upon process content to the exclusion of product content (or vice versa) is not only existentially impossible, he argues, it is totally insufficient for the content of religious instruction. "Probably the most effective way to successfully teach the overall substantive content of religious instruction is to structure the pedagogical situation in such a manner that the learners can live religiously. Central in the successful teaching of overall substantive content, then, is heavy emphasis on religious conduct, on holistic religious performance."[31]

The religion teacher, then, structures the learning situation most fruitfully when one content or another is selected and given special salience on the basis of the kinds of outcomes desired from a particular lesson. Although the conceptualization of content as a bundle of interactive contents (rather than as a unitary product-content) is relatively new in the field of religious education, Lee maintains that such a perspective will enable the religion teacher to teach more efficaciously. Additionally, he argues that this approach to the substantive content of religious instruction makes it possible for the curriculum designer, as well as the teacher, to move more easily toward performance based instructional criteria.[32]

Content-Method

Although religious instructional *content* and religion teaching *method* are commonly dichotomized, the social-science model asserts that these two concepts are one reality fused together in the instructional act itself. Lee remarks that earlier understandings of the religious instructional process have tended to look upon religious instruction as a "messenger boy," or at best a "translator," for theology. He insists that these earlier views contribute to the maintenance of a totally artificial breach between content and method. By so doing, these views have also contributed inadvertently, but nonetheless effectively, to a misplaced emphasis—sometimes upon content and sometimes upon method—which has all too often resulted in something less than maximally effective religion teaching.

Lee proposes that this breach between content and method may be healed and, more importantly, that religion teaching may be rendered more fruitful by the adoption of a model in which the religious instructional process is looked upon as a process of *mediation*. In this mediational activity, both theology and instructional method are subsumed in a sophisticated relationship in which any dichotomy between content and method is existentially impossible. He maintains that, within this dynamic relationship, method and content do not simply add their own properties to the instructional act. Rather, they take on the new dimensions of a religious instructional compound. (The elements in a compound do not retain their own identity whereas in a mixture they do.) For this reason, Lee observes that "the age-old method-content duality never really existed except in the heads of religious instruction theorists."[33]

Teacher

From the viewpoint of Lee's social-science model, the teacher is fundamentally a professional specialist who is able to facilitate religious learning. As a professional, the teacher consciously anchors teaching practices in a theory of teaching derived not alone from the facts of learning but also from the facts of teaching. Perhaps the most essential characteristic of an effective religion teacher, according to this model, is a functional competence to modify learner behavior along desired religious lines.

The Nature of Teaching

Like most other contemporary specialists in the teaching-learning dynamic, Lee regards teaching as the overall act which causes a desired change in an individual's behavior. He has defined teaching as "that orchestrated process whereby one person deliberatively, purposively, and efficaciously structures the learning situation in such a manner that specified learning outcomes are thereby acquired by another person."[34] Lee notes that this definition is complex precisely because the teaching act is complex. Indeed, his elaboration of this definition distinguishes among no less than fifteen discrete elements in teaching.[35]

Thus perceived, teaching is, at bottom, a facilitational process. It is an enabling, helping activity by which the teacher, having analyzed both teaching and learning behavior, controls his or her teaching behavior with the specific intention of producing desired outcomes in the life processes of the learner. The key to optimum teaching of religion, then, is threefold: (1) religion teachers must pay careful attention to their own pedagogical behaviors; (2) they must pay careful attention to learner behavior; (3) they must exercise skill in controlling their own behavior so that it leads to acquisition of desired outcomes on the part of learners.[36]

Teaching as prediction. Lee maintains that because the teacher seeks to produce desired (rather than "happenstance") learning outcomes, he or she places within the learning situation those variables that it can be predicted will be efficacious in bringing about these outcomes. He states, by way of example: "A teacher opts to use pedagogical practice X rather than pedagogical practice Y to produce the desired learning outcome precisely because he predicts practice X will be more effective than practice Y."[37] A number of theorists seem to believe that deliberately injecting a predictive element into the instructional setting plays down God's part in the religious instructional process. To the contrary, Lee argues that prediction is as crucial to effective religion teaching as it is to any other kind of teaching. He views the utilization of scientifically verified facts as the basis for prediction as a kind of cooperation with God which will result in more fruitful religious instruction. Enhancement of the potency of prediction is, not surprisingly, regarded as one of the most important early benefits to be derived from the social-science model of religious education.[38]

Teaching as a cooperative art-science. Lee considers teaching to be an art-science because it employs both artistic and scientific elements in such a way that the creativity (art) and validity (science) of the pedagogical act is preserved. He observes that teaching which is thus viewed as an art-science has a "built-in generator for peda-gogical improvement" since the artist-scientist will have developed the sensitivities and skills necessary both to observe the consequences of one's own instructional behavior and to adjust this behavior in accordance with a scientific evaluation about how well these consequences meet stated performance objectives.[39]

Furthermore, Lee asserts that teaching, in addition to being an art-science, is a *cooperative* art-science (an "operative art" being one which is exercised upon passive matter, a "cooperative art" being one which is exercised together with an interactive agent). As a cooperative art-science, teaching is a single activity in which the several elements of the teaching situation (teacher, learner, subject matter, and environment) interact in such a way that the desired outcome is facilitated. Another reason for regarding teaching as a cooperative art-science is that it is a social activity involving persons. Lee contends that the teacher-centeredness which is obvious in much religious instructional practice stems from the tendency of theologically oriented theorists to consider teaching as an operative rather than as a cooperative activity. He believes that an un-derstanding of teaching as a cooperative art-science will contribute to a desirably learner-centered religious instructional process in which feedback from the learner becomes an "absolutely indispensable" part of the overall teaching act. To suggest, then, that teaching is a cooperative art-science implies (1) that teaching is directed toward persons as persons rather than toward persons as objects and (2) that teaching is a joint enterprise between learner and teacher.[40]

The teacher as pure function. From the social-science standpoint, a teacher is a teacher purely because of the *function* that is performed and not because of the kind of person that he or she is. To state that a person is a teacher is to denote that certain kinds of goal-directed activities are to be expected of that individual. For example, one has a right to take for granted that a religion teacher is able to facilitate the modification of learner behaviors along desired religious lines. This characterization of the teacher as pure function makes it possible for any kind of capable, willing individual to become a religion teacher—providing that "he is able to adequately deploy his personality toward achieving the function which is teaching."[41] From this perspective, the teacher is effective or ineffective according to the degree to which his or her knowledge, skills, and behaviors are placed at the service of the facilitation process. In addition, it should be noted that stress upon the teacher-as-function underscores the helping relationship of the religion teacher. It also places added emphasis upon the fact that religion teachers do not exist for themselves, they exist to help other persons learn to live in a Christian manner. For this reason, "The religion teacher ought not to be in the profession for what he can get out of it in terms of personal satisfaction but for what he can give, for what he can facilitate."[42]

The Teacher's Training

As is true of many religious educators, Lee considers adequate training for religion teachers to be among the most pressing of the many needs in the field. Although he assumes that theology and other forms of religiously related knowledge are indispensable to the religion teacher, Lee contends that training programs will dependably lead to more fruitful religion teaching only as they are focused upon improving the actual pedagogical skills of persons intending to teach religion.

In the concluding chapter of *The Flow of Religious Instruction*, Lee concretizes a program model for the improvement of religion teaching.[43] The concepts incorporated in this two-phase model appear to be implicit throughout his educational writings. *The first phase* of Lee's program model suggests that the religion teacher can be brought to a higher level of understanding with respect to pedagogical behavior through: (1) being helped to become aware of the theoretical components which operate during a religion lesson, (2) being aided in identifying as specifically as possible those outcomes which learners are expected to attain, (3) being assisted in ascertaining the degree to which specified learning outcomes are products of one's own pedagogical behaviors, and (4) being enabled to analyze the overall instructional act in a critical manner. Lee maintains that this phase of a training program will generate the self-sharpening activity of focusing attention upon the effects of pedagogical behaviors as the teacher interacts with the learner, the subject matter, and the environment. At the conclusion of this first phase of training, a teacher should be able (1) to intelligently critique his or her own pedagogical behaviors and (2) to begin to distinguish those behaviors which are effective from those which are ineffective in bringing about desired consequential learning outcomes.

The second phase of Lee's program model suggests that the religion teacher can be enabled to achieve more fruitful results as improvement is made in pedagogical behavior. In the *first* stage of this phase, the religion teacher personally experiments with pedagogical behaviors in contrived situations which usually become progressively congruent with a typical instructional setting. As the teacher tries out certain pedagogical behaviors (antecedents) he or she progressively works toward shaping them so that they become more productive of the desired learning outcomes (consequences). In the *second* stage, the teacher trainee continues self-experimentation in a practicum or classroom setting under normal, or near normal, conditions. During the *third* stage, regular practice leads to new and growing analytical insights which in turn initiate the *fourth* stage, namely a heightened awareness of the teacher's own pedagogical behavior. This new awareness serves a dual purpose. It brings about a deeper insight into the actual underlying teaching dynamic and it serves as a reentry device propelling the teacher back into the first phase of the instructional closed-loop feedback system. Lee's model of instruction as a closed-loop feedback system insures that a teacher training program will be self-generating—at least theoretically.[44]

In summary, training programs for religion teachers offered under the social-science model (1) give the teacher an adequate knowledge and understanding of theory and (2) they provide the teacher with the instructional skills (behaviors) by which this theory may be implemented. Lee believes that training programs rooted in the social sciences rather than in theological science offer the major hope for the future of religious education because "it is only from a social-science base that a theory and practice unique to teaching can be developed."[45]

The Teacher's Instructional Practice

As mentioned previously in this chapter (under Content), Lee takes the position that religion is the *substantive content* of religious instruction while instructional practice constitutes the *structural content*. The *real content*, he argues, is an "existential compound" of both religion and instructional practice. In the present section, Lee's rather extensive treatment of instructional practice (i.e., structural content) will be described under four more-or-less discrete headings developed from (1) his distinction between learning theory and teaching theory; (2) his proposed taxonomy of the teaching act; (3) his treatment of the structure of teaching; and (4) his analysis of approaches to teaching religion.

Learning theory and teaching theory. Along with certain other educational researchers, Lee takes sharp issue with the point of view which regards teaching as merely an application of learning theory. He holds that a teaching theory distinct from, but not divorced from, learning theory is a primary need in the field of religious education. Lee regards *learning* as a hypothetical construct, a reality which is presumed to exist because it can be inferred from observed changes in an individual's behavior. *Teaching*, on the other hand, is considered a distinct activity with a particularized set of goal-directed activities. Learning theory which attempts to explain what happens when a student learns is a very different kind of theory than is teaching theory which deals directly with the ways in which one person influences another person to learn. Learning theory which treats of occurrences is a form of *event* theory;

whereas teaching theory which is concerned with the means (practices) by which desirable ends may be attained is a form of praxeological theory.[46] Lee remarks that: "Only confusion results when praxeological theory is equated with or reduced to event theory."[47] Nonetheless, teaching and learning are highly related activities which exert a mutual influence on each other in the total instructional experience. For this reason, Lee employs throughout his writings the term "teaching-learning act" to simultaneously indicate the separateness, the relatedness, and the reciprocity of the two functions.

An adequate *theory of learning* assists the religion teacher principally in two ways: (1) it provides the necessary data about which variables are affecting learning (performance) at a given moment, and (2) it guides in selecting (predicting) those variables which will aid him or her in promoting the desired learning (performance). In elaborating upon the problems associated with identifying an adequate theory of learning, Lee condemns those theories which have been constructed solely on theological grounds by theorists who perceive religious learning to be in some way different from other kinds of learning. The fundamental form of these so-called "Christian learning theories" (Lee's term) assumes that it is God who in some mysterious, ineffable way causes the student to learn. Such theologically based theories are held to be so fuzzy and vague as to be of little practical help to the teacher because the theoretical variables that purportedly affect religious learning (e.g., grace, divine-human encounter) are well beyond the teacher's control. A more fruitful approach to learning theory is to construct a theory from the facts and laws of human learning as these facts and laws have been discovered by the social sciences. Lee holds that this kind of learning theory, grounded in learning itself, is adequate to provide practical help enabling the teacher to work effectively with students in the here and now.[48]

An adequate *theory of teaching* which enables the teacher to see that religion teaching is a form of behavioral chaining rather than a mysterious, quasi-mystical event is regarded as of even greater helpfulness than is an adequate theory of learning. What such a teaching theory does is to suggest which general kinds of pedagogical practice are most likely to be fruitful in certain situations. A teaching theory generates, but does not stipulate, pedagogical practice. The teacher fashions specific pedagogical behaviors from the several interactive clusters of an overall teaching theory. Put another way, a teaching theory makes the teaching act intelligible by enabling one to make sense of what happens in the lesson. It provides a reasonable basis for predicting the consequences of one's pedagogical behavior.[49]

A taxonomy of the teaching act. Because of his strongly held conviction that religious instructional practice must be viewed as an important content element rather than as merely a method of carrying out the task of conveying content, Lee has suggested that a more complete analysis of the teaching act might well put theorists in a better position to work toward enhancing the pedagogical effectiveness of religion teaching. To this end he has proposed the development of a taxonomy of the teaching act. Lee believes that such a taxonomy, arranged along a generality-specificity continuum, would: (1) create a deeper understanding of the teaching-learning act; (2) allow for more effective design of instructional practices; (3) enable the development of more effective teaching modes; and (4) help bring consistency to the various levels of the teaching act—so that, for example, substantive and structural content will be mutually reinforcing, instead of working at cross-purposes.[50]

A tentative, preliminary taxonomy of the teaching act bridges the gap between theory and practice in six sequential categories: approach, style, strategy, method, technique, and step.[51] *Approach* is the most basic orientation toward the teaching act; it is normally inferred from the activities proposed as comprising the instructional act (examples, theological approach, social-science approach). *Style* is the overall pattern or mode of instruction which determines the more general direction and form of learning activities (teacher-centered or learner-centered modes). *Strategy* may be viewed as the overall plan or blueprint for deploying pedagogical methods and techniques (transmission, discovery, and structured learning are examples). *Method* is the set of pedagogical procedures which furnishes the larger tactical units of the teaching-learning act (problem-solving, teacher-pupil planning, affective teaching). *Technique* refers to the structuring of a given learning situation (lecturing, telling, role-playing). *Step* is the (here and now) enactment of sequenced pedagogical behavior upon which particularized consequent student response depends (praise, question, giving direction).

Theoretically, the use of this kind of taxonomy should lead to more effective instructional practice as the steps and techniques used by individual teachers in specific situations become more consciously rooted in wider pedagogical laws. Lee states: "By means of the taxonomy, the religion teacher can radicate his technique in method or strategy, thereby developing a technique which will be effective in his here-and-now lesson."[52]

The structure of teaching. Lee has identified four major clusters of variables (teacher, learner, subject matter, and environment) which interact during the teaching act in such a way as to bring about a particular learning outcome (a dependent variable). By deliberatively arranging these four independent variables in as skillful a manner as possible, the religion teacher works toward attaining desired outcomes. The goals (aims) of the religion lesson then, determine the way in which the teacher (or curriculum designer) structures the independent variables. Consequently, a major function of the religion teacher is to be able to identify those goals which are both desirable and attainable. In addition, the teacher must be skilled in the use of instructional practices which have shown themselves fruitful in producing these outcomes.

Lee claims that the four major variables mentioned above may be architected into an overall teaching structure by using the following sequential steps. *First*, the instructional objectives must be specified in operational terms. *Second*, an instructional system (curriculum, lesson), based upon the best available data about the kinds and sequence of experiences likely to produce the desired objectives, must be designed. *Third*, the system must be tried out under conditions as close to normal as possible. *Fourth*, the system will be put into normal operation after making necessary adjustments. *Finally*, the effectiveness of the system will be evaluated by measuring progress toward instructional goals. Lee emphasizes that this teaching structure incorporates a closed-loop feedback system[53] which generates in-system correctives. Thus, the system is made continually more effective in terms of actualizing the desired goals.[54] This sequential structure of teaching is further developed into a teaching model which utilizes the same essential variables, namely teacher, learner, subject matter, environment, and goal.[55]

Careful attention to the structure of teaching, according to Lee, will highlight the significance of the antecedent-consequent dimension of the teacher's pedagogy. The teacher will then be in a position to use the available means[56] to analyze pedagogical behaviors with a view to controlling them in order to make his or her instructional activity more successful.

A prime benefit of paying close attention to the structure of teaching is that the religion teaching process will be more clearly seen for the complex, cause-effect process that it is. The "veils of mystery" can then be removed from religious instruction as teaching is demonstrated to be a process made up of a series of identifiable, improvable acts. Lee remarks that "the sooner religious instruction 'despookifies' the teaching act and concentrates on identifying and improving the teacher's pedagogical behavior, the sooner will the Lord, the church, the teacher, and the learner reap the harvest."[57]

Theoretical approaches to teaching religion. In view of his assertion that "a theory of teaching religion is one of the most important determinants of both the kind and the quality of the practice of teaching religion,"[58] it is not surprising that Lee's analysis of major theoretical approaches ("theories") to teaching religion is a central feature in his *The Flow of Religious Instruction*. (It should be recalled that in Lee's taxonomy, an approach is the most basic orientation toward the teaching act.) The major theoretical approaches to religious instruction theories which are analyzed by Lee in *The Flow of Religious Instruction* are the "personality" theory, the "authenticity" theory, the "witness" theory, the "blow" theory, the "dialogue" theory, the "proclamation" theory, the "dedication" theory, and the "teaching" theory.[59] Lee remarks at the outset of his discussion that, of these eight theories, only the teaching theory specifies the relevant variables in such a way that it has sufficient explanatory and predictive power to merit being called a *theory* in the strict sense of the term.

The *personality* theory is said to hold that the sole basic variable in teaching religion is the religion teacher's personality. Lee argues that a winning personality is an important quality in a religion teacher, but he contends that other, more controllable, variables are necessary for an adequate theory of teaching religion. The *authenticity* theory holds that the authentic, here-and-now manifestation of the religion teacher's genuine personality is the basic variable involved in modifying the student's behavior along religious lines. This position, in spite of some empirical support, "imprisons the teacher in the web of his own presently experienced feelings."[60] Therefore it is said to be inadequate as an overarching theory for the teaching of religion. The *witness* theory holds that as the religion teacher witnesses to the Christian message in word, deed, and lifestyle the student's behavior will be modified along religious lines. There is the implicit notion in this theory that it is the teacher's personal holiness rather than his skill in facilitating religious learning which is the supreme criteria of the good religion teacher. Lee rejects the witness theory on the grounds that, among other weaknesses, it is too vague in its delineation of antecedent-consequent relationships in the teaching act. The fourth theoretical approach to teaching religion noted by Lee is the *blow* theory. This theory holds that the incomprehensible action of the Holy Spirit is the basic causal variable involved in the teaching of religion. Lee maintains that the blow theory is not adequate as a macrotheory for religious instruction because "its power of prediction is little or nothing, and its explanatory capability is shrouded in opacity and mystery."[61]

The *dialogue* theory suggests that modification of the student's behavior along desired religious lines grows out of an interactive teacher-pupil relationship—a deep personal encounter. Lee argues that despite a number of praiseworthy aspects (such as an emphasis upon both teacher-student interaction and process content) the dialogue theory is deficient as a macrotheory for explaining and predicting effective religious instruction because it fails to generate a consistent, interconnected series of pedagogical practices targeted toward the specifically religious aims characteristic of religious instruction.

The *proclamation* theory of teaching religion is based upon the notion that announcing or heralding the good news of salvation is the primary variable in bringing about religious learning; its emphasis is upon transfer of solid product content. This theory incorporates a number of weaknesses in that it pays little attention to learner behavior or to the environment and also that it requires the learner to be largely inactive during the religion lesson. In addition, it generates mostly transmission strategy and lecture techniques. Thus the proclamation theory fails to meet the criteria of multidimensionality which must characterize an adequate theory of religious instruction.

The *dedication* theory of religious instruction holds that the teacher's dedication is the most important in religion teaching. Lee suggests that this theory merits little consideration as a religious instructional theory because it generates few, if any, educational practices. Furthermore, it fails to specify antecedent-consequent relationships at any level in the religious instructional act. Dedication can, however, be a helpful variable in the religion teacher's personality structure, Lee notes.

The *teaching* theory of religious instruction, espoused by Lee, is based upon the empirically demonstrated causal relationships which exist between the teacher's antecedent pedagogical behaviors and the student's consequent performance behaviors. Possibly the most distinctive characteristic of this theory is that it regards religious instruction as being the purposeful and deliberative modification of the student's behavior along religious lines. The four major variables by which the teaching theory exerts its multidimensional explanatory and predictive powers include: (1) all of the pedagogical behaviors utilized by the teacher in the instructional setting; (2) learner variables which embrace such characteristics as intelligence, creativity, affective level, and value orientation; (3) course variables which are comprised of subject matter area, level, and orientation; and (4) environmental variables which include the physical setting, the teacher, and the other students. Lee claims that the teaching theory weaves these four variables into one fabric which both explains their dynamic interaction and predicts teaching effectiveness on the basis of how they are deployed. He states: "The teaching theory of religiou instruction...raises to the highest level of intelligibility and usefulness the basic multidimensionality of the religious instruction act."[62]

In addition, the *teaching theory* of religious instruction not only allows for but also delineates a closed-loop system of religion teaching. The function of such a closed-loop (feedback) system is to allow for each of the variables involved in the total religiou instructional act to interact with all of the other variables "so that the effects of which any single variable has on the next linked variable in the behavioral chain eventually return to the original variable to modify, reinforce, or enhance it."[63] Theoretically, the feedback generated from within an operative closed-loop system leads to a continual self-correction and renewal of the religiou instructional process. Evaluation obviously plays a vital role in the processing of feedback within such a closed-loop system.

Finally, the teaching theory of religious instruction is directly generative of the structured learning strategy of teaching religion because teaching is regarded as the deliberative arrangement of those conditions which are productive of learning.[64]

Learner

The learner is quite possibly the key theoretical element in the social-science perspective on religious instruction. From this perspective the learner is at the center of the pedagogical act because learning, of which religious learning is an instance, begins and end with him or her. Lee holds it to be axiomatic that religion must be taught according to how the learner learns rather than according to the logical structure of theology as many advocates of the theological approaches assert. In this connection, Lee's favorite sentence (since it seems to appear in all of his books) may well be this one: "All learning is according to the mode of the learner."[65] I should be emphasized again that learning, for those who adopt the social-science viewpoint, is a construct, an inference drawn from observing behavioral changes in individuals. Hence, Lee states

"Effective religion teaching is that which focuses on performance and behavioral change rather than on learning as such. In the final analysis, performance is all the religion teacher has to work with."[66]

The Learner as a Person

It is crucial to Lee's position on religious instruction that both the natural and supernatural dimensions of humankind are interwoven together in the learner's actual existence as a person in such a way that she or he is a whole self, an integer. This inseparable structural relationship between the natural and supernatural dimensions of man affords a rationale for Lee's insistence that religious behavior can be ascertained and modified by using the methods of the social sciences. Religious learning, from this point of view, does not occur within some mystical, amorphous, magical, supernatural dimension of personality; it occurs within the context of an individual's whole personality structure. Lee argues, then, that an optimally effective religious instruction must recognize (and actualize) this wholeness in the makeup of the personality of the learner.[67]

The Learner as Learner

Because of the empirical research data which indicate that learning religion is not fundamentally different from learning any other behavior, Lee asserts that the facts of learning which have been discovered and described by the social sciences constitute a reliable fund of theoretical and practical information which is as relevant to the teaching of religion as it is to the teaching of any other subject. For this reason he devotes an extensive chapter in *The Flow of Religious Instruction* to a survey of these findings about human learning and to an analysis of their potential application in the teaching of religion.[68] Lee warns his readers, however, that such findings are not uniformly applicable and that they do not operate in exactly the same way with all learners; rather, they are generalizations which function with differing force according to the particularized, concrete learning situation. Among the most important findings about learning which are touched upon by Lee in his carefully documented survey and analysis are those which relate to an individual's early family life, total experience, overall environment, corpus of attitudes, and personal development. In the extensive body of research literature surveyed by Lee, the weight of evidence suggests that *early family life* constitutes the single most powerful, pervasive, and enduring variable which affects substantially all aspects of an individual's learning and most especially of attitudes and values. Indeed, moral conduct, emotional life, social behavior, and the entire structure of personality have been found to be determined in major part by those learnings associated with early family living—particularly during the first six years of a child's life. This finding seems to pinpoint the family as the primary agent of religious instruction. Accordingly, its major significance for religious education is that "the religion teacher's role must be regarded as basically a reinforcer and amplifier of the family's work in the religious sector."[69]

A second key finding is that the directness, immediacy, quality, and texture of an individual's *experience* have much to do with the richness, impact, and lasting quality of learning. Lee concludes that this finding indicates that religion teaching must be saturated with experience which is as direct, as immediate, and as rich as the teacher can possibly make it. The religion teacher must therefore learn to structure learning situations so that the learner's environment provides stimuli of a rich and varied nature which contribute to the depth and lasting quality of religious learning.

A third example of the findings from this investigation of the empirical research on learning is that the *environment* in which an individual develops exerts such a powerful influence that the extent of his or her learning is actually dependent upon the environment's composition and structure. Because the composition and structure of the learning group environment are controllable aspects of the learner's total environment, Lee argues that much more thought should be given to the direct control of the learning environment than is commonly the case in religious instructional settings. The deliberative structuring of the physical, emotional, and social aspects of the learning environment may well be the "most important single pedagogical activity the teacher does."[70]

A fourth finding is that the total group of *attitudes* held both shapes and conditions what the individual will and will not learn.

For this reason, teaching for attitudes may well be one of the two or three principal pedagogical tasks of religious instruction. Since the hard research evidence indicates that attitudes tend to be acquired at three pivotal points in life, namely, early childhood, adolescence, and young adulthood, Lee argues that great dividends in effective religious teaching would be gained if the overall development of personnel and resources for teaching religion were so ordered as to take advantage of these pivotal points in attitudinal learning.

A final example of these findings on learning is that both moral and religious development are deeply linked with the whole process of human learning and development. This finding is so basic as to be almost axiomatic, but it is of overarching significance for the teaching of religion in that "religious and moral development takes place according to the normal interactive growth patterns of human maturation and learning."[71] This means that religious and moral development does not take place in a magical, mystical, or supernaturally unfathomable manner but according to a discernible cause-and-effect pattern. It should also be noted that this finding underscores the need to "take the learner where he is." Therefore, religion teaching must become a process in which the teacher continually assesses the learner's developmental state in order to skillfully adapt the various contents of one's teaching to their present here-and-now state of existence.

Lee holds that constant reference to these, and other examples of empirically verified findings on human learning, will enable the religion teacher to devise and to deploy pedagogical practices which are, in fact and not in fancy, conducive to bringing about the desired learning outcomes. Stated another way, this reference to the findings on human learning will help the teacher to know "where the learner is at all times" thereby enabling her to become a more effective artist-scientist partner with the learner in the unfoldment of the "teaching-learning act."[72]

Environment

Whereas the environment typically plays an inconsequential role in theologically oriented theorizing about religious education, it is a critical element in the social-science model. The rationale for Lee's viewpoint on this matter is grounded in his conviction that revelation, in addition to being a historical phenomenon, is an "ongoing, present, flesh-and-blood experiencing." He maintains that experience is not a low level human activity which is inferior to intellectual activity as many theologically oriented theorists assert; rather, it involves the *whole* self in living contact with one's milieu. In the act of experiencing, then, the intellect coordinates with the spirit as well as with the other components of the self. It follows that experience revelationally involves the whole person, including one's spiritual, intellectual, and affective dimensions. On this account Lee argues that the religion lesson can be most fruitfully conceptualized as a deliberatively structured environment within which the learner's experience is recast in a form whereby ongoing revelation is consciously incorporated into one's pattern of living. The religion lesson, then, is ideally "an environment whose conditions are so shaped by the teacher that a personal living encounter between the learner and Jesus is facilitated."[73]

Facilitation of Religious Learning by Shaping the Environment

The primary mark of a learning environment which has been deliberatively structured so as to produce desired learning is that it is facilitational. "Facilitation is the total helping process of enabling the individual to learn for himself all the various 'contents,' the process content as well as the product content, the affective content as well as the cognitive content, the nonverbal content as well as the verbal content."[74] Thus, facilitation involves the careful arrangement of all the conditions (i.e., the total environment) by which an individual is enabled to learn according to his or her developmental level—here and now. In religious instruction the goal of the facilitation process is to provide the kinds of experiences which have been empirically shown to be effective in empowering individuals to acquire behaviors that are truly Christian. The religion teacher's function is to so shape the learning environment by arranging the several facilitational elements (curriculum, social environment, affective climate, the teacher, etc.) that the conditions will work together to bring about the intended (and predicted) learning outcome. "It is this structuring of the learning situation to most effectively facilitate the modification of behavior along religious lines which constitutes the very heart of the religious instruction process."[75]

The pedagogical problem when viewed from the facilitational perspective is not to control the actions of the Holy Spirit; it is rather to manipulate the environment (not the learner) in such a way that the Spirit will be enabled to operate most fruitfully. The facilitating teacher, accordingly, bases pedagogical decisions upon "hard" empirical data about teaching and learning rather than upon theological speculation. For this reason Lee states that "the facilitation process in religious instruction is a uniquely social-science activity."[76]

In connection with this discussion, it should be noted that Lee's definition of the religion class as a "laboratory for Christian living" is a practical way of putting the pedagogical principles of environmental shaping into operation in a particularized religious instructional setting. Lee is convinced that religion can best be learned in a personalized interactive milieu. In other words, in a laboratory which stresses such pedagogical elements as primary experience, the here-and-now situation, and person-centeredness. A laboratory for Christian living, then, connotes a learning situation in which the learner "hammers out in a deeply existential manner his own personal form of operationalizing the revelation experience in his own life."[77] By way of further explanation, Lee emphasizes throughout his writings that structured environments do not produce desired learnings automatically; they merely facilitate learning.

Environments Affecting Religious Instruction

Within the larger environment which includes all stimuli to which an individual consciously or unconsciously responds, Lee identifies seven environments that seem to be of special relevance to the teaching of religion: (1) the overall cultural climate which influences many aspects of behavior; (2) the local environment which profoundly affects levels of school achievement; (3) the school environment which has the power to stimulate (or stifle) the quality and texture of learning; (4) the classroom or learning environment which exerts a significant impact upon a wide range of learning; (5) the peer group environment which affects the direction of learning; (6) the home environment which exerts a determining influence on value learning; and (7) the immediate physical environment (composed of a host of variables, the most notable of them being the affective climate) which affects the rate and character of learning. Lee suggests that the skillful teacher, attuned to the probable effects of these seven environments, can actually capitalize on their effects in order to sharpen the goal-directedness of learning.[78]

Although the effective teacher will be concerned with all of those environments which bear upon the teaching and learning of religion, the greatest attention should be focused upon the learning environment (often a classroom, but not necessarily so) since this is the environment which is obviously most susceptible to deliberative structuring. Lee's analysis suggests that the learning environment itself has many properties such as the physical, the social, the affective climate, and the teacher. The *physical environment,* sometimes simplistically viewed as *the* environment, can usually be altered by the religion teacher in such a way as to positively support the desired learning outcomes. The *social environment* is an especially useful variable in religious instructional settings because it can generally be selectively structured in a manner that tends to promote specified religious learnings, for example, social awareness. On the basis of empirical evidence, Lee considers the *affective climate* to be among the more important aspects of the learning environment because it has been demonstrated that it is well within the power of the informed and skillful teacher to control both the form and the thrust of the affective climate so as to predictively facilitate a variety of highly desirable learning outcomes. Finally, the *teacher* is "without a doubt" the most significant aspect of the learning environment because the pedagogical behaviors the teacher employs are more highly correlated with successful learning than is the case with any other environmental factor. The significance of the teacher in this regard is underscored by the fact that it is the teacher who gives salience to other characteristics of the environment by the structuring of the environment itself.

Evaluation

Although actual evaluation of the learner's learning as a significant aspect of religious educational theory has historically played a very small part in the thinking of most religious educators, it has been assigned a vital role by Lee. According to his social-science model, truly purposive evaluation of student learning (1) must be based upon scientific rather than impressionistic evidence; (2) must be a positive and continuous process; and (3) must be targeted toward assisting the student to attain desired goals rather than merely measuring final learning outcomes. Furthermore, this perspective on evaluation requires that learning goals be envisioned in terms of student behavior and be framed in terms of student performance (i.e., stated as behavioral objectives). It should also be recalled that religious instructional objectives are most meaningful when they are determined by the teacher in active collaboration with the parents, the learner, and representatives of the larger church community.

Evaluation as an Integral Part of Religious Instruction

Lee maintains throughout his writings that evaluation of learning should not be considered the final end of teaching. Rather, it should be regarded as a part and parcel of teaching itself. Thus, in his first book, Lee states a pedagogical dictum: "Testing does not follow teaching; rather testing is an integral part of teaching."[79] It is on this basis that Lee's previously discussed vision of an optimally effective instructional system incorporates evaluation as an integral factor in its closed-loop, goal-setting, goal-achieving cycle. This whole closed-loop feedback system of antecedent-consequent behaviors as (1) analyzed and (2) controlled by the teacher clearly indicates that evaluation is going on at every moment in the religion lesson.[80]

Measurement in Evaluation of Religious Instruction

Measurable observations of Christian living (the goal of religious instruction) are obviously not always easy to make because of the numerous natural and supernatural variables which affect those behaviors that are commonly identified as Christian. For this reason, Lee believes that a scientifically developed taxonomy of objectives for religious education might well be the key in enabling the teacher (1) to operationalize and state religious instructional goals in a uniform way and (2) to evaluate religious learning according to a reliable and validated standard. By measuring learner performance and comparing it with the validated taxonomical standard, the teacher would know the extent of the learning and would thus be able to evaluate the effect of selected pedagogical behaviors. Lee contends that this kind of process by which religious instructional goals are rendered into performance outcomes is necessary because it is only as these outcomes are observed that inferences can be made which allow the religion teacher to know with any sort of validity whether the student has actually learned what was intended. There are, however, some internal behaviors for which there is typically neither time nor opportunity for the teacher to establish performance criteria. Lee holds that by teaching for process content, the teacher can help the learner evaluate these internal behaviors by putting them in performance terms outside the time-space frame of the religion lesson.

Lee contends that the kind of sophisticated evaluation described above has never been accorded its proper place in religion teaching for at least three reasons. *First,* the theories of instruction upon which most religious education is based actually do not deeply value any kind of evaluation. *Second,* religious instruction is typically a low-budgeted, low priority undertaking staffed by inadequately trained, nonprofessional personnel who lack the skills and inclination to engage in meaningful (to say nothing of sophisticated) evaluation. *Third,* many theorists hold the implicit (and sometimes explicit) belief that religious instruction deals with the spiritual outcomes that cannot be measured by humanly devised means.[81]

Because of his strongly held conviction, supported by a considerable body of research evidence, that adequate evaluation is an integral and indispensable part of religious instruction, Lee proposes that: (1) religious instruction must be rooted in a multi-dimensional teaching theory that makes integral use of information feedback, rather than in such unidimensional "theories" as the witness "theory" or the personality "theory"; (2) religious instruction must be placed on a professional base with adequate levels of financial, personal, and institutional support; (3) religious instruction must be "despookified" by recognizing that religious behaviors are identifiable and measurable; and (4) religious instruction must flow out of a new level of cooperation between teacher, parent, learner, pastor, and all who recognize that evaluation is not necessarily threatening but that it offers the potentiality of new and higher levels of fruitful teaching in the field.[82] Thus, Lee states that "if religious instruction is to move forward, it must make heavy use of scientific, objective evaluation which puts the teacher or administrator in constant touch with his own instructional behavior."[83]

SUMMARY

The social-science model is properly set apart from the theological models in that it considers the findings of the social sciences normative for instructional decisions. This viewpoint enables the body of empirically validated facts and laws pertaining to the teaching-learning act to play a central role in religious instructional decisions. The model assumes that a learner's religious behavior is learned in essentially the same way as any other human behavior. Accordingly, a heavy responsibility falls upon the teacher, as a professional, to be in command of relevant religious and educational variables. Lee's vision is that the value of freedom inherent in the social-science model will be recognized by religious educators so as to enable deployment of the social-science model in a broad range of religious education settings. Such deployment might well, in turn, enable more fruitful cooperation leading to greater vitality in the practice of religious education.

CHAPTER 7

CELEBRATING A FRUITFUL FIELD:

A Conclusion

UPON REFLECTION

Almost exactly a quarter of a century ago a chance reading of D. Campbell Wyckoff's *The Gospel and Christian Education* brought clearer focus to my search for a better understanding of the process of Christian religious education. As stated in chapter 1, Wyckoff challenged me to attend to theory as a means of self-understanding, insight, and improvement. Attention to theory directly contributed to my becoming a better teacher and, I firmly believe, a better parent. Indirectly, Wyckoff's challenge led me into the profession that my own pietistic tradition chooses to call Christian education.

A quarter of a century ago I was a young college instructor. My wife and I were parents of two pre-teenage daughters. Now, I am a graying seminary professor and we are grandparents of six pre-teenage children. We sometimes pause to reflect, appreciatively, upon the vital Christian faith of our daughters and upon the budding faith we see unfolding in our grandchildren. At such times I am grateful for the fellowship, insights, and wisdom received from religious educators of a number of schools of thought, many of them well outside the boundaries of my own tradition. In my case, an aphorism borrowed from a theologian friend seems to pinpoint an important aspect of truth: "even theories are sometimes a means of grace." Thus, theories that I have adopted, and sometimes adapted, from colleagues have often provided resources for making sense of those educational, spiritual, and interpersonal experiences that make all of life an adventure. Such experiences contribute to my firm conviction that careful attention to theory is a powerful stabilizing force in many areas of life, especially in times of crisis and change.

In the last quarter of a century, especially since 1970, the range of scholarship in the field of religious education has broadened markedly, the focus has shifted in a number of ways, and the pace of publication has accelerated dramatically. As in so many other dimensions of our culture, change has been the order of the day. However, the focal point of the changes affecting the field seems to be the pluralism which is rapidly becoming a defining aspect of the larger religious environment.

The implications of pluralism for religious education have been rather thoroughly considered from a number of perspectives; but perhaps the most important scholarly study is that planned, implemented, and edited by Norma Thompson in her *Religious Pluralism and Religious Education* (1988). Thompson adduces data to suggest that there has been an intermingling of cultures and religions on a scale that could not have been imagined even a generation ago. Americans and other Western societies that for centuries have thought of themselves as Christian, with perhaps a small Jewish minority, have at the end of the twentieth century become pluralistic. Such changes have obvious implications for the theory and the practice of religious education. In an insight that is of particular relevance for this book, Thompson suggests that pluralism profoundly affects patterns of theoretical discourse that are in any sense public.[1]

IN REVIEW

The modest goal of this book remains to invite interested persons to work together toward a better understanding of the relationship between theory and practice in the broad field of religious education. As promised in the introduction, the primary scholarly task is limited to description. Accordingly, little effort has been expended in drawing conclusions concerning the relative merits of the models analyzed in earlier chapters.

Nonetheless, especially in the context of the growing pluralism mentioned above, it seems worth asking whether or not any one model may prove especially hopeful for the long-term future of the field and of the profession. In this context, a number of observers believe that *some construction of the social-science model makes increasing sense.* In the light of its capacity for finding and for communicating better answers to a wide range of questions, it may offer unique advantages for answering queries about how to improve the teaching of religion, even when evaluated from different theological perspectives. Then too, as presented in the version offered in the writings of James Michael Lee, there is at least the promise of a process of discourse that allows (even requires) teachers and other practitioners to be faithful to denominational and theological commitments.[2] It seems possible that this model may offer a professional environment in which discourse regarding theoretical (even theological) issues can be pursued with minimal distortion in a pluralistic context.[3] Even more to the point, and to repeat a prospect mentioned in the introduction, the social-science model may offer a milieu in which there might be developed a body of reliable, validated information pertinent to the goals of a wide range of religious education settings. Such information, readily accessible, might well enable theorists to make meaningful strides toward establishing a more defined field.

In some contrast, early stages of the research which undergirded the writing of this book yielded arresting evidence that an extraordinary amount of energy has been expended by proponents of the several theological models in denouncing (commonly on theological grounds) all religious educational viewpoints which differed from their own. Within Protestantism, for example, during the first three decades of the twentieth century the evangelical model was a favorite target for liberal writers. Naturally, evangelicals vociferously defended their position. Writers from both models regularly accused the other of not being "fully Christian."[4] Meaningful theoretical discourse between these two schools of thought was, quite naturally, nearly nil. About the middle of the century, with the rise of neo-orthodoxy as a vehicle of model making, battle lines were somewhat redrawn. Even so, the outcome of theoretical discourse across models was all too little changed.

During earlier decades of the twentieth century, then, discourse in the field seemed to be characterized more by verbal exchanges delivered in a petulant and often defensive spirit than by any spirit of wholehearted, cooperative seeking. Scant effort was expended, for example, in deliberatively assessing acts of teaching so as to identify outcomes which might conceivably enable teachers to improve (as judged from the perspective of whatever model). Worse still, uninformed borrowing of teaching practices (whether strategies, methods, or techniques) devised to serve the goals of any particular model sometimes yielded counterproductive results when applied, untested, from within another model.[5]

CELEBRATING A FRUITFUL FIELD

In the concluding days of writing this final chapter, and frankly upon a whim, I queried the library computer for a list of books published in the field of religious education since 1970.[6] I was unprepared for the list of nearly 8,000 titles offered to me by two smiling librarians.[7] On average, that number amounts to a completed book for every working day since January of 1970. It was an exhilarating experience to hold in my hands such evidence of vitality and scholarly fruitfulness. However, it was also a reminder that this study leaves unconsidered the work of many productive writers: scholars, thinkers, theorists.

Accordingly, I conclude this book by celebrating this fruitfulness with brief essays recognizing four contemporary writers who are active contributors to the field in the 1990s. Each has added significantly to the current dialogue across denominational and theological boundaries. Furthermore, each offers a varying blend of theological speculation and interaction with the social sciences. In each case I have at least considered treating these authors under one or another of the models described in the body of this book, but the field is obviously growing, changing. As the field grows, so perhaps must the models used to describe it, but that is a matter for the future.

Timothy Lines (Louisville, Ky.)

Timothy Lines' two books add substantially to any extended, theoretical discussion of religious education. A Southern Baptist, with a confessedly passionate commitment to the church, Lines probably fits best within some version of the social-science model. He proceeds upon the conviction that improvement in religious education is more dependent upon discovering and utilizing the social-science underpinnings of effective education than upon reworking theological structures. Accordingly, his *Systemic Religious Education* (1987) offers a "fresh perspective" that seeks a workable, interactive, communicable integration of religion and science. In pursuit of this high goal, Lines develops a four-element thesis rooted in "systems theory." The structure of the book follows these elements:

> *(1) the systemic perspective is composed of a paradigm, a worldview, models, and simulations; (2) a systemic paradigm can be developed from a study of open systems; (3) a systemic worldview is emerging that is conducive and amenable to the overall systemic perspective; (4) systemic models of religion, education, and religious education can be constructed which reflect the systemic paradigm and which organically and cybernetically influence the systemic worldview.*[8]

Functional Images of the Religious Educator (1992) creatively "actualizes" the systemic pattern of thought initiated in Lines' earlier book. Admittedly, it takes a certain amount of preparation to appreciate the nuances of his impressive scholarship. Even so, his second book is important reading for volunteers as well as for those contemplating professional careers. The "heart of the book" is given to investigating ten roles of the religious educator. Examples of these roles include "Parent," "Scientist," "Coach," "Storyteller," "Visionary," and "Minister." Faithful to his "systemic promise," Lines explores the typical dimensions, aims, functions, teaching procedures, and representative educators (contemporary as well as historical). Thus, in the context of considering each "role," the reader is exposed to a carefully planned learning sequence. Consequently, Lines introduces such historic educators as Horace Bushnell, Ulrich Zwingli, and Ignatius Loyola; together with such diverse contemporaries as James Michael Lee, John H. Westerhoff III, and Mother Teresa of Calcutta. In both of his books, Lines takes a number of opportunities to offer directions as to how his readers are to harvest his thought. Accordingly, in the concluding passages of *Functional Images of the Religious Educator*, he appeals for his readers to seek a harmonious integration of his carefully drawn "roles" which, Lines suggests, have the potential of "coming together to make wonderful, magical music," constituting a "wholeness" within individual religious educators and within the profession.[9]

Richard Robert Osmer (Princeton Theological Seminary)

Richard Osmer's key contribution to the study of religious education is *A Teachable Spirit: Recovering the Teaching Office in the Church* (1990). For this title, Osmer reaches back to John Calvin's confession that, at his conversion, God subdued his obstinate devotion to the Roman Catholic Church and brought alive within him "a teachable frame"; interpreted in the title as "A Teachable Spirit."[10] Osmer's argument begins with a recognition that thoughtful persons within the church have begun to raise serious questions about whether churches have not lost the kind of vitality that it takes to sustain a culture-transforming vision of religion. His speculative, theologically framed, prescription for revitalizing the church is rooted in his assessment of mainline Protestantism: deenergized by various forms of pluralism and characterized by (1) declining membership, (2) declining influence, and (3) increasing ambiguity in regard to its relationship to society. In the light of these myriad problems, Osmer calls to mind H. Richard Niebuhr's argument that the church might benefit from periodic retreat from engagement with the "surrounding culture in order to sort out the boundaries by which it defines its identity." Osmer opines that, given time to reflect, individuals in the church might well be able to "rid themselves of any frantic attempt to recapture the dominant role they once played in American life," with the hope that they could "encounter" once again the "classic resources of their faith" and hence recover "the message of scripture and tradition as they search for the way forward."[11]

It follows, then, that the heart of Osmer's vision for such a revitalized church would be a recovery of the "teaching office." This "office," recognized as a necessary "function" of the church from ancient times and, for Osmer, focused in the writings of Luther and Calvin, is identified with three primary tasks: (1) determination of normative beliefs and practices; (2) reinterpretation of these norms in changing contexts; and (3) the formation of appropriate means of education.[12] Reconstructing the teaching office in the context of the voluntary pattern of American denominations is an obvious challenge. However, Osmer expresses optimism that the Reformer's vision may be actualized in this context even more fully than in the past. His operational plan calls for the identification of three centers of teaching "authority" closely linked to the pattern laid down in Reformation thought: (1) centers (seminaries) for training clergy in the context of scholarly inquiry; (2) centers (congregations) that offer lay education in the context of practical theological reflection; and (3) centers that train denominational personnel for leadership in addressing socioethical issues "in the light of the insight and wisdom of the entire church."[13]

Osmer's *Teaching for Faith* is directed to teachers of adult classes. With obvious roots in Reformed theology, it calls for the principles enunciated in *Teachable Spirit* to be actualized in the church's congregational life, arguing that, as a means of grace, teaching does not directly cause faith. Rather, teaching serves as a "human agency" by which God comes to persons. Osmer charges adult teachers with the task of creating a "context in which faith can be awakened, supported, and challenged." In pursuit of this "ministry," he offers four lenses for bringing adult teaching into sharper focus: (1) *belief* that serves as a basis of trust, (2) *relationship* with God that generates relationship with persons, (3) *commitment* to God that shapes life's investments, and (4) *mystery* that limits our understanding of God and our temptation to control him.[14]

Thomas H. Groome (Boston College)

Thomas Groome's widely read *Christian Religious Education: Sharing Our Story and Vision* (1981)[15] builds upon insights rooted in his own "great awakening" while teaching religion in a Catholic boy's high school. His foundational proposals are extended and refined in *Sharing Faith: A Comprehensive Approach to Religious Education and Pastoral Ministry* (1991).[16] A certain immediacy, one might say "a kind of evangelistic urgency," adds to the effect as Groome conducts his readers on a guided tour of his theologically dimensioned quest for a better way of teaching religion. Groome, a confessed Catholic Christian, seeks to practice pluralism by welcoming readers of other traditions to draw insights helpful to their own needs as they "wrestle with ideas" and reflect upon the several "intersections of theory and practice" visited along the way. The imagery in the book conveys an atmosphere indebted to existential thought, within which Groome's vision for "shared Christian praxis" comes into focus. This vision is informed by a wealth of concepts drawn from classical disciplines, but it is sustained by his creative interaction with liberation theology.

Christian religious education by shared praxis can be described as "a political activity with pilgrims in time that deliberately and intentionally attends with them to the activity of God in our present, to the Story of the Christian faith community embodied in that present, and to the future Vision of God's Kingdom, the seeds of which are already among us."[17] The actual process may be understood as "a group of Christians sharing in dialogue their critical reflection on present action in the light of the Christian Story and its Vision toward the end of lived Christian faith."[18] The heart of Groome's analysis of teaching is developed in terms of five main components: *Present Action* refers to one's expression of deliberate, intentional, human engagement in the world; *Critical Reflection* calls upon one's critical faculties to evaluate the present, recall and critically link the present and the past; and to envision the future in the present; *Dialogue* highlights the aspect of building and responding to Christian community through communicating (listening and telling) the group's individual stories and visions; *The Story*, an activity which Groome intends should move beyond bald narrative so as to examine the authentic, active dimensions of the Christian faith tradition; and *The Vision*, conceived as a vital response toward faithfulness to wholehearted participation in the kingdom of God.[19]

Groome argues that, properly executed, Christian religious education will foster both Christian faith and human freedom. These, he identifies as "parts of the same piece" which will be supportive of a life lived in response to the kingdom of God in Jesus Christ. Groome commonly, and consciously, employs the language of freedom as a way of discoursing about the conditions and consequences of living a life in tune with the values of the kingdom of God. Accordingly, he proposes that *freedom* together with its related terms, *liberation* and *emancipation*, may be "the most adequate words in our time for talking about the historical consequences and responsibilities for Jesus' disciples of his life, death, and resurrection."[20]

Mary C. Boys (Union Theological Seminary, N.Y.)

In addition to a number of scholarly articles, edited works, and scholarly lectures, Mary Boys has offered two substantial books to the field: *Biblical Interpretation in Religious Education* (1980)[21] and *Educating in Faith: Maps and Visions* (1989).[22] Boys writes as a Christian, a Roman Catholic woman, a feminist, and a scholar informed in biblical studies as well as religious education. In addition to her thought provoking contributions for those of us who work more or less exclusively in Christian settings, Boys plays an important role at the cutting edge of Christian dialogue with the Jewish community.

Biblical Interpretation in Religious Education proceeds upon the fundamental assumption that, as a direct result of the information and insights available through responsible biblical scholarship, the discipline of religious education is strategically located so as to bear fruit in the pastoral, as well as the educational, arena. Relatedly, Boys perceives the discipline to be situated at the point of convergence between academic and pastoral interests. She directs attention to "a particular way of interpreting the Bible that clearly manifests this convergence: the Bible as salvation history."[23]

Accordingly, Boys examines the roots of salvation history (*heilsgeschichte*) and its later ally, the biblical theology movement. Focused in the biblical theology movement, this stream of thought played a significant role in the years following World War II: functioning as (1) "a way to navigate through the Scylla of liberalism and the Charybdis of fundamentalism," (2) "a mediating theology among Protestants in the 1945-1960 era," and (3) a shaping force in the development of Protestant curricula, especially in the Presbyterian Church U.S.A. through the leadership of James Smart.[24] Within Catholicism, Boys traces the circuitous development of salvation history (*heilsgeschichte*) as a hermeneutical principle undergirding the influence of kerygmatic theology. Flowing from this theology, and reaching the zenith of its influence in the early 1960s, the kerygmatic model was thrusted to "present the full view of God's plan for us."[25] In a long chapter, Boys sketches the factors that, from 1966, influenced the decline of salvation history as a guiding principle of Catholic religious education. Included among these, and of special interest to earlier chapters of this book, were the developing views of revelation expressed in the writings of Gabriel Moran and in James Michael Lee's forceful presentation of his social-science model of religious education.[26]

Boys argues that the demise of *heilsgeschichte*, as a primary hermeneutical principle, unveiled the truly interdisciplinary religious education, especially of its Catholic expression. This opened the opportunity for reconstituting religious education as a "configuration of disciplines" situated at the convergence of theology and education. The chasm existing between, for example, religious educators and Scripture scholars may accordingly be bridged; enabling, in Boys' view, the fruits of biblical criticism to more adequately permeate the life of the church. In the light of this envisioned configuration, the ability to synthesize would be a requirement for scholars working in the field. Boys concludes this provocative book with a brief agenda for well-trained religious educators (e.g., able to read biblical texts in the original languages) to work together with scholars representing a range of classical disciplines as a "collaborative team" to "document, assess, and publish" the fruits of this "network of scholarship."[27]

Boys' *Educating in Faith* actualizes her vision for the religious educator to function in a synthetic capacity. Utilizing a number of scholarly tools and disciplines, she analyzes four classic ways of understanding the mission and process of religious education. These analyses ("maps") are offered as heuristic devices for maintaining a sense of direction while navigating the field as one assesses the implications and consequences of religious education. For herself, Boys employs the "map" of her own tradition not merely to maintain it (or to let it become an idol), but ultimately that it might serve as a pattern by which God's involvement with creation may be recognized in a manner which ultimately fosters conversion and transformation. The goal of such "transformative education" has a concommitant political goal: "changing society to make it more just."[28]

AFTERWORD

Just as this book was being readied for print, my editor suggested the inclusion of a brief "afterword." Since I have written what I wish concerning objective substance in the text, I eagerly seized this opportunity to make a personal response. The field of Christian religious education has been my milieu for just over a quarter of a century. Research for this book has given me occasion to wander anew over the field, exploring its fence rows, furrows, and fruit. It is a grand and multidimensional field where, in a wondrous way, the past blends with the now and with the future. Perhaps as much as any field in which one might be called upon to labor, the work of those who have gone before has been preserved, not only in manuscripts, books, and curricula; but also in the spirit of the traditions and in the lives which it has molded. The broad field of church education is clearly indebted to Augustine, Gerson, Luther, Comenius, and Wesley. Higher Christian education will never be free from the influence of Origen, Aquinas, Calvin, Ignatius, and Newman. Of those mentioned above, Comenius and Wesley come closest to the Brethren tradition that marks my personal religious identity. The twentieth-century writers are, of course, much more diverse; even so, we are a community and we do our work within the boundaries of the same productive field.

It is true, however, that in writing these final words I must confess to a certain pain. Partially, perhaps, it stems from years of working in academic settings where professors of Christian education are not as highly regarded as, for example, professors of Greek (who happen to be among my best friends). I do not expect these mere words to change the culture in which I choose to live, for I am aware of good reasons why Christian education is so lightly regarded. This book, then, does represent my effort to contribute to an upgrading of the field. I have sought to speak to a number of the more critical needs in the field, arguing, in particular, (1) for an appreciation of the relationship of the educational endeavor to the wholeness of the church and (2) for a more effective grasp of theory and of its power to improve practice.

NOTES

Chapter 1

1. D. Campbell Wyckoff, *The Gospel and Christian Education* (Philadelphia: Westminster, 1959), 7.

2. James Michael Lee, *The Flow of Religious Instruction* (Birmingham, Ala.: Religious Education Press, 1973), 27.

3. See James Michael Lee's helpful deliberation on terminology in *The Shape of Religious Instruction* (Birmingham, Ala.: Religious Education Press, 1971), 6-8; also Thomas H. Groome's discussion in *Christian Religious Education* (San Francisco: Harper & Row, 1980), 20-29.

4. William Bedford Williamson, *Language and Concepts in Christian Education* (Philadelphia: Westminster, 1970), 33-41.

5. Georgia Harkness is rumored to have remarked that, since she could not understand what they were supposed to be saying, she would read no more books on religious education lest she "go mad."

6. Charles F. Melchert, "Hope for the Profession," *Religious Education* 67 (September-October 1972), 360. Also see his "Theory in Religious Education" in *Foundations of Christian Education in a Time of Change*, ed. Marvin J. Taylor (Nashville: Abingdon, 1976), 20-29. One could easily wish that Melchert had published a book expanding upon these articles.

7. Nicholas Lobkowicz, *Theory and Practice: History of a Concept from Aristotle to Marx* (Notre Dame, Ind.: Univ. of Notre Dame Press, 1967), 31. Lobkowicz is a political scientist, but his discussion is pertinent.

8. It would be easy to press this matter too far. While some writers in *Religious Education* have indeed expressed this unfortunate point of view, overall, careful attention has been given to the integration of theory and practice.

9. For a summary of the report of the Character Education Inquiry, see Hugh Hartshorne and Mark A. May, "A Summary of the Work of the Character Education Inquiry," *Religious Education* 25 (September 1930 and October 1930). The full report was published by Macmillan in three volumes (1928, 1929, and 1930).

10. James Michael Lee's trilogy includes *The Shape of Religious Instruction*, 1971; *The Flow of Religious Instruction*, 1973; and *The Content of Religious Instruction*, 1985. The subtitle for each volume is "A Social Science Approach." The trilogy is published by Religious Education Press, Birmingham, Alabama.

11. James W. Fowler, *Stages of Faith: The Psychology of Human Development and the Quest for Meaning* (San Francisco: Harper & Row, 1981).

12. Timothy Arthur Lines, *Functional Images of the Religious Educator* (Birmingham, Ala.: Religious Education Press, 1992).

13. Lawrence O. Richards, *Christian Education: Seeking to Become Like Jesus Christ* (Grand Rapids: Zondervan, 1988), 190-227.

14. For a helpful discussion of the role of models in research, especially as it relates to the behavioral sciences, see Abraham Kaplan, *The Conduct of Inquiry* (San Francisco: Chandler, 1964), 256-93. James Michael Lee's discussion of the role of theory is particularly germane to the role of models in religious education; see "The Authentic Source of Religious Instruction," in *Religious Education and Theology*, ed. Norma H. Thompson (Birmingham, Ala.: Religious Education Press, 1982), 117-21.

15. Adapted from Martin Heidegger, *What Is Called Thinking*, trans. Fred D. Wieck and J. Glenn Gray (New York: Harper and Row, 1968), 3-12.

16. To name but few among many, the writings of Thomas H. Groome, John H. Westerhoff III, D. Campbell Wyckoff, James Michael Lee, and Timothy Arthur Lines support the notion that descriptive research is an essential need for the advancement of religious education theory. See also, Carter V. Good and Douglas E. Scates, *Methods of Research* (New York: Appleton-Century-Crofts, 1954), 259; and Robert Dubin, *Theory Building* (New York: Free Press, 1969), 85.

17. George A. Coe, *A Social Theory of Religious Education* (New York: Scribner's, 1917), 9-10.

18. Lewis Joseph Sherrill, *The Rise of Christian Education* (New York: Macmillan, 1944), 2.

19. D. Campbell Wyckoff, "Toward a Definition of Religious Education as a Discipline," *Religious Education* 62 (September-October 1967): 392-93.

20. *Contemporary Approaches to Christian Education*, ed. Jack L. Seymour and Donald E. Miller (Nashville: Abingdon, 1982), 11-34.

21. *Theological Approaches to Christian Education*, ed. Jack L. Seymour and Donald E. Miller (Nashville: Abingdon, 1992), 7-24.

22. Lee, *Flow of Religious Instruction*, 232-40.

23. There is one change in terminology from my earlier work. I have elected to employ the term "learner" rather than "student." The reason is that "student" has a strong identification with the notion of "schooling." As here discussed, religious education may, or may not, take place in a school.

24. Wayne R. Rood, *Understanding Christian Education* (New York: Abingdon, 1970), 38-40.

25. Ibid., 41.

Chapter 2

1. *The American Heritage Dictionary*, 3rd ed. (Boston: Houghton Mifflin, 1993), 1457.

2. These descriptors are derived from a reading of primary and secondary literature. Obviously, there is considerable diversity in how they are fleshed out.

3. Lewis Joseph Sherrill, *The Rise of Christian Education* (New York: Macmillan, 1944), 2-3.

4. Adolf von Harnack, *The Mission and Expansion of Christianity in the First Three Centuries*, trans. James Moffatt (New York: Putnam, 1908), 1-72.

5. Robert Ulich, *History of Educational Thought* (New York: American Book, 1945), 70; also Findley B. Edge, *Teaching for Results* (Nashville: Broadman, 1956), 1-13; and H.H. Horne, *Jesus the Master Teacher* (New York: Association, 1920).

6. F.F. Bruce, *The Dawn of Christianity* (London: Paternoster, 1950), 90-100.

7. Joseph A. Grassi, *The Teacher in the Primitive Church and the Teacher Today* (Santa Clara, Calif: Univ. of Santa Clara Press, 1973), 15-17.

8. See Werner Wilhelm Jaeger, *Paideia: The Ideals of Greek Culture*, trans. Gilbert Highet (New York: Oxford Univ. Press, 1945); also Edwin Hatch, *The Influence of Greek Ideas on Christianity* (New York: Harper, 1957).

9. Pierre Joseph Marique, *History of Christian Education* (New York: Fordham Univ. Press, 1924), 3-25. Also see Charles Norris Cochrane, *Christianity and Classical Culture: A Study of the Thought and Action from Augustus to Augustine* (New York: Oxford Univ. Press, 1957).

10. Sherrill, *Rise of Christian Education*, 137-210.

11. Michael Dujarier, *A History of the Catechumenate*, trans. Edward J. Haasl (New York: Sadlier, 1979), 11-40.

12. Ibid., 19-21. Also see Leonel L. Mitchell, "The Ancient Church" in *A Faithful Church: Issues in the History of Catechesis*, ed. John H. Westerhoff III and O.C. Edwards (Wilton, Conn.: Morehouse-Barlow, 1981), 749-78.

13. James Donald Butler, *Religious Education: The Foundations and Practice of Nurture* (New York: Harper & Row, 1962), 27.

14. For an informative treatment of Clement's life and contributions, see John Ferguson, *Clement of Alexandria* (New York: Twayne, 1974); also Salvatore Romano Clemente Lilla, *Clement of Alexandria: A Study in Christian Platonism* (London: Oxford Univ. Press, 1971). For a contrasting perspective on Clement, consult Richard Bartram Tollinton, *Clement of Alexandria* (London: Williams and Northgate, 1914).

15. Clement of Alexandria, *Christ the Educator*, trans. Simon P. Wood (New York: Fathers of the Church, 1954).

16. Clement of Alexandria, *Miscellanies*, Book 7, trans. John Anthony Fenton (New York: Garland, 1987).

17. Henri Crouzel, *Origen: The Life and Thought of the First Great Theologian*, trans. A.S. Worrall (San Francisco: Harper and Row, 1989), 1-58.

18. See "The Works of St. Cyril of Jerusalem" in *The Fathers of the Church: A New Translation*, 2 vols., trans. Leo P. McCauley, S.J. and Anthony A. Stevenson (Washington, D.C.: Catholic Univ. of America Press, 1968).

19. For an essay relevant to my treatment of Cyril's lectures, see "The Primitive Baptismal Catechesis and the Teacher" in Grassi, *The Teacher in the Primitive Church*, 89-91.

20. M.L.W. Laistner, *Christianity and Pagan Culture in the Later Roman Empire: Together with an English translation of John Chrysostom's Address on Vainglory and the Right Way to Bring up Children* (Ithaca, N.Y.: Cornell Univ. Press, 1951), 85-122.

21. Chrysostomus Baur, *John Chrysostom and His Time*, trans. M. Gonzoga (Westminster, Md.: Newman, 1960). For a study that gives special attention to the spirit of the times, see Donald Attwater, *St. John Chrysostom: Pastor and Preacher* (London: Harvill, 1959), 11-77.

22. Aurelius Augustinus, "The Teacher," in *Ancient Christian Writers*, trans. H. Colleran (New York: Newman, 1951), 9:129-86.

23. St. Augustine, *First Catechetical Instruction*, trans. Joseph P. Christopher in *Ancient Christian Writers*, vol. 2 (Westminster, Md.: Newman, 1946), 13-51.

24. Gerard Stephen Sloyan, "Religious Education: From Early Christianity to Medieval Times" in *Shaping the Christian Message*, ed. Gerard Stephen Sloyan (New York: Macmillan, 1958), 17.

25.   Ibid., 26.

26.   Andrew Fleming West, *Alcuin and the Rise of the Christian Schools* (New York: AMS, 1971), 4-30; also Ulich, *History of Educational Thought*, 89-101.

27.   Sloyan, *Shaping the Message*, 34.

28.   Augustine, *City of God*, trans. D.B. Fema, et al., in *Fathers of the Church*, vols. 8, 14, 24 (New York: Fathers of the Church, 1950).

29.   Josef Andreas Jungmann, "Religious Education in Late Medieval Times," in Sloyan, *Shaping the Message*, 48.

30.   Ibid., 49.

31.   *The Holy Rule of Our Most Holy Father Saint Benedict*, ed. The Benedictine Monks of St. Meinrad Archabbey (St. Meinrad, Ind.: Grail, 1956).

32.   T.F. Lindsay, *St. Benedict: His Life and Work* (London: Burns and Oates, 1949), 136-94; also John Chapman, *St. Benedict and the Sixth Century* (Westport, Conn.: Greenwood, 1971), 1-36.

33.   West, *Alcuin and the Rise of the Christian Schools*, 89-116; 165-79.

34.   Hrabanus Maurus, *On the Education of the Clergy* (New York: American Book, 1905). For a more readily available reading from this text, see Robert Ulich, *Three Thousand Years of Educational Wisdom* (Cambridge: Harvard Univ. Press, 1947), 174-80.

35.   Marique, *History of Christian Education*, 106.

36.   Thomas Aquinas (Saint), *Summa Theologica*, Latin text and English translation, notes, appendices, and glossaries (New York: McGraw-Hill, 1964).

37.   Ulich, *History of Educational Thought*, 93.

38.   For an English translation of "De Magistro," see Mary Helen Mayer, *The Philosophy of Teaching of St. Thomas Aquinas* (Milwaukee: Bruce, 1929), 39-86.

39.   For a comprehensive treatment of Aquinas and his contributions to education, see James A. Weisheipl, *Friar Thomas D'Aquino: His Life, Thought, and Work* (Garden City, N.Y.: Doubleday, 1974); also Etienne Gilson, *The Christian Philosophy of St. Thomas D'Aquinas* (New York: Random House, 1956), 187-99.

40.   Thomas Aquinas, "Questiones disputatae de veritate," trans. from the definitive Leonine text in *Living Library of Catholic Thought*, 3 vols. (Chicago: Regnery, 1952-1954).

41.   I was exposed to the disputation as a method of teaching while in graduate studies at the University of Notre Dame. When one student strenuously opposed a point of view I had taken, the Dominican professor took control of the highly emotional argument that erupted and smoothly moved us into one of the most dynamic learning sessions I have ever experienced. At the close of the session he explained that the issues I had raised, together with the response of the other class member, had given him an excellent opportunity to employ "an important medieval method of teaching/learning/inquiry, the disputation."

42.   Ulich, *History of Educational Thought*, 101. For a larger segment of this work, see Ulich, *Three Thousand Years*, 181-90.

43.   James L. Connolly, *John Gerson, Reformer and Mystic* (Dubuque, Ia.: William C. Brown, 1962), 51-89.

44.   For a provocative treatment of Erasmus and his relation to the Reformation period, see Marjorie O'Rourke Boyle, *Rhetoric and Reform: Erasmus' Civil Dispute with Luther* (Cambridge: Harvard Univ. Press, 1983).

45.   I am in debt to Robert Ulich for the selection of these particular heroes, see his *A History of Religious Education*, 102.

46.   Roland Herbert Bainton, *Here I Stand: A Life of Martin Luther* (New York: Abingdon-Cokesbury, 1950), 60-67. For a more recent interpretation of Luther's faith and life work, see Walther Von Loewenich, *Martin Luther: The Man and His Work*, trans. Lawrence W. Denef (Minneapolis: Augsburg, 1986). For a Roman Catholic perspective on

Luther and other reformers, see Joseph Lortz, *The Reformation in Germany*, 3 vols., trans. Ronald Walls (London: Darton, Longmans & Todd, 1968).

47. This widely quoted statement is found in Luther's "Letters to the Mayors and Aldermen of All the Cities of Germany in Behalf of Christian Schools," in F.V.N. Painter, *Luther on Education* (Philadelphia: Concordia, 1890), 186.

48. Ibid., 169-209.

49. Richard Friedenthal, *Luther. His Life and Times*, trans. John Nowell (New York: Harcourt Brace Jovanovich, 1970), 305-13; also Bainton, *Martin Luther*, 326-35.

50. Martin Luther, *Large Catechism*, trans. Robert Fischer (Philadelphia: Muhlenberg, 1959).

51. Martin Luther, *Small Catechism: The Five Parts with a Selection of Occasional Prayers*, intersynodical trans. (Minneapolis: Messenger, 1929); also Loewenich, *Martin Luther*, 311.

52. Ibid., 314-17; also Bainton, *Luther*, 340-47.

53. Harold J. Grimm, "Luther and Education" in *Luther and Culture*, ed. George W. Forell, Harold J. Grimm, and Theodore Hoelty-Nickel (Decorah, Ia.: Lutheran College Press, 1960), 73-90.

54. Loewenich, *Luther*, 66-67.

55. John Calvin, *Institutes of the Christian Religion*, 2 vols., in *Library of Christian Classics*, vols. 20 and 21, trans. John T. McNeill (Philadelphia: Westminster, 1960).

56. Calvin, *Institutes*, vol. 1, 72.

57. William J. Bouwsma, *John Calvin: A Sixteenth-Century Portrait* (New York: Oxford Univ. Press, 1988). For a study of Calvin that gives helpful attention to his views on education in the context of the Geneva Academy, see Williston Walker, *John Calvin: Organizer of Reformed Protestantism* (New York: Schoken, 1969), 360-75.

58. Loyola's older brother actually traveled with Columbus on his second journey to the New World, 1493.

59. Ignatius Loyola, Saint, *The Spiritual Exercises*, trans. W.H. Longridge (London: A.R. Mowbray, 1955).

60. Ignatius Loyola, *Constitutions of the Society of Jesus* (St. Louis: Institute of Jesuit Resources, 1970).

61. George E. Ganss, *Saint Ignatius' Idea of a Jesuit University: A Study in the History of Catholic Education* (Milwaukee: Marquette Univ. Press, 1956), 52-80; 191-258.

62. For a helpful assessment of the life and work of Loyola in brief compass, see George E. Ganss, "Ignatius of Loyola," in Elmer L. Towns, ed., *A History of Religious Educators* (Grand Rapids: Baker, 1975), 136-43.

63. J. Brodrick, *Saint Peter Canisius* (London: Sheed and Ward, 1935), 224-52.

64. James Hastings Nichols, *History of Christianity 1650-1950: Secularization of the West* (New York: Ronald, 1956), 3-14; Kenneth Scott Latourette, *Three Centuries of Advance: 1500-A.D. 1800*, vol. 3 of *A History of the Expansion of Christianity* (New York: Harper & Brothers, 1939), 13-32; and Gerald R. Cragg, *The Church and the Age of Reason: 1648-1789* (New York: Penguin, 1981), 9-16; 37-49.

65. In this regard, it is extremely interesting that John Wesley began field preaching, for decades typical of Methodism, in the same year, 1739, that David Hume published *A Treatise of Human Nature*, in some sense the bible of Enlightenment thought.

66. Matthew Spinka, *John Amos Comenius, That Incomparable Moravian* (Chicago: Univ. of Chicago Press, 1943), 22.

67. Ibid., 23.

68. John Amos Comenius, *The Great Didactic*, part 2, trans. and ed. M.W. Keatinge (London: A. & C. Black, 1923), 194.

69. Ibid., 81.

70. Ibid., 52.

71. Johann Amos Comenius, *The Gate of Languages Unlocked* (Printed by T.R. and N.T. for the Company of Stationers, 1673); available in microfilm.

72. Spinka, *Comenius, Incomparable Moravian*, 65-71.

73. Wesley Tracy, "Christian Education in the Wesleyan Mode," *Wesleyan Theological Journal* (Spring 1982): 32.

74. John Wesley, *The Works of the Reverend John Wesley, A.M.*, ed. John Emory (New York: J. Collard, Printer, 1831), 1:52. For a fascinating treatment of early Methodist education, see, John W. Prince, *Wesley on Religious Education* (New York: Methodist Book Concern, 1926), 132-36.

75. Wesley, *Works*, 7:32; also see Tracy's "Christian Education in the Wesleyan Mode," 35-40.

76. *The Journal of the Rev. John Wesley*, ed. Nehemiah Curnock (London: Charles H. Kelly, 1909), 8:3.

77. Christopher Hollis, *Newman and the Modern World* (London: Hollis & Carter, 1967), 115.

78. For a reliable edition, with preface and introduction by C.F. Harrold, see John Henry Cardinal Newman, *The Idea of a University* (London: Longmans, Green and Co., 1947).

79. Owen Chadwick, *Newman* (New York: Oxford Univ. Press, 1983), 23.

80. In the following analysis, the historical progression of the writers will generally be maintained within each category.

81. St. Cyril of Jerusalem, "Procatechesis" in *The Works of Saint Cyril of Jerusalem*, trans. Anthony A. Stephenson in *The Fathers of the Church: A New Translation* (Washington, D.C.: Catholic Univ. of America Press, 1969), 1:79.

82. "Catecheses" in *Works of Saint Cyril*, 92.

83. Augustine, *First Instruction*, 13.

84. Benedict, *Rule*, 165-67.

85. Maurus, *Education of Clergy*, 175.

86. Gerson, *On Leading Children to Christ*, 185.

87. Martin Luther, "Sermon on Mark 8:1-9," in *Luther on Education in the Christian Home and School*, comp. P.E. Kretzmann (Burlington, Ia.: Lutheran Literary Board, 1940), 112.

88. Ibid., 112-13.

89. George Ganss, *Saint Ignatius' Idea of a Jesuit University* (Milwaukee: Marquette Univ. Press, 1956), 191.

90. S.S. Laurie, *John Amos Comenius, Bishop of the Moravians: His Life and Educational Works* (Cambridge: University Press, 1893), 73.

91. John Amos Comenius, *School of Infancy: An Essay on the Education of Youth During the First Six Years*, ed. Will S. Monroe (Boston: D.C. Heath, 1901), 70-71.

92. John Amos Comenius, *The Great Didactic: Setting Forth the Whole Art of Teaching All Things to All Men*, trans. M.W. Keatinge (London: A. & C. Black, 1923), 225.

93. Wesley, *Works*, 7:32. Also relevant is Tracy's treatment of Wesley's schools in "Christian Education in the Wesleyan Mode," 35-40.

94. Clement of Alexandria, "On Spiritual Perfection," in *Miscellanies*, Book 7, trans. and rev. J.B. Meyer in *The Library of Christian Classics*, vol. 2 (Philadelphia: Westminster, 1954), 93.

95. Cyril, *Catecheses*, 120.

96. Ibid., 120.

97. Augustine, *Christian Doctrine*, 42.

98. Ibid., 42-43.

99. Augustine, *First Instruction*, 18.

100. Benedict, *Rule*, 215.

101. Hrabanus Maurus, *On the Education of the Clergy,* trans. F.V.N. Painter in Robert Ulich, *Three Thousand Years of Educational Wisdom: Selections from the Great Documents* (Cambridge: Harvard Univ. Press, 1947), 174.

102. Martin Luther, "Address to the Christian Nobility of the German Nation Respecting the Reformation of the Christian Estate," trans. Wace and Buchheim, in Frederick Eby, *Early Protestant Educators* (New York: McGraw-Hill, 1931), 41-42.

103. Martin Luther, "Foreword to the Small Catechism," trans. J.N. Lenker in *Luther's Catechetical Writings: God's Call to Repentance, Faith and Prayer* (Minneapolis: Luther Press, 1907), 17.

104. Calvin, "Academy By-laws," in Eby, *Early Educators,* 267.

105. Comenius, *Great Didactic,* 223.

106. Ibid., 226.

107. John Henry Cardinal Newman, *The Idea of a University: Defended and Illustrated* (1852; reprint, Westminster, Md.: Christian Classics, 1973), 42.

108. Clement, *Christ the Educator,* 51.

109. Ibid., 50.

110. Ibid., 4.

111. Augustine, *On Christian Doctrine,* 7.

112. Augustine, *First Instruction,* 34.

113. Augustine, *The Teacher,* 175-76.

114. Ibid., 177.

115. From Martin Luther's *Commentary on the Epistle to the Galatians,* trans. Henry Barnard, in *German Teachers and Educators* (Hartford: Brown, 1878), 152.

116. From the "By-laws of the Academy of Geneva," in Eby, *Early Educators,* 254-55.

117. Comenius, *Great Didactic,* 120-21.

118. Ibid., 127.

119. Newman, *Idea of a University,* 460.

120. Clement, *Christ the Educator,* 199.

121. Ibid., 13.

122. Augustine, *On Christian Doctrine,* 142.

123. George Howie, *Educational Theory in Augustine* (New York: Teachers College Press, 1969), 64.

124. Augustine, drawn from "Against the Manichean Conception of Two Souls" and quoted in Howie, *Educational Theory in Augustine,* 83.

125. Augustine, *First Instruction,* 24.

126. Howie, *Educational Theory in Augustine,* 152.

127. Benedict, *Rule,* 189.

128. Eby, *Early Educators,* 266.

129. Comenius, *Great Didactic,* 256.

130. Cyril, *Catecheses,* 79.

131. Benedict, *Rule,* 219.

132. Ibid., 187.

133. Gerson, *Leading Children to Christ,* 186.

134. Comenius, *The Great Didactic,* 216.

135. Ibid., 216.

136. Clement, *On Spiritual Perfection,* 95.

137. Cyril, *Catecheses,* 18.

138. Augustine, *Christian Doctrine,* 135.

139. Augustine, *First Instruction,* 82.

140. Augustine, *Christian Doctrine,* 138.

141. Ibid., 168.

142. Luther, "Foreword to the Large Catechism."

143. Comenius, *Great Didactic*, 263.

144. Ibid. Also see Jean Piaget, *John Comenius on Education* (New York: Teacher's College Press, 1967), 77.

Chapter 3

1. These hypothetical criteria are derived from examining the literature.

2. Austen K. DeBlois, "The Value to the Minister of the Study of Religious Education," *Religious Education* 1 (June 1906): 42-46.

3. Harrison S. Elliott, *Can Religious Education Be Christian?* (New York Macmillan, 1940), 3-4.

4. Wayne R. Rood, *Understanding Christian Education* (Nashville: Abingdon 1970), 41.

5. George Albert Coe, "Religious Education and General Education," *Religious Education* 12 (April 1917): 123.

6. Jean-Jacques Rousseau, *Emile; ou, de l'education* (Paris: Garnier, 1961), 3 translation mine.

7. Michael Heafford, *Pestalozzi: His Thought and Its Relevance for Today* (London Methun, 1967), 39-78.

8. Friedrich Froebel, *The Education of Man*, trans. W.N. Hailmann (New York Appleton, 1905), 1-36.

9. Horace Bushnell, *Christian Nurture* (New Haven: Yale Univ. Press, 1967), 4.

10. A.J. William Myers, *Horace Bushnell and Religious Education* (Boston Manthorne & Burrack, 1937), 144.

11. Rood, *Christian Education*, 10-84.

12. Rood, *Christian Education*, 92-138; also, Dominique Parodi, "Knowledge and Action in Dewey's Philosophy," trans. Walter Geiske, in *The Philosophy of John Dewey*, ed Paul Arthur Shilpp (New York: Tudor, 1951), 229-42.

13. For an excellent treatment of this distinction, see Lawrence A. Cremin, *Th Transformation of the School: Progressivism in American Education, 1876-1957* (New York Knopf, 1961), 115-17, 234-50.

14. Elliott, *Can Religious Education Be Christian?* 1-11.

15. "The Purpose of the Association," *Religious Education* 1 (April 1906): 2.

16. A more or less authoritative account of the association is Stephen A. Schmidt' *A History of the Religious Education Association* (Birmingham, Ala.: Religious Education Press, 1983). Schmidt's highly readable, even entertaining, study details the events persons, ideas, politics, and cultural forces that were a part of its founding and it continuing story. John H. Westerhoff III has also provided a most helpful volume fo those interested in getting a sense of perspective concerning the Religious Education Association. See his edited book, *Who Are We?: The Quest for a Religious Education* (Birmingham, Ala.: Religious Education Press, 1978). This book contains a fascinating selection of eighteen articles that have appeared in *Religious Education*. Westerhof provides an introduction and conclusion.

17. George Albert Coe, *A Social Theory of Religious Education* (New York Scribner's 1917).

18. George Albert Coe, *What Is Christian Education?* (New York: Scribner's, 1929), 23

19. Ibid., 13-37.

20. Sophia Lyon Fahs, *Today's Children and Yesterday's Heritage: A Philosophy o Creative Religious Development* (Boston: Beacon, 1952).

21. William Clayton Bower, *The Curriculum of Religious Education* (New York Scribner's, 1925).

22. William Clayton Bower, *A Survey of Religious Education in the Local Church* (Chicago: Univ. of Chicago Press, 1919).

23. William Clayton Bower, *Moral and Spiritual Values in Education* (Lexington, Ky.: Univ. of Kentucky Press, 1952).

24. Adelaide Teague Case, *Liberal Christianity and Religious Education* (New York: Macmillan, 1924).

25. George Herbert Betts, *The Social Principles of Education* (New York: Scribner's, 1912).

26. George Herbert Betts, *How to Teach Religion: Principles and Methods* (New York: Abingdon, 1919).

27. George Herbert Betts, *Method in Teaching Religion* (New York: Abingdon, 1925).

28. Walter Scott Athearn, *A National System of Education* (Boston: Pilgrim, 1920).

29. Ernest J. Chave, *A Functional Approach to Religious Education* (Chicago: Univ. of Chicago Press, 1947).

30. James D. Smart, *The Teaching Ministry of the Church: An Examination of the Basic Principles of Christian Education* (Philadelphia: Westminster, 1954), 59-61.

31. Chave, *Functional Approach*, 1-16.

32. George Albert Coe, "The Idea of God," *Religious Education* 6 (June 1911): 178.

33. Chave, *Functional Approach*, 3.

34. Sophia Lyon Fahs, "Changes Necessary in Elementary Religious Education Due to Conflicts Between Science and Religion," *Religious Education* 23 (April 1928): 333; also Coe, *What Is Christian Education?* 31.

35. Case, *Liberal Christianity*, 11.

36. Coe, *What Is Christian Education?* 31.

37. Bower, *Character Through Creative Experience* (Chicago: Univ. of Chicago Press, 1930), 13.

38. Coe, *Social Theory*, 6.

39. Fahs, *Today's Children and Yesterday's Heritage*, 152-53.

40. Coe, *Social Theory*, 383-92; also Coe, *What Is Christian Education?* 240-62; also Bower, *Moral and Spiritual Values*, 10.

41. Case, *Liberal Christianity*, 41.

42. Bower, *Curriculum of Religious Education*, 226-33; also George Albert Coe, "Virtue and the Virtues," *Religious Education* 6 (January 1912): 485.

43. Coe, *Social Theory*, 55.

44. Ibid., 53.

45. Ibid., 55-57.

46. Ibid., 41-59.

47. William Clayton Bower, *Christ and Christian Education* (New York: Abingdon-Cokesbury, 1943), 38-39. An even more extensive treatment of aim by the same author may be found in *Religious Education in the Modern Church* (St. Louis: Bethany, 1929), 28-56.

48. Chave, *Functional Approach*, 17-34. Chave elaborates upon these "functional" categories throughout the remainder of the book.

49. Betts, *How to Teach Religion*, 43-47.

50. Case, *Liberal Christianity*, 33.

51. Fahs, *Today's Children and Yesterday's Heritage*, 176-97; Bower, *Religious Education in the Modern Church*, 101.

52. Coe, *What Is Christian Education?* 46.

53. Ibid., 46-59.

54. Fahs, *Today's Children and Yesterday's Heritage*, 22-29.

55. Betts, *How to Teach Religion*, 2.

56. Chave, *Functional Approach*, 2.

57. Coe, *Social Theory*, 67.

58. Bower, *Religious Education in the Modern Church*, 101-23; Fahs, *Today's Children and Yesterday's Heritage*, 15-30; and Chave, *Functional Approach*, 1-16.

59. Coe, *Social Theory*, 74-84; 97-116.

60. Ibid., 18-24; also Fahs, *Today's Children and Yesterday's Heritage*, 176-97.

61. Bower, *Religious Education in the Modern Church*, 115-21.

62. Betts, *How to Teach Religion*, 48-57.

63. Fahs, *Today's Children and Yesterday's Heritage*, 76.

64. Coe, *Social Theory*, 113-16.

65. Ibid., 19, 29, 65. Also see Bower, *Religious Education in the Modern Church*, 133-37; and Fahs, *Today's Children and Yesterday's Heritage*, 156.

66. Coe, *Social Theory*, 65.

67. Ernest J. Chave, *Supervision of Religious Education* (Chicago: Univ. of Chicago Press, 1931), 166.

68. George Albert Coe, *Education in Religion and Morals* (New York: Revell, 1904), 310-11.

69. Coe, *Social Theory*, 270-73.

70. Chave, *Supervision*, 2, 270-73; Coe, *Social Theory*, 235-36.

71. Chave, *Functional Approach*, 141; also Bower, *Moral and Spiritual Values*, 186.

72. Coe, *Social Theory*, 28-30.

73. Bower, *Character Through Experience*, 107-23.

74. Coe, *Social Theory*, 23-24.

75. George Albert Coe, "Religious Education as a Part of General Education," in *The Proceedings of the First Convention of the Religious Education Association* (Chicago: n.p., 1903), 45; also see Bower, *Moral and Spiritual Values*, 39.

76. Bower, *Moral and Spiritual Values*, 39.

77. Fahs, *Today's Children and Yesterday's Heritage*, 31-46.

78. Coe, *Education in Religion and Morals*, 33-64; also Betts, *How to Teach Religion*, 30-40.

79. Bower, *Moral and Spiritual Values*, 39-47.

80. Coe, *What Is Christian Education?* 68.

81. Ibid., 60-128.

82. Ibid., 196.

83. Coe, *Social Theory*, 6, 38-56.

84. Fahs, *Today's Children and Yesterda y's Heritage*, 176-78.

85. Case, *Liberal Christianity*, 64.

86. Coe, *Social Theory*, 13-15.

87. Bower, *Moral and Spiritual Values*, 48-60.

88. See George Herbert Betts, *The New Program of Religious Education* (New York: Abingdon, 1921), 14; George Albert Coe, *The Spiritual Life: Studies in the Science of Religion* (New York: Eaton & Mains, 1900), 5; and Coe, *Social Theory*, 36.

89. Bower, *Curriculum of Religious Education*, 99-119.

90. Betts, *How to Teach Religion*, 39-40, 91.

91. William Clayton Bower, *Christ and Christian Education* (New York: Abingdon-Cokesbury, 1943), 38.

92. Coe, *What Is Christian Education?* 178.

93. Chave, *Supervision*, 305.

94. Coe, *Social Theory*, 238-40.

95. Chave, *Supervision*, 305-33.

96. Bower, *Survey of Religious Education*, 13.

97. William Clayton Bower, *The Educational Task of the Local Church* (St. Louis: Front Rank, 1921), 114.

98. Coe, *What Is Christian Education?* 136-40.

Chapter 4

1. Karl Barth, *The Epistle to the Romans*, 6th ed., trans. Edwyn C. Hoskyns (London: Oxford Univ. Press, 1933).

2. Reinhold Niebuhr, *Moral Man and Immoral Society: A Study in Ethics and Politics* (New York: Scribner's, 1932).

3. D. Campbell Wyckoff, *The Task of Christian Education* (Philadelphia: Westminster, 1955), 13-16.

4. Harrison S. Elliott, *Can Religious Education Be Christian?* (New York: Macmillan, 1940), 9.

5. Ibid., 307-21.

6. H. Shelton Smith, *Faith and Nurture* (New York: Scribner's, 1941), vii.

7. An informative treatment of this reassessment, including an extended treatment of Elliott's and Smith's contributions, is in Stephen A. Schmidt, *A History of the Religious Education Association* (Birmingham, Ala.: Religious Education Press, 1983), 120-29. That the dynamic forces unleashed in the debates of this period still affect the field may be observed in Mary Elizabeth Moore, *Education for Continuity & Change: A New Model for Christian Religious Education* (Nashville: Abingdon, 1983), especially Part 1, "Seeking a New Model."

8. Paul H. Vieth, ed., *The Church and Christian Education* (St. Louis: Bethany, 1947), 7.

9. James D. Smart, *The Teaching Ministry of the Church: An Examination of the Basic Principles of Christian Education* (Philadelphia: Westminster, 1974), 65.

10. Sara Little, *The Role of the Bible in Contemporary Christian Education* (Richmond, Va.: John Knox, 1961), 12.

11. Randolph Crump Miller, *The Clue to Christian Education* (New York: Scribner's, 1950).

12. Randolph Crump Miller, "How I Became a Religious Educator—Or Did I?" in *Modern Masters of Religious Education*, ed. Marlene Mayr (Birmingham, Ala.: Religious Education Press, 1983), 71.

13. Miller, *The Clue*, 16.

14. Randolph Crump Miller, ed., *Empirical Theology: A Handbook* (Birmingham, Ala.: Religious Education Press, 1992).

15. Lewis Joseph Sherrill, *The Rise of Christian Education* (New York: Macmillan, 1944).

16. Lewis Joseph Sherrill, *The Gift of Power* (New York: Macmillan, 1955).

17. Ibid., x-xi.

18. Ibid., 82, also 65-91, 105.

19. Sara Little, *The Role of the Bible in Contemporary Christian Education* (Richmond, Va.: John Knox, 1961).

20. Sara Little, *To Set One's Heart: Belief and Teaching in the Church* (Atlanta: John Knox, 1983).

21. James D. Smart, *The Teaching Ministry of the Church* (Philadelphia: Westminster, 1974).

22. James D. Smart, *The Creed in Christian Teaching* (Philadelphia: Westminster, 1962).

23. Iris V. Cully, *The Dynamics of Christian Education* (Philadelphia: Westminster, 1958).

24. Iris V. Cully, *Change, Conflict, and Self-Determination* (Philadelphia: Westminster, 1972).

25. Iris V. Cully, *Education for Spiritual Growth* (New York: Harper & Row, 1984).

26. Iris V. Cully, *The Dynamics of Christian Education* (Philadelphia: Westminster, 1958), 13-35.

27   D. Campbell Wyckoff, "From Practice to Theory—And Back Again," in Mayr, *Modern Masters*, 96.

28   D. Campbell Wyckoff, *The Task of Christian Education* (Philadelphia: Westminster, 1955).

29.   D. Campbell Wyckoff, *The Gospel and Christian Education* (Philadelphia: Westminster, 1959).

30.   Howard Grimes, *The Church Redemptive* (New York: Abingdon, 1958), 7.

31.   Howard Grimes, "How I Became What I Am," in Mayr, *Modern Masters*, 135-73.

32.   C. Ellis Nelson, *Where Faith Begins* (Richmond, Va.: John Knox, 1967).

33.   C. Ellis Nelson, *How Faith Matures* (Louisville: Westminster/John Knox, 1989).

34.   See Robert Wood Lynn's "Introduction" to John H. Westerhoff III, *Values for Tomorrow's Children: An Alternative Future for Education in the Church* (Boston: Pilgrim, 1970), viii-x.

35.   John H. Westerhoff III, "A Journey into Self-Understanding," in Mayr, *Modern Masters*, 124-25.

36.   John H. Westerhoff III, *Will Our Children Have Faith?* (New York: Seabury, 1976), 27.

37.   John H. Westerhoff, "Fashioning Christians in Our Day," in *Schooling Christians: "Holy Experiments" in American Education*, ed. Stanley Hauerwas and John H. Westerhoff (Grand Rapids: Eerdmans, 1992), 262-81.

38.   J. Gordon Chamberlin, *Freedom and Faith: New Approaches to Christian Education* (Philadelphia: Westminster, 1965).

39.   Rachel Henderlite, *The Holy Spirit in Christian Education* (Philadelphia: Westminster, 1964).

40.   Gabriel Moran, *Religious Education as a Second Language* (Birmingham, Ala.: Religious Education Press, 1989), 1-3.

41.   Gabriel Moran, *Religious Body: Design for a New Reformation* (New York: Seabury, 1974).

42.   Gabriel Moran, *Religious Education as a Second Language* (Birmingham, Ala.: Religious Education Press, 1989).

43.   Gabriel Moran, *Catechesis of Revelation* (New York: Herder and Herder, 1966), 13.

44.   Ibid., 70.

45.   Gabriel Moran, *Design for Religion* (New York: Herder and Herder, 1970), 11-28.

46.   Moran expressed reservations about my earlier analysis of his contributions, especially the way that this model treats "revelation" as a theological rather than a religious category. I fully agree that his quest as a Roman Catholic assumes a very different trajectory than does that of the Protestant thinkers I have included in this model. Even so, it is my judgment that this model is flexible enough to accommodate the obvious differences that exist between him and, e.g., James Smart. See Gabriel Moran, "Philosophies Among Roman Catholics" in *Changing Patterns of Religious Education*, ed. Marvin J. Taylor (Nashville: Abingdon, 1984), 43-44; and Harold Burgess, *An Invitation to Religious Education* (Birmingham, Ala.: Religious Education Press, 1975), 94-126.

47.   Maria Harris, *Fashion Me a People: Curriculum in the Church* (Louisville: Westminster/John Knox, 1989).

48.   Maria Harris, *Teaching & Religious Imagination* (San Francisco: Harper & Row, 1987).

49.   Cully, *Dynamics of Christian Education*, 16.

50.   Miller, *The Clue*, 54.

51. A brief, yet helpful, discussion of revelation pertinent to this discussion may be found in Randolph Crump Miller, *Education for Christian Living* (Englewood Cliffs, N.J.: Prentice-Hall, 1956), 12-13.

52. Sherrill, *Gift of Power*, 83-84.

53. Harris, *Fashion Me a People*, 50-51.

54. Westerhoff, *Values for Tomorrow's Children*, 9-10.

55. Smart, *Teaching Ministry*, 88.

56. Miller, *The Clue*, 37.

57. Nelson, *Where Faith Begins*, 34.

58. Grimes, *Church Redemptive*, 104.

59. Little, *To Set One's Heart*, 90.

60. Randolph Crump Miller, *Education for Christian Living*, 2nd ed. (Englewood Cliffs, N.J.: Prentice-Hall, 1963), 55.

61. Moran, *Catechesis of Revelation*, 72-73.

62. J. Gordon Chamberlain, *Freedom and Faith* (Philadelphia: Westminster, 1965), 19.

63. Sherrill, *Gift of Power*, 95; Miller, *The Clue*, 34, 170; and Little, *Role of the Bible*, 67-89.

64. Sherrill, *Gift of Power*, 79-86.

65. Smart, *Teaching Ministry*, 108.

66. Wyckoff, *The Gospel*, 51.

67. Ibid., 51-54.

68. Chamberlain, *Freedom and Faith*, 124-26.

69. Sherrill, *Gift of Power*, 83-84.

70. Moran, *Vision and Tactics*, 75.

71. Henderlite, *Holy Spirit in Christian Education*, 16.

72. See Randolph Crump Miller, *Christian Nurture and the Church* (New York: Scribner's, 1961), 48-64; also Miller, *The Clue*, 18-36.

73. Wyckoff, *The Task*, 23-24.

74. Ibid., 24.

75. Smart, *The Teaching Ministry*, 107.

76. Harris, *Teaching and Religious Imagination*, 69-70.

77. Grimes, *Church Redemptive*, 103. Also see Nelson, *Where Faith Begins*, 204.

78. Westerhoff, *Values for Tomorrow's Children*, 29-30.

79. Miller, *The Clue*, 5.

80. Ibid., 6.

81. Miller, *Education for Christian Living*, 44.

82. Wyckoff, *The Task*, 52-56.

83. Sherrill, *Gift of Power*, 79-91, 174-75.

84. Grimes, *Church Redemptive*, 104-6.

85. See Moran, *Design for Religion*, 11-28; *Catechesis of Revelation*, 30-40; *Vision and Tactics*, 57-68.

86. Miller, *Education for Christian Living*, 173.

87. Ibid., 171-74; also Wyckoff, *The Task*, 50-60.

88. Smart, *Teaching Ministry*, 131-53.

89. Henderlite, *Holy Spirit in Christian Education*, 48-58.

90. Sherrill, *Gift of Power*, 92-118, 174-84.

91. Randolph Crump Miller, *Biblical Theology and Christian Education* (New York: Scribner's, 1956), 1-31.

92. Grimes, *Church Redemptive*, 103.

93. Westerhoff, *Values for Tomorrow's Children*, 52.

94. Westerhoff, *Will Our Children Have Faith?* 34-35.

95. Moran, *Catechesis of Revelation*, 76-89.

96. Wyckoff, *The Task*, 121.

97. Little, *To Set One's Heart*, 30.

98. Miller, *Education for Christian Living*, 369.

99. Reuel L. Howe, "A Theology for Education," *Religious Education* 54 (November-December 1959): 494-96.

100. Harris, *Teaching and Religious Imagination*, 65-68.

101. Smart, *Teaching Ministry*, 12, 41, 154-67.

102. Moran, *Vision and Tactics*, 38-68; and Moran, *Catechesis of Revelation*, 30-40.

103. Wyckoff, *The Task*, 122.

104. Ibid., 154.

105. Grimes, *The Church Redemptive*, 8; Westerhoff, *Values for Tomorrow's Children*, 29; and Harris, *Teaching and Religious Imagination*, 71.

106. Wyckoff, *The Task*, 111.

107. Wyckoff, *The Gospel*, 147-51.

108. Smart, *Teaching Ministry*, 168-69, also see 11-23.

109. Miller, *Christian Nurture*, 76-80.

110. Sherrill, *Gift of Power*, 184-86.

111. Moran, *Catechesis of Revelation*, 13, 67.

112. Miller, *The Clue*, 17, 55.

113. Smart, *Teaching Ministry*, 157.

114. Nelson, *Where Faith Begins*, 39.

115. Moran, *Vision and Tactics*, 112.

116. Smart, *Teaching Ministry*, 158; Sherrill, *Gift of Power*, 114-15; and Miller, *The Clue*, 55-70.

117. Miller, *The Clue*, 5.

118. Sherrill, *Gift of Power*, 82.

119. Ibid., 65-91; also Miller, *Christian Nurture and the Church*, 33-47 and *Education for Christian Living*, 7.

120. Westerhoff, *Will Our Children Have Faith?* 41-42.

121. Grimes, *Church Redemptive*, 90-91.

122. Sherrill, *Gift of Power*, 1-119; Wyckoff, *The Task*, 95-102; and Grimes, *Church Redemptive*, 8, 91-93.

123. Wyckoff, *The Task*, 96; also Smart, *Teaching Ministry*, 154-60.

124. Smart, *Teaching Ministry*, 156-60; Sherrill, *Gift of Power*, 145-62; and Miller, *Education for Christian Living*, 41-42.

125. Moran, *Catechesis of Revelation*, 70.

126. Smart, *Teaching Ministry*, 77-80, 103-7.

127. Miller, *Christian Nurture and the Church*, 61-62.

128. Miller, *The Clue*, 9.

129. Wyckoff, *The Task*, 104.

130. Ibid., 120.

131. Smart, *Teaching Ministry*, 168-69.

132. Sherrill, *Gift of Power*, 82-83; also Lewis Joseph Sherill, *The Opening Doors of Childhood* (New York: Macmillan, 1939), 33.

133. Miller, *Education for Christian Living*, 396.

134. Grimes, *Church Redemptive*, 27.

135. Westerhoff, *Will Our Children Have Faith?* 23.

136. Miller, *Education for Christian Living*, 102-3.

137. Grimes, *Church Redemptive*, 92.

138. Harris, *Teaching and Religious Imagination*, 131.

139. Wyckoff, *The Task*, 38; also Wyckoff, *The Gospel*, 144.

140. Henderlite, *Holy Spirit in Christian Education*, 114.

141. D. Campbell Wyckoff, *How to Evaluate Your Education Program* (Philadelphia: Westminster, 1962). This book presents an elaborate plan for evaluating the total educational ministry of almost any local church.

142. Miller, *Education for Christian Living*, 393-94.

143. Smart, *Teaching Ministry*, 70.

144. Westerhoff, *Values for Tomorrow's Children*, 114.

Chapter 5

1. Aurelius Augustinus, *De Catechizandis Rudibus*, trans. Joseph Patrick Christopher in *The Catholic University of America Patristic Studies*, vol. 8 (Washington, D.C.: Catholic Univ. of America, 1926).

2. Gerard S. Sloyan, "The Relation of the Catechism to the Work of Religious Formation," in *Modern Catechetics: Message and Method in Religious Formation*, ed. Gerald S. Sloyan (New York: Macmillan, 1963), 95.

3. "Evangelical," as the term is employed in this chapter, designates a point of view which emphasizes the authority of the Scriptures. Evangelicals typically endorse doctrinal formulations common to orthodox Christianity, placing particular stress upon the importance of a personal reconciliation to God through Christ. See Frank E. Gaebelein, *Christian Education in a Democracy* (New York: Oxford, 1951), 15-17; and Kendig Brubaker Cully, *The Search for a Christian Education—Since 1940* (Philadelphia, Westminster, 1965), 94-99.

4. Harold Carlton Mason, "The History of Christian Education," in *An Introduction to Evangelical Christian Education*, ed. J. Edward Hakes (Chicago: Moody, 1964), 31-33. An alternative perspective may be seen in William Clayton Bower and Percy Roy Hayward, *Protestantism Faces Its Educational Task Together* (Appleton, Wis.: Nelson, 1949), 1-65.

5. See *50 Years Serving Christ through Leadership Training* (Wheaton, Ill.: Evangelical Teacher Training Association, 1980).

6. Gaebelein, *Christian Education in a Democracy*, 116-17.

7. This purpose statement is given on the copyright page of each issue of the journal; see, e.g., *Christian Education Journal* 15/3 (Spring 1995): 2.

8. John T. McMahon, *Some Methods of Teaching Religion*, and Klemens Tilman, "Origin and Development of Modem Catechetical Methods," in *Teaching All Nations*, trans. Clifford Howell (New York: Herder and Herder, 1961), 1-25; 81-94.

9. Valerian Cardinal Gracias, "Modem Catechetical Renewal and Missions," in *Teaching All Nations*, 11-14.

10. The most accessible version for English readers is Josef Andreas Jungmann, *The Good News Yesterday and Today*, trans. William A. Huesman (New York: Sadlier, 1962). This twenty-fifth anniversary edition of Jungmann's classic includes four essays in appraisal of the original work.

11. *Lumen Vitae* is published by *Centre international detudes de leformation religieuse*, Brussels, Belgium.

12. See "Supernaturalism" in *Sacramentum Mundi: An Encyclopedia of Theology*, 6, ed. Karl Rahner (New York: Herder and Herder, 1970), 191.

13. Gabriel Moran's criticism of my earlier work is instructive on this matter. See his "Philosophies of Religious Education among Roman Catholics," in *Changing Patterns of Religious Education*, ed. Marvin J. Taylor (Nashville: Abingdon, 1984), 43-44. I am appreciative of Moran's argument, but remain convinced that whatever their specifically theological differences, the views of both Protestants and Catholics discussed in this chapter are of the same genre insofar as their model of Christian religious education is concerned. See my *An Invitation to Religious Education*, 27.

14. Frank E. Gaebelein, *Christian Education in a Democracy* (New York: Oxford, 1951).

15. Lois E. LeBar, *Education That Is Christian* (Old Tappan, NJ.: Revell, 1955). This book continues in print and is available in an updated version (Wheaton, Ill.: Victor Books, 1995).

16. Clarence H. Benson, *Introduction to Child Study* (Chicago: Bible Institute Colportage Association, 1942).

17. Clarence H. Benson, *The Christian Teacher* (Chicago: Moody, 1950).

18. Clarence H. Benson, *A Popular History of Christian Education* (Chicago: Moody, 1943).

19. C.B. Eavey, *History of Christian Education* (Chicago: Moody, 1964).

20. C.B. Eavey, *Principles of Teaching for Christian Teachers* (Grand Rapids: Zondervan, 1968).

21. Harold Carlton Mason, *Abiding Values in Christian Education* (Westwood, NJ.: Revell, 1955).

22. Herbert W. Byrne, *A Christian Approach to Education: Education Theory and Application* (Milford, Mich.: Mott Media, 1977).

23. Herbert W. Byrne, *Christian Education for the Local Church: An Evangelical and Functional Approach* (Grand Rapids: Zondervan, 1963).

24. Kenneth O. Gangel, *Building Leaders for Church Education* (Chicago: Moody, 1981).

25. Kenneth O. Gangel & Warren S. Benson, *Christian Education: Its History & Philosophy* (Chicago: Moody, 1983).

26. Roy B. Zuck, *The Holy Spirit in Your Teaching* (Wheaton, Ill.: Scripture Press, 1963), 87-100.

27. James DeForrest Murch, *Christian Education and the Local Church: History-Principles-Practice*, rev. ed. (Cincinnati: Standard, 1958).

28. Lawrence O. Richards, *A Theology of Christian Education* (Grand Rapids: Zondervan, 1975).

29. Donald M. Joy, *Meaningful Learning in the Church* (Winona Lake, Ind.: Light and Life, 1989), 9.

30. Donald M. Joy, ed., *Moral Development Foundations* (Nashville: Abingdon, 1983).

31. Donald M. Joy, *Bonding: Relationships in the Image of God* (Nappanee, Indiana: Evangel Publishing House, 1999).

32. Findley B. Edge, *Teaching for Results* (Nashville: Broadman, 1956).

33. Robert W. Pazmiño, *Foundational Issues in Christian Education: An Introduction in Evangelical Perspective* (Grand Rapids: Baker, 1988).

34. Robert W. Pazmiño, *Principles and Practices of Christian Education: An Evangelical Perspective* (Grand Rapids: Baker, 1992), esp. 37-57.

35. Josef Andreas Jungmann, *Die Frohbotschaft und unsere Glaubensverkundigung* (Regensburg: Pustet, 1936).

36. Josef Andreas Jungmann, *Handing on the Faith: A Manual of Catechetics*, trans. and rev. by A.N. Fuerst (New York: Herder and Herder, 1962).

37. Johannes Hofinger, *The Art of Teaching Christian Doctrine* (Notre Dame, Ind.: Univ. of Notre Dame Press, 1962).

38. Marcel van Caster, *The Structure of Catechetics* (New York: Herder and Herder, 1965).

39. Marcel van Caster, *Themes of Catechesis* (New York: Herder and Herder, 1966).

40. Jean Le Du and Marcel van Caster, *Experiential Catechetics* (New York: Newman, 1969).

41. G. Emmett Carter, with contributing editor William J. Reedy, *The Modern Challenge to Religious Education: God's Message and Our Response* (New York: Sadlier, 1961).

42. Josef Goldbrunner, *New Catechetical Methods*, trans. M. Veronica Riedl (Notre Dame, Ind.: Univ. of Notre Dame Press, 1965).

43. Alphonso M. Nebreda, *Kerygma in Crisis?* (Chicago: Loyola Univ. Press, 1965).

44. Alfred McBride, *Catechetics: A Theology of Proclamation* (Milwaukee: Bruce, 1966).

45. Michael Warren, *Sourcebook for Modern Catechetics* (Winona, Minn.: Saint Mary's, 1983).

46. Berard L. Marthaler, *Catechetics in Context: Notes and Commentary on the General Catechetical Directory Issued by the Sacred Congregation for the Clergy* (Huntington, Ind.: Our Sunday Visitor, 1973).

47. Josef Andreas Jungmann, *Announcing the Word of God,* trans. R. Walls (New York: Herder and Herder, 1967), 7-65.

48. Zuck, *Holy Spirit in Your Teaching*, 5.

49. Gaebelein, *Christian Education in a Democracy*, 259.

50. Van Caster, *Structure of Catechetics*, 13.

51. Hofinger, *Art of Teaching Doctrine*, 65.

52. Mason, *Teaching Task*, 25.

53. Jungmann, *Handing on the Faith*, xii.

54. Zuck, *Holy Spirit in Your Teaching*, 101.

55. Mason, *Abiding Values*, 15-33; also LeBar, *Education That Is Christian*, 135-38.

56. Gaebelein, *Christian Education in a Democracy*, 227.

57. Byrne, *Christian Approach to Education*, 39.

58. Eavey, *Art of Effective Teaching,* 15.

59. Van Caster, *Themes of Catechesis*, 203.

60. Josef Goldbrunner, "Catechesis and Encounter," in *New Catechetical Methods*, 22.

61. Hofinger, *Teaching All Nations*, 403.

62. Jungmann, *Handing on the Faith*, 94.

63. Hofinger, *Art of Teaching Christian Doctrine*, 17.

64. C.B. Eavey, "Aims and Objectives of Christian Education" in Hakes, *Introduction to Evangelical Christian Education*, 62.

65. Edge, *Teaching for Results*, 16-17.

66. Benson, *Christian Teacher*, 87-89.

67. Jungmann, *Good News Yesterday and Today*, 166.

68. LeBar, *Education That Is Christian*, 27-30.

69. Mason, *The Teaching Task*, 12; and Gaebelein, *Christian Education in a Democracy*, 260-62.

70. Gaebelein, *Christian Education in a Democracy*, 1-3.

71. Edge, *Teaching for Results*, 222-23, also 23-26.

72. Zuck, *Holy Spirit in Teaching*, ii.

73. For example, Jungmann, *Announcing the Word*, 53-58.

74. Jim Wilhoit, *Christian Education and the Search for Meaning* (Grand Rapids: Baker, 1991), 68-70.

75. Murch, *Christian Education and the Local Church*, 100.

76. Gangel, *Building Leaders*, 30.

77. Benson, *The Christian Teacher*, 77-91.

78. Ibid., 14.

79. Hofinger, *Art of Teaching Christian Doctrine*, 12-14.

80. Gaebelein, *Christian Education in a Democracy,* 13-14.

81. Eavey, *Principles of Teaching*, 13.

82. Byrne, *Christian Approach to Education*, 61.

83. Zuck, *Holy Spirit in Teaching*, 99.

84. Goldbrunner, "Catechetical Method as Handmaid of Kerygma," in *Teaching All Nations*, 112-18.

85. Van Caster, *Themes of Catechesis*, 205.

86. Marcel van Caster, "The Spirit of the Religion Course," *Lumen Vitae* 6 July-September 1951): 438-39.

87. Jungmann, *Announcing the Word of God*, 59-60; also Jungmann, *Good News Yesterday and Today*, 7-8.

88. Hofinger, *Art of Teaching Christian Doctrine*, 92.

89. Gaebelein, *Christian Education in a Democracy*, 92.

90. LeBar, *Education That Is Christian*, 203-7.

91. Lois E. LeBar, *Children in the Bible School* (Westwood, N.J.: Revell, 1952), 193-94.

92. Eavey, *Art of Effective Teaching*, 49.

93. Hofinger, *Art of Teaching Christian Doctrine*, 11.

94. Jungmann, *Good News Yesterday and Today*, 9.

95. Ibid., 11.

96. Jungmann, *Announcing the Word of God*, 28.

97. Benson, *Christian Teacher*, 223.

98. Mason, *Teaching Task*, 25.

99. Jungmann, *Handing on the Faith*, xii.

100. Van Caster, *Themes of Catechesis*, 203-7; also van Caster, *Structure of Catechetics,* 168-214.

101. LeBar, *Education That Is Christian*, 30.

102. Edge, *Teaching for Results*, 8.

103. Hofinger, *Art of Teaching Christian Doctrine*, 51.

104. Clarence H. Benson, *The Sunday School in Action* (Chicago: Moody, 1952), 138.

105. George M. Marsden, *Fundamentalism and American Culture: The Shaping of Twentieth Century Evangelicalism: 1870-1925* (New York: Oxford Univ. Press, 1980), 60.

106. Byrne, *Christian Approach to Education*, 125.

107. Gaebelein, *Christian Education in a Democracy*, 185.

108. Eavey, "Aims and Objectives of Christian Education," in Hakes, *Introduction to Evangelical Christian Education,* 61.

109. Mason, *Abiding Values*, 131-41.

110. Carter, *Modern Challenge to Religious Education*, 333-37.

111. Jungmann, *Handing on the Faith*, 70-71.

112. Johannes Hofinger, "The Catechetical Apostolate of Lay Teachers," *Lumen Vitae* 12 (October-December 1957): 652. Hofinger makes a similar point in *The Art of Teaching Christian Doctrine*, 205-6.

113. Lois E. LeBar, *Focus on People in Church Education* (Westwood, N.J.: Revell, 1968), 23-24. Also on this matter, see Johannes Hofinger with William Reedy, *The ABC's of Modern Catechetics* (New York: Sadlier, 1962), 29.

114. Jungmann, *Handing on the Faith*, 75; also Benson, *Christian Teacher*, 49-57; and LeBar, *Children in the Bible School*, 35-37.

115. Gaebelein, *Christian Education in a Democracy*, 187.

116. Hofinger, *Art of Teaching Christian Doctrine*, 197.

117. Jungmann, *Handing on the Faith*, 71; also see Gaebelein, *Christian Education in* a *Democracy*, 186; and Carter, *Modern Challenge to Religious Education*, 342-43.

118. Hofinger, *Art of Teaching Christian Doctrine*, 200; LeBar, *Children in the Bible School*, 33-34; and Carter, *Modern Challenge to Religious Education*, 343.

119. Ibid., 342.

120. Hofinger, *Art of Teaching Christian Doctrine*, 201.

121. Gaebelein, *Christian Education in a Democracy*, 201

122. D.K. Reisinger, "Teacher Training," in *An Introduction to Evangelical Christian Education*, 98.

123. Benson, *Sunday School in Action*, 122.

124. Benson, *Christian Teacher*, 209.

125. Zuck, *Holy Spirit in Your Teaching*, 64-65.

126. Edge, *Teaching for Results*, 65-88.

127. Byrne, *Christian Approach to Education*, 128.

128   Reisinger, "Teacher Training," in Hakes, *Introduction to Evangelical Christian Education*, 96-106; and Eavey, *Principles of Teaching for Christian Teachers*, 96-123.

129. Jungmann, *Handing on the Faith*, 72.

130. Ibid., 70-76, and Hofinger, *Art of Teaching Christian Doctrine*, 197-260. Also see Frank B. Norris, "The Catechetics Course in the Major Seminary"; Mary Carol Francis, "Catechetics Formation of Religious"; and Raymond Lucker and Theodore Stone, "Formation and Training of Lay Catechists," in *Pastoral Catechetics*, ed. Johannes Hofinger and Theodore Stone (New York: Herder and Herder, 1964), 213-25; 226-38; 239-62.

131. Jungmann, *Handing on the Faith*, 174-217.

132. Hofinger, *Art of Teaching Christian Doctrine*, 62-73.

133. Marcel van Caster, "The Spirit of the Religion Course," *Lumen Vitae* 6 (July-September 1951): 438.

134. Gaebelein, *Christian Education in a Democracy*, 198.

135. LeBar, *Education That Is Christian*, 230-45.

136   Mason, *Abiding Values*, 98.

137. LeBar, *Education That Is Christian*, 230.

138. Edge, *Teaching for Results*, 29-50.

139. Byrne, *Christian Approach to Teaching*, 193.

140. Eavey, *Art of Effective Teaching*, 70-74.

141. LeBar, *Focus on People in Church Education*, 23-24.

142. Joy, *Meaningful Learning*, 10.

143. Jungmann, *Handing on the Faith*, 79.

144. Gaebelein, *Christian Education in a Democracy*, 227.

145. Gangel, *Building Leaders*, 33.

146. Zuck, *Holy Spirit in Your Teaching*, 129.

147. Eavey, *Art of Effective Teaching*, ii.

148. Jungmann, *Handing on the Faith*, 79.

149. Gaebelein, *Christian Education in a Democracy*, 259.

150. LeBar, *Education That Is Christian*, 135.

151. Ibid., 136.

152. Gaebelein, *Christian Education in a Democracy*, 270.

153. LeBar, *Education That Is Christian*, 26.

154. Jungmann, *Handing on the Faith*, 125.

155. Gaebelein, *Christian Education in a Democracy*, 269-70.

156. Jungmann, *Handing on the Faith*, 77.

157. Eavey, *Art of Effective Teaching*, 20.

158. Ibid., 20-23.

159. Gaebelein, "Toward a Philosophy of Christian Education," in Hakes, *Introduction to Evangelical Christian Education*, 45.

160. Hofinger, *Art of Teaching Christian Doctrine*, 199-202.

161. Byrne, *Christian Approach to Education*, 152.

162. Gangel, *Building Leaders*, 189-203.

163. Eavey, *Art of Teaching*, 243-65.
164. Edge, *Teaching for Results*, 167-70.

Chapter 6

1. James Michael Lee, *The Shape of Religious Instruction: A Social Science Approach* (Birmingham, Ala.: Religious Education Press, 1971), 182-218.

2. Lee employs the term "religious instruction" rather than "religious education" or "Christian education" to designate a focus upon the teaching-learning dimension.

3. See, e.g., James Michael Lee, *Principles and Methods of Secondary Education* (New York: McGraw-Hill, 1963); James Michael Lee and Louis J. Putz, eds., *Seminary Education in a Time of Change* (Notre Dame, Ind.: Fides, 1965); and James Michael Lee, "Professional Criticism of Catholic High Schools," *Catholic World* (October 1961), 7-12.

4. James Michael Lee, "The Third Strategy: A Behavioral Approach to Religious Education" (three parts), *Today's Catholic Teacher* (September, October, and November, 1969).

5. James Michael Lee, "The Teaching of Religion," in *Toward a Future for Religious Education*, ed. James Michael Lee and Patrick C. Rooney (Dayton, Ohio: Pflaum, 1970), 67.

6. For example, "Compassion in Religious Instruction," in *Compassionate Ministry*, ed. Gary L. Sapp (Birmingham, Ala.: Religious Education Press, 1992); "Facilitating Growth in Faith through Religious Instruction," in *Handbook Of Faith*, ed. James Michael Lee (Birmingham, Ala.: Religious Education Press, 1990); and "The Blessings of Religious Pluralism," in *Religious Pluralism and Religious Education*, ed. Norma H. Thompson (Birmingham, Ala.: Religious Education Press, 1988).

7. James Michael Lee, "The Authentic Source of Religious Instruction," in *Religious Education and Theology*, ed. Norma H. Thompson (Birmingham, Ala.: Religious Education Press, 1982), 100-197.

8. Ibid., 184.

9. Ibid.

10. Lee suggests that persons working from a purely theological perspective typically reject, or may not understand, the language of religious instruction. See Lee, "Authentic Source of Religious Instruction," 188.

11. Lee argues that the religion teacher should be a fully trained professional who works out a sound theoretical framework. See James Michael Lee, *The Flow of Religious Instruction* (Birmingham, Ala.: Religious Education Press, 1973), 290-91.

12. For an extended treatment of these positions, see James Michael Lee, *The Purpose of Catholic Schooling* (Dayton, Ohio: National Catholic Education Association/Pflaum, 1968).

13. Lee, *The Flow*, 11.

14. Ibid., 13.

15. Charles Y. Glock, "On the Study of Religious Commitment," *Religious Education*, research supplement 57 (July-August 1962): s98-s110. For Lee's application of Glock's five dimensions of religiosity, see *The Shape*, 11-13.

16. Lee, *The Shape*, 11-13.

17. Ibid.

18. Ibid., 204-7.

19. Lee, *The Flow*, 23. One long-used taxonomy in the field of education is Benjamin S. Bloom, et al., *Taxonomy of Educational Objectives: Handbook I: Cognitive Domain* (New York: McKay, 1956).

20. Lee, *The Shape*, 67-69.

21. James Michael Lee, "Towards a Dialogue in Religious Instruction," *The Living Light* 8 (Spring 1971): 11.

22. Lee, *The Shape*, 63; and *The Flow*, 289-90.

23. James Michael Lee, *The Content of Religious Instruction: A Social Science Approach* (Birmingham, Ala.: Religious Education Press, 1985), 8. A brief discussion of Lee's understanding of content is in his chapter "The Authentic Source of Religious Instruction," in *Religious Education and Theology*, ed. Norma H. Thompson (Birmingham, Ala.: Religious Education Press, 1982), 115-16. Also see Lee's application of this concept in "Compassion in Religious Instruction," in Sapp, *Compassionate Ministry*, 172-73, 186-87.

24. Lee, *The Content*, 8-13.

25. Ibid., 13-17.

26. Ibid., 35-128.

27. Ibid., 129-275.

28. Ibid., 276-474.

29. Ibid., 475-607.

30. Lee, *The Shape*, 10; also *The Content*, 608-735.

31. Lee, *The Content*, 738.

32. Ibid., 736-45.

33. Ibid., 8, 25-26; and *The Flow*, 19.

34. Lee, *The Flow*, 206.

35. Ibid., 206-10.

36. Ibid., 211.

37. Ibid., 212.

38. Ibid., 212-15. See also, James Michael Lee, "Prediction in Religious Instruction," *The Living Light* 9 (Summer 1972): 43-45.

39. Lee, *The Flow*, 215-18.

40. Ibid., 218-21.

41. Ibid., 226.

42. Ibid., 229.

43. Ibid., 277-89.

44. Ibid., 279-82.

45. Ibid., 294.

46. "Speculation may be about forms, events, values, or practices. Consequently, there are four kinds of theory: formal theory, event theory, valuational theory, and praxeological theory" (Elizabeth Steiner Maccia, "Curriculum Theory and Policy" [Bureau of Educational Research and Services, The Ohio State University, 1965], 3). Lee's reference here is to the distinction made by Maccia between event theory and praxeological theory.

47. Lee, *The Flow*, 57.

48. Ibid., 43-47.

49. Ibid., 47-57.

50. Ibid., 32.

51. Reflecting the fact that this taxonomy is only a preliminary one, Lee admits that these categories are less than watertight and that they await further development and testing.

52. Lee, *The Flow*, 230-33.

53. The notion of a closed-loop feedback system reflects Lee's application of cybernetic principles toward an understanding of the structure of teaching.

54. Lee, *The Flow*, 230-33.

55. For a pictorial presentation of this model, see Lee, *The Flow*, 234.56.   Lee gives a usable summary of a number of available rating, sign, and category systems for accomplishing this analysis. See Lee, *The Flow*, 252-68.

57. Lee, *The Flow*, 268.

58. Ibid., 149.

59. Ibid., 149-205.

60. Ibid., 162.

61. Ibid., 179.

62. Ibid., 198.

63. Ibid., 199.

64. An overview of Lee's perspective on teaching religion may be found in "The Teaching of Religion," in *Toward a Future for Religious Education*, 55-92.

65. Lee's views on this matter are treated extensively in *Principles and Methods of Secondary Education*, 111-43.

66. Lee, *The Flow*, 59.

67. Lee, *Principles and Methods*, 120-28; and *The Shape*, 258-93.

68. Lee, *The Flow*, 58-148. This long chapter, with 422 footnote references, is a veritable mine of information about the empirical research on human learning and its practical application in religious instruction.

69. Ibid., 63.

70. James Michael Lee, *Forward Together: A Preparation Program for Religious Education* (Chicago: Thomas More Association, Meditape Program, 1973), twelve one-half hour cassette tapes and instructor's guide, see tape number five.

71. Lee, *The Flow*, 135-36.

72. Ibid., 147-48.

73. Lee, *The Shape*, 17.

74. Ibid., 49.

75. Ibid., 78.

76. Ibid., 75.

77. Ibid., 81.

78. Lee, *The Flow*, 65-72.

79. Lee, *Principles and Methods*, 438-39.

80. Lee, *The Flow*, 232.

81. Ibid., 275.

82. Ibid., 275-76.

83. Ibid., 277.

Chapter 7

1. Norma H. Thompson, "The Challenge of Religious Pluralism," in *Religious Pluralism and Religious Education*, ed. Norma H. Thompson (Birmingham, Ala.: Religious Education Press, 1988), 7-36.

2. James Michael Lee, "The Blessings of Religious Pluralism," in Thompson, *Religious Pluralism*, esp. 65-98.

3. Ibid., 57-124.

4. See, e.g., George Albert Coe's *What Is Christian Education?* (New York: Scribner's, 1929) and Harrison Elliott's *Can Religious Education Be Christian?* (New York: Macmillan, 1940).

5. This extremely important point is made in Lee, *The Flow*, 27.

6. It will be remembered that a key limitation of this study is that it gives attention solely to theorists who have published books important to the field of religious education.

7. The smiling librarians were Donald Butterworth and Dorothy James, professional staff members of the B.L. Fisher Library, Asbury Theological Seminary. The two of them, together with John Seery (who also smiles a lot), have aided research on this book in ways too numerous to mention. Each of them seems to have the "gift of helps" and they know how to make research a pleasure.

8. Timothy Arthur Lines, *Systemic Religious Education* (Birmingham, Ala.: Religious Education Press, 1987), 3.

9. Timothy Arthur Lines, *Functional Images of the Religious Educator* (Birmingham, Ala.: Religious Education Press, 1992), 149, 501-10.

10. Richard Robert Osmer, *A Teachable Spirit: Recovering the Teaching Office of the Church* (Louisville: Westminster/John Knox, 1990), 52.

11. Ibid., 12.

12. Osmer, *A Teachable Spirit*, 3-23.

13. Ibid., 175-211.

14. Richard Robert Osmer, *Teaching for Faith: A Guide for Teachers of Adult Classes* (Louisville: Westminster/John Knox, 1992), 9-38.

15. Thomas H. Groome, *Christian Religious Education: Sharing Our Story and Vision* (San Francisco: Harper and Row, 1980).

16. Thomas H. Groome, *Sharing Faith: A Comprehensive Approach to Religious Education and Pastoral Ministry: The Way of Shared Praxis* (San Francisco: Harper, 1991).

17. Groome, *Christian Religious Education*, 140.

18. Ibid., 184.

19. Ibid., 184-95.

20. Groome, *Sharing Faith*, 22.

21. Mary C. Boys, *Biblical Interpretation in Religious Education: A Study of the Kerygmatic Era* (Birmingham, Ala.: Religious Education Press, 1980).

22. Mary C. Boys, *Educating in Faith: Maps and Visions* (San Francisco: Harper, 1989).

23. Boys, *Biblical Interpretation*, 9.

24. Ibid., 13-61.

25. Ibid., 62-139.

26. Ibid., 140-273.

27. Ibid., 274-338.

28. Boys, *Educating in Faith*, esp. 192-218.

SELECT INDEX

A

Aim

as an analytical category, 13, 23-27, 29, 56, 65-68, 85, 89-95, 114, 122-28, 162-68, 191-95

behavioral aspect of, 193

conversion, role in, 166-67

creative aspect of, 90-91

focus of, 123-25, 191-92

integralist position on, 192

intellectualist position on, 191

knowledge of faith and Christian living, an aspect of, 164-65

moralist position on, 192

scope of, 91-92, 125-26, 165-66, 191-92

social and moral dimensions of, 91-95, 126-28

supernatural element in, 163-64

transmissive aspect of, 162-63

Albert the Great, 47

Alcuin, 43, 45-47

Alexandria, catechetical school of, 37-38

Ambrose, 41

Analysis, descriptive, 23

Analytical matrix, as a descriptor for religious education theory, 13